effective learning
& teaching in

LAW

Edited by **roger burridge, karen hinett,
abdul paliwala, tracey varnava**

**the institute for learning and teaching
in higher education**

THE TIMES
HIGHER
EDUCATION SUPPLEMENT

First published in 2002

Kogan Page Limited   Stylus Publishing Inc.
120 Pentonville Road   22883 Quicksilver Drive
London N1 9JN   Sterling VA 20166 2012
UK   USA

The views expressed in this book are those of the authors and are not necessarily
the same as those of *The Times Higher Education Supplement*.

British Library Cataloguing in Publication Data

A CIP record for this book is available from the British Library.

ISBN 0 7494 3568 2

Typeset by Saxon Graphics Ltd, Derby
Printed and bound in Great Britain by Biddles Ltd, Guildford and King's Lynn
www.biddles.co.uk

Contents

About the editors

Roger Burridge is Director of the UK Centre for Legal Education. He is also Director of Warwick Law School's Legal Proceedings Training, which provides investigative and prosecution training for the Health and Safety Executive, and teaches Law in Practice and Legal Action and Social Justice as part of Warwick's postgraduate Law in Development programme. His research interests are in legal education (particularly clinical legal education), law and community action and the role and practices of lawyers, with a particular interest in advocacy. Previously Roger practised as a barrister in chambers in London and in Newham Rights Centre, a community law centre.

Dr Karen Hinett is Education Developer at the UK Centre for Legal Education. She is responsible for the events programme, supporting legal education networks and the Project Development Fund. Karen is also responsible for the evaluation of the Centre, and is a member of the LTSN Steering Committee for Evaluation. Karen has published a number of articles related to learning and teaching in higher education including assessment, emotion and learning and failure. Previously Karen worked as the Assistant Project Manager of an FDTL project looking at the use of Self and Peer Assessment in Professional and Higher Education (Saphe) focusing on law and social work, based at the University of Bristol.

Abdul Paliwala is Professor of Law at the University of Warwick. He is the C&IT Director at the UK Centre for Legal Education and Director of the Law Courseware Consortium, which produces the Iolis courseware for the UK legal education community, and of the Electronic Law Journals project, which publishes *JILT* (the *Journal of Information Law and Technology*) and *LGD* (*the Journal of Law, Social Justice and Global Development*). Abdul is a founder member of the British and Irish Law, Education and Technology Association and is responsible for the BILETA secretariat. Previously Abdul taught at the Universities of Papua New Guinea (where he was Head of Department and Dean of Faculty), Dar-es-Salaam and the Queen's University of Belfast.

Tracey Varnava is Coordinator of the UK Centre for Legal Education. Tracey is the editor of *Directions in Legal Education*, the newsletter of the UKCLE, and also edits the Government and Education News section of *The Law Teacher*. To date, she has been involved in commissioning and editing six learning and teaching publications funded by the NCLE and the UKCLE and has co-authored (with Paul Greatrix) the UKCLE *Guide to QAA subject review for law teachers*. In her spare time she studies for a PhD in Educational Research at Lancaster University. Previously Tracey was employed as the Coordinator of the National Centre for Legal Education and as a Lecturer in Law at the University of Leicester.

About the specialist contributors

Alison Bone is a principal lecturer at the University of Brighton where she is head of the law subject group. Alison has published widely and undertakes training and consultancy activity in the field of management development and employment law. A former Chair of the Association of Law Teachers, she is currently the Honorary Secretary. She is a member of the Governing Body of the University of Brighton, the ILT and of the CIPD. She was educated at the universities of London, Leeds and Warwick.

Linda Byles is a Senior Lecturer at Bournemouth University. She works in staff and educational development and is year one tutor for the University's MA in Professional Development (Post Compulsory Education). She has a background in student skills development, in particular supporting student capability. She has contributed to the development of the learning and teaching resource *The Intellectual Property Micromodule* for the UK Patent Office. Her current research interests include the disciplinary differences in approaches to teaching and examining ways staff can be assisted in reflecting on learning and assessment strategies for their students.

Nigel Duncan is a Principal Lecturer at the Inns of Court School of Law within the Institute of Law, City University. He formerly taught on undergraduate courses at South Bank Polytechnic, where he introduced the country's first Law Access course and developed experiential learning methods. He is editor of *The Law Teacher*, a past Chair of the Association of Law Teachers, a founder member of the Clinical Legal Education Organisation, the Practice, Profession and Ethics subject section of the Society of Public Teachers of Law and the Global Alliance for Justice Education and is a member of the Advisory Board of the UK Centre for Legal Education. He is currently researching lawyers' and law students' perceptions of their values.

Dr Julie Macfarlane is a tenured half-time Full Professor at the Faculty of Law of the University of Windsor (on leave). During 2001/2002, she is Visiting Professor at Osgoode Hall Law School, Toronto, where she is heading up a new research initiative on dispute resolution and is Co-Director of the Masters in Law (ADR) Program. Dr Macfarlane devotes the other half of her time to her consulting practice, which offers conflict resolution service, training, facilitation and systems design for a range of public and private sector clients. Dr Macfarlane is the editor of *Dispute Resolution: Readings and Case Studies* (Emond Montgomery, 1999) a student text used widely in ADR courses in Canadian law schools. She is also the editor of *Rethinking Disputes: the Mediation Alternative* (Emond Montgomery, 1997), as well as numerous periodical articles on dispute resolution and mediation.

Dr Paul Maharg is Senior Lecturer in Law at the University of Strathclyde and Co-Director of Legal Practice courses in the Glasgow Graduate School of Law, University of Strathclyde. Paul has acted as Scottish Coordinator at the UK Centre for Legal Education, is an Executive Member of the British and Irish Legal Education Technology Association (BILETA), and of the Legal Education Technology Association. He is also a member of the Education and Training Committee, Law Society of Scotland. He has published in fields of legal education, educational technology, jurisprudence, legal critique and law and literature.

Ruth Soetendorp teaches intellectual property law and management to lawyers and non-lawyers at Bournemouth University, where she is Joint Director of the Centre for Intellectual Property Policy and Management. Her teaching includes short courses to IP Managers in UK universities and research councils, and to IP professionals in Eastern Europe, as part of the European Commission's Regional Industrial Property Programme. Her outputs include a learning and teaching resource, *The Intellectual Property Micromodule*, developed for the UK Patent Office, and a software-based interactive introduction to IP developed for a major UK public limited company. Ruth authors the IP chapter of Gee's *Company Secretary Fact Book*, and is the European Correspondent of *Intellectual Property Forum*, the journal of the Australian and New Zealand Society of IP Lawyers. She was awarded an ILT National Teaching Fellowship in 2001.

Andrew Williams is a lecturer in law at the University of Warwick. He teaches a series of courses there on Law in Practice and is also engaged in the research and delivery of human rights outreach programmes in India, Africa and South East Asia. He is an experienced solicitor and continues to work within the Law Centre and human rights movements both in the UK and internationally. He is currently a trustee/director of Coventry Law Centre and is a founding member of Peacerights. He has also published in the field of human rights law with particular emphasis on the activities of the European Union.

Acknowledgements

Many more people have been involved in the writing of this book than its editors and authors. A wide range of colleagues, to whom we are indebted, have read and commented upon individual chapters. Students helped enormously by responding, commenting, engaging or criticizing our efforts as teachers, from which many of our reflections have derived; we have all learnt from their learning. Anonymous reviewers of an early draft of the book gave invaluable guidance; we hope that this final version does justice to the points that they raised and confirms their faith in our ability to produce a useful and thought-provoking contribution to the progress of legal education. The editors and various authors have also benefited from advice from each other. Tracey Varnava and Karen Hinett contributed above and beyond the call of the other editors by chasing and generally coordinating the rest of us. We are greatly indebted to their industry and organization. The efforts of other colleagues have indirectly contributed to the book. The editors particularly appreciate the support of Ann Priestley and Hansa Surti from the UKCLE and Lisa Mann from Warwick Law School. Finally, the editors and authors all wish to acknowledge their families, partners and pets who have stayed with them during the book's preparation.

Forewords

I am delighted to see this latest volume in the Effective Learning and Teaching series in print. The editors are to be congratulated on the immense amount of hard work they have invested in putting together this important contribution to the literature on learning and teaching in law. Teaching law is a complex task and I am sure that readers will find much useful information and advice in this book, as well as useful contact information and references to further reading. I am particularly happy to see a high level of involvement of the LTSN subject centre for law in shaping this volume, since it is imperative that the ILT and subject centres collaborate and provide a 'joined up' approach to supporting staff working in teaching and the support of learning.

The ILT is now at an important stage in its development, with more than 10,000 members as we go to press, 112 programmes in higher education teaching and learning accredited by the ILT and a full programme of publications, activities and events on offer. Now with members in the majority on our governing Council, active on all our committees and working parties and getting involved in running our members' forums and other events, members are increasingly taking charge of shaping and directing the policy and direction of the organisation.

This book has a part to play in the ILT's mission to enhance the status of teaching, improve the experience of learning and support innovation in higher education. I commend it to you, whether you are an ILT member or not and welcome the contribution it makes to the higher education context.

Sally Brown
Director of Membership Services
Institute for Learning and Teaching

We have witnessed considerable progress for change in legal education over the last five years or so. The Lord Chancellor's Advisory Committee's First Report on Legal Education and Training (1996), after several years of deliberation by the committee, came to the conclusion that we should seek to maintain the law degree as a source of liberal education.

This conclusion did not necessarily assuage the concerns of the Professional Bodies and there have been, and continue to be, protracted discussions on the content of a qualifying law degree. Add to this the Lord Chancellor's Department's apparent *volte-face* in 2000, with regard to the concept of law as liberal education and its brief flirtation with the idea of requiring law degrees to contain a practical element, and the tensions surrounding the delivery of law as a discipline become obvious.

In addition, along with the rest of our colleagues in HE, we have had to wrestle with the intricacies of Subject Benchmarks, Programme Specifications and Learning Outcomes etc. We are also taking up the exciting challenges presented through the potential to deliver to new audiences of students via computer and information technology.

Given all these drivers, this book is a most welcome addition to the ILT/Kogan Page stable. It will be of immense assistance to both new and experienced teachers of law and is destined to become a key reference work for all of us in legal education.

Professor Richard W Painter
Dean of Staffordshire University Law School
Chair of the UKCLE Advisory Board
Secretary/Treasurer of Committee of Heads of University Law Schools

Preface

This book has been written as part of the series of publications commissioned by the Institute for Learning and Teaching and Kogan Page on effective learning and teaching across disciplines in higher education. The editors are all members of staff at the UK Centre for Legal Education (UKCLE), the subject centre for law funded through the Teaching Quality Enhancement Fund. The UKCLE supports a range of activities and resources designed to promote discussion, review and innovation in legal education. This book is a contribution to that enterprise and is written with the UK law teacher in mind in the belief that the future success of legal education lies with individual law teachers more than their institutions. It is the practices and ideas of the law teacher that shape how and what students will learn, although their role can only be effective if they are provided with the support, resources and rewards that are commensurate with the task.

The book addresses teachers in 'old' and 'new' universities and considers the particular challenges facing those who teach law to students for whom the subject is only a subsidiary part of their studies. While there are no chapters specifically on postgraduate law teaching (other than on the vocational courses), Further Education and schools, the editors hope that anybody involved with the teaching or learning of law will find something provocative, useful or enlightening amongst these pages.

Aims of the book

The book's primary aim is to promote an approach to legal education that is founded on the development and recognition of the law teacher as a professional educator. This professionalism, it is argued, encompasses a commitment to teaching and the support of learning evidenced by the approach taken to assessment, the design and planning of learning activities and the provision of suitable learning environments.

Underpinning this professional practice is the adoption of a reflective and developmental approach to teaching. Thus the chapters that follow suggest a professional identity for law teachers, which observes the tenets of a reflective practice that we often urge upon our students. If at present our roles are largely determined by the expert knowledge of law that we profess, the authors of this book urge the development of a complementary knowledge and expert practice in the ways of teaching law and the knowledge of learning.

The book also aims to explore ideas and approaches that transcend arguments about the content and delivery of the curriculum. It focuses upon the process and culture of learning what law is and how it works. It sees the primary objective of legal education as a means of equipping students with the intellectual and practical wherewithal to progress in whatever role they wish to fulfil. Student experiences are therefore a central concern of this book although we will be (pleasantly) surprised if they comprise a significant portion of its readership.

What is in the book?

The topics are inevitably selective, but the contributions cover the main issues confronting UK legal education and include some discrete areas of legal teaching practice. Chapter 1 explains the context of UK legal education and analyses the factors influencing its recent development, specifically the effect of higher education policy, the professions, and the law schools themselves. These change agents have often had competing agendas, which have tended to result in disagreement about the direction and purpose of legal education. Tracey Varnava and Roger Burridge suggest that a less divisive way forward is to encourage law teachers to assert and develop their own identity and expertise as professional educators to enable the evolution of legal education founded upon scholarship and expert practices.

The way that students learn law and how it operates lies at the centre of debates about the curriculum. In place of haggling over the content of the law degree or vocational programmes, Chapter 2 advocates the consideration of method as a determinant of message. Conventional approaches to law teaching conceive of the enterprise as essentially a cognitive task. Students learn rules, how to apply them and hence the process by which law can solve problems. The undergraduate programme has as its core aspiration the assimilation of a prescribed quantity of rules and the accomplishment of an 'expert' way of applying legal principle and established precedent or statute to alternative social circumstances. Roger Burridge argues such a process is committed to failure in that the intellect alone is unable to explain how law and lawyers work. It reviews the development of active learning in law, and promotes experiential learning in the curriculum as the only means to inculcate a problem-solving methodology and ethical sensitivity amongst those who study law, at any stage, and regardless of whether they will practice law or not. The author argues that understanding how law works and its propensity or otherwise to effectively pursue justice values or promote a human rights discourse is inextricably linked to the way law is encountered by students.

Modern education research has exposed the importance of evaluation and feedback. Without guidance, commentary, suggestions, critique or praise from others, our efforts at self-reflection lack any external reference. Chapter 3 explores the importance of assessment strategies and the utilisation of the variety of approaches suited to the complexity of programme objectives and their learning outcomes. Karen Hinett and Alison Bone address the strengths and importance of a comprehensive approach to student feedback to support learning. They outline the value of self- and peer assessment and provide valuable examples of how good practices can be implemented. The chapter includes guidance on how to cope with plagiarism and other obstacles to successful assessment.

The comprehensive exploration of the way we teach and assess and students learn is given a new dimension by information and communication technologies (ICT). In Chapter 4, Paul Maharg and Abdul Paliwala explore the potential of electronic learning resources and suggest that their value depends on the pedagogic context within which they are used. The historic dependence of students upon the stored knowledge of tutors and their programmed pathways for navigating the syllabus can be replaced by the relative freedom of resource-based learning, the outcome of which is independent student learning. In these circumstances, electronic learning systems, which support structured group work as well as negotiation, provide exciting possibilities for student learning. Their radical potential is explained through experiences of a personal injuries project at the University of Strathclyde and an electronic negotiation class between students at the EDHEC Business School in France and the Warwick Law School.

In Chapter 5, Nigel Duncan engages the challenge of introducing ethical responsibility into a vocational programme. He describes ways of introducing ethical issues into a vocational course that exposes the individual significance of codes as well as the difficulties of interpretation and practical challenges that can arise. In doing so, he draws upon examples from courses at the Inns of Court School of Law. The objective is to embed ethical concerns within the course as a whole, without reducing the topic to a somewhat sterile application of Frank's equation: Rule $\times$ Facts = Decision. The author argues that values, whether professional or individual, can only be successfully approached through course design and the learning opportunities created. Chapter 5 is especially valuable for the examples that accompany Duncan's commentary.

The significance of human rights teaching extends far beyond its incorporation in the undergraduate curriculum following the revised Joint Statement on the Qualifying Law Degree by the Bar and Law Society in 1999. It is arguably the most significant legal and constitutional development in the United Kingdom in the last century. In Chapter 6, Andrew Williams maintains the theme of the indivisibility of substance and process in his account of observing the principles of human rights when teaching the subject. He suggests that human rights is more than a framework for apportioning responsibility or restraining the oppressive exercise or power. Whilst it may be a discrete topic or a pervasive value system in the curriculum, it also requires a rethinking of our approach to the teaching of law and the experiences of students in the education system. His proposals for a pedagogy that reflects a human rights ethos are illustrated in his account of a course that he teaches at Warwick University.

The vast majority of writing about legal education focuses upon its efficacy or otherwise as a nursery for legal practitioners. Law is now taught to students with a wide variety of career aspiration (including those without any specific career), as well as an increasing number of undergraduates who wish to study it as an adjunct to their main subject. In Chapter 7, Linda Byles and Ruth Soetendorp address learning and teaching for those whose main interest and discipline is not law. As the authors explain, the expectations, abilities and purposes of such students are very different from those who study law as a single or even mixed honours programme. Their chapter provides a firm foundation and valuable examples for law teachers who are involved in teaching law as a subsidiary subject.

Julie Macfarlane, in Chapter 8, takes on an even more ambitious project. Previous contributors suggest significant reforms but confine their attention to specific areas of the curriculum, special needs of students or approaches to a new challenge. Chapter 8 considers the effect that the professional fixation with adversarial dispute resolution holds for legal education. Macfarlane bases her critique of traditional legal education on her experiences in teaching mediation in Ontario. This contribution reminds us that not only is learning moulded by content but that curriculum and professional culture is founded on fixed and possibly flawed beliefs and practices inherited from bygone communities. For all its imagination, however, it deals with the real world and existing experiences of Canadian commercial law practice.

In the final chapter, Abdul Paliwala interconnects changes in relationships between students, academics and institutions; in physical and virtual learning spaces and props; in learning times and in ideologies of learning with wider environmental factors such as commodification, globalization and digitisation. In a context in which changes can be either constructive or destructive of educational values, he considers ways in which creative teaching/learning strategies can protect and promote values in legal education. Law academics have a crucial role in the mediation of change in safeguarding the values of academic responsibility and freedom, in promoting student development and liberation and in supporting ethical values in the legal system. Relying on the issues raised in the chapter as well as in previous chapters in the book, he suggests guidelines to academics involved in the negotiation of change.

The authors hope you appreciate all or some of their contemplation and commentary, or at least are moved to object. They make the usual admissions of responsibility and, where appropriate, acknowledgements of support. If a few readers are provoked to experiment with the suggestions proposed, the book will have served some purpose. If, upon reflection, some readers develop their own responses and solutions to their teaching and their students' learning, it will be a more significant success.

1

Revising legal education

Tracey Varnava and Roger Burridge

Introduction

There are certain enduring features of the landscape inhabited by legal education in the United Kingdom that are commonly reprised in writings on the subject. Often presented in oppositional terms, the features described generally include: academic/vocational; new/old university; teaching/research; skills/knowledge; City/citizen; Bar/Law Society and so on. Whilst analysis of sources of tension is useful to highlight trends and challenge positions, it suffers from a tendency to oversimplification and may obscure, rather than illuminate, alternative strategies. Not faint-hearted, the purpose of this book is to move beyond the conflict between the disparate agendas of those with an interest in the form and content of the law degree, to sketch fresh identities for law teachers. This chapter will set out to meet this objective by revising legal education: both by reassessing the arguments proposed by the main protagonists and by proposing new ambitions for law teachers in the 21st century.

The leading contenders for influence over legal education development are the legal professions, the law schools and Higher Education theorists and policy-makers. Despite the claims of some of their representatives, it is important to recognise at the outset that there is no unanimously supported agenda attributable to these bodies. The professions are riven by the competing needs of the high street and the City, barristers and solicitors and the struggle for market share and graduate supply. The law schools are aligned largely according to their ability to attract the best quality entrants; the recruitment potential of their graduates amongst leading City firms; and the vagaries of HE funding that ensure the ruins of the binary divide stay visible years after the formal wall has been demolished.

Higher Education policy is produced amid struggles between institution and state over audit, accountability and sustainable funding. The purpose and function of universities is gradually being reshaped, prompting questions and anxieties about the status and role of the individual academic. It is not the purpose here to attempt to re-present the respective positions of these different factions. Not only would this merely serve to retread old ground but it would also no doubt provoke further dispute about the accuracy of any description offered. We seek instead to draw, from the debate core issues that need to be addressed if progress is to be made towards building a consensus about the future development of legal education. We advocate a more proactive and influential role for the law teacher as a professional exponent of effective learning and teaching practice. Our assessment of what are the core issues and our depiction of the development of the role of the law teacher are, of course, also subject to challenge. However, it is based on our experience of working with law teachers and listening to their perspectives on the current and future shape of legal education.

In Section 1 we look at the context within which any attempt to reformulate the debate about the future direction of legal education must be set. We examine in particular the influence of Higher Education policy, the legal professions, and the law school. We extract what we see as the key issues to be addressed if progress is to be made beyond the familiar points of contention between these various stakeholders in legal education. The combination of these influences creates peculiar challenges for legal education and, we would suggest, unique opportunities for responding to current trends and developing needs. Section 2 examines how law schools are currently responding to these issues and suggests the adoption of fresh perspectives to enable new responses to old problems. Section 3 explores the role of the law teacher as a reflective professional and argues that the development of this identity is central to asserting a leading, rather than subordinate, role in the future of legal education.

Section 1
Setting the context

Higher Education policy

The past decade has witnessed major upheaval in the Higher Education system, characterised by a number of initiatives that seek to remodel universities for new and more diverse purposes. We concentrate here on the effects of revisions that have particular significance for the learning and teaching of law since they bring with them the potential for development beyond the bounds of the traditional law degree.

Access to Higher Education

By 2010, the government aims to enable 50 per cent of young people to benefit from Higher Education. Law remains popular with those applying to study at university. It is notable, however, that despite attempts to benchmark degrees and reassure employers, parents and students that all honours degrees in law are equal, the reality within the current funding climate is destined to be different. Students are well aware that a second class degree from one of the élite universities is more marketable than the equivalent or better from a new university. The legal professions are known to prefer to recruit from the 'old' university sector. In this sense, therefore, students do not have a wider choice than previously: there are just more students vying for places in the 'best' law schools.

The irony of the application of this 'fitness for the professions' criterion is not lost on those who teach law in newer universities. It is they on the whole who are most proactive in equipping their students with vocational skills and it is they who are more interested in professional legal education, both by providing the lucrative LPC and BVC and being more ready to undertake research in the field (Leighton, 1998). Since the newer universities tend to be more successful at recruiting from educationally and otherwise disadvantaged sections of society, the professions' insistence on seeking their entrants primarily from the older, established law schools has grave implications for the administration of justice.

If we are to take these implications seriously and genuinely seek to widen access, not only to Higher Education but also to the legal professions, a radical change in attitude is called for. Policy-makers need to add weight to their professed commitment to widening access by providing recognition, through additional funding, to those universities that recruit students from less privileged backgrounds. The status and contribution of these institutions needs to be promoted. In an increasingly diverse system, there should be room for institutions that fulfil different needs and interests with each being recognised for the value added by their endeavours. The recruitment policies of the legal professions may be harder to influence through direct intervention but it is clear that the legitimacy and relevance of the law is compromised without adherence by the professions to principles of fairness and equality.

The expansion in the proportion of students entering Higher Education has had other effects in terms of the disorientation of the curriculum, as programmes and courses are adjusted to appeal to a wider range of interests and experience. The widespread adoption of a modular system has had a tendency to dislocate the student's experience of the degree programme, undermining the holistic approach to learning that 'seeks to identify and preserve the overall framework and structure of knowledge' (Webb, 1996: 38. See also Marton, 1988 and below). If law schools ever sought to provide a coherent undergraduate curriculum in accordance with their own rather than the professions' concept of core content, such an objective is less attainable in a modular world than previously. This fracturing of the degree programme also raises concerns about the depth of knowledge that can be fostered and the piecemeal and disconnected understanding that results. The increase in assessment tasks exacerbates this problem and promotes a surface, and instrumental approach to learning (see Chapter 3).

However, despite these concerns, modularization can be the vehicle for positive progress through the redesign of the curriculum and the increase in choice available to the individual student. The change to a modular system should prompt a complete review of the curriculum to enable students to both choose a route to suit their individual interests and also to graduate with a degree that continues to reflect achievement in areas of knowledge that are fundamental to the understanding of law. This is no easy task and demands that law teachers discuss and plan the curriculum and have a shared idea of what they value as the fundamentals of a law degree. Chapter 3 describes this process in relation to assessment and suggests the use of learning matrices to ensure coverage of essential elements of the degree. Another positive outcome of the competition resultant upon the drive for more students and more funding has been the expansion of the range of options offered by law schools, providing more mixed degrees and generally developing more opportunities for law teaching.

RAE and subject review

Whilst the more intrusive aspects of subject review have been modified and a new approach is contemplated, the previous approaches had exerted considerable pressure for documenting and tracking learning and teaching procedures. The future form of the Research Assessment Exercise is also uncertain but efforts to evaluate the research value of university departments are likely to continue in some form. The Law panel significantly revised their criteria for RAE to include legal education scholarship following consultation with their colleagues. It may take much more than acknowledgement by the RAE panel of the possibility that learning and teaching are capable of becoming the object of research and scholarship to effect a cultural shift in career focus amongst teachers and law schools. The panel's acknowledgement is nonetheless a signal to university administrations that teaching and learning development can be compatible with research prowess.

Published reflection within the legal education community on teaching quality evaluation has been critical of the tendency towards a more prescriptive curriculum. According to some writers, subject review in particular, and HE audit in general, is antithetical to the aspirations of liberal intellectual enquiry and undergraduate learning. Specifically, the drive to equip graduates with knowledge and competencies for employment is seen as no part of the purpose of Higher Education (see, for example, Bradney, 2001). These sentiments will find some support amongst colleagues, as much for the resentment that teachers may feel for the cumulative chores involved in quality assurance and the audit trail. Against this, the positive fallout from subject review has included attention to learning outcomes, clear articulation of degree and module programmes and a general focus on the process of learning that many would argue was long overdue.

Graduate skills and abilities

The creation, on 8 June 2001, of the Department for Education and Skills under-lines the government's commitment to placing skills firmly within the education brief. Skills are variously preceded with words such as 'key', 'core' and 'transferable' and the lists of the skills that these terms encompass vary depending on who has put them together. For our purposes here, the law benchmark statement, as the most recent consideration of the kinds of skills that may properly be found within the law graduate's armoury, will be relied upon.

The law benchmark statement identifies what may be termed 'abilities' as well as skills that are labelled as 'key'. The abilities include: application and problem solving; sources and research; analysis, synthesis, critical judgement and evaluation; autonomy and the ability to learn. The last of these is described as '… perhaps the key feature of graduateness' (QAA, 2000: 7). The key skills set out in the benchmark statement include: communication and literacy; numeracy; infor-mation technology; teamworking. Some commentators have questioned the value of skills teaching and suspect that it both narrows the focus of academic inquiry as well as diverting it from its proper mission; the pursuit of knowledge in its own right (see for example, Bradney, 1992, 1995; Toddington, 1995).

Despite criticism from some quarters, the teaching of skills in the under-graduate curriculum has a fairly robust history (Gold et al, 1989; Webb and Maughan eds, 1996). The ACLEC report (1996) confirmed the role for skills development in the undergraduate curriculum:

[a] liberal and humane legal education… implies that students are engaged in active rather than passive learning, and are enabled to develop intellectually by means of significant study *in depth* of issues and problems… and that the

teaching of appropriate and defined skills is undertaken in a way which combines practical knowledge with theoretical understanding

(ACLEC, 1996: 23. Emphasis in the original.)

Indeed, many believe that law as a discipline is uniquely suited to the development of skills, however defined. Being able to 'think like a lawyer' is considered one of the main aims of undergraduate study both by those who espouse the liberal education ideal and by those who see it as the first step on the road to a career in law. However, the skills that 'thinking like a lawyer' encompasses (analysis, synthesis, reasoning, communication and problem solving) are not, in fact, uniquely promoted within law but are emblematic of Higher Education more generally (see, for example, Twining, 1994: 181).

Employability

The report of the National Committee of Inquiry into Higher Education (the Dearing Report, 1997) clearly recognised the role of Higher Education in the development of people, society and the economy. The value of a university education is now more clearly judged by how employable graduates are, rather than some less defined appreciation of the general good of Higher Education. In legal education there have been ongoing debates between the academy and the professions about the form and content of the undergraduate degree as a preparation for a professional career in law. The concentration in Higher Education policy, too, on the appropriate outcomes of a degree programme, has required some further consideration of the role of the various stages of legal education in contributing to the acquisition of the knowledge and skills required for the practice of law. We turn now, therefore, to a consideration of the influence of the legal professions on the form and content of legal education, particularly at the undergraduate stage.

Influence of the legal professions

It is clear that since the Dearing Report the face of Higher Education is firmly set in the vocational direction. During the 1990s the legal professions promoted competence and lawyer performance in place of programmes that had required the assimilation of additional knowledge of procedures (Boon, 1998). They devolved responsibility for the delivery of these programmes to accredited providers, many of whom were the law schools of the newer universities. These moves focused professional training on the competent accomplishment of discrete legal tasks. In doing so they tended to deprive the vocational stage of reflective practice and theoretical enquiry (Nathanson, 1996). By taking on the role of practical lawyering, the new programmes also obviated any interest for legal practice in the academic stage. As a result, the significance of the law degree has arguably diminished so far as the training of professional lawyers is concerned. Twining observes that in comparison with other countries, law schools in the United Kingdom are endowed with a considerable amount of academic autonomy since they play a relatively limited role in the production of professional lawyers (Twining, 1994: 37). In their search for 'quality' graduates from established universities, the professions have also placed less store by the possession of a law degree and have instead sought non-law graduates from the same narrow band of universities (Hodgson and Bermingham, 2001).

Despite this, the professions are still keen to regulate the content of the law degree and the Joint Statement on Qualifying Law Degrees specifies seven core subjects that must be studied at the undergraduate stage if the degree is to exempt the holder from further study before joining one of the professional training courses. The professions are also keen to ensure that the standard of law degrees is maintained. The recent announcement by the QAA that subject review was to be reformed and the degree of external scrutiny would be significantly reduced resulted in the Bar suggesting that, if HE was not exerting sufficient regulation of quality in the professions' view, then the professions might themselves feel obliged to take on a greater regulatory role (Bastin, 2001).

The Bar's renewed concern about the quality of the undergraduate degree is echoed in the Law Society's review of training for solicitors. In response to the demands of globalization and new technology, a new competency-based framework of all stages of legal education has been advocated (Law Society, 2001: 4–5). The review is prompted by 'widespread concern amongst the profession that, for whatever reason, the pre-admission training process, taken as a whole, is insufficiently rigorous and produces a lower standard of legal knowledge and analysis than was previously the case' (2001: 2). Leaving aside the empirical evidence for such a statement, it underlines in its singling out of legal knowledge and analysis as a cause for concern, the felt inadequacy of undergraduate law programmes. Such specific inadequacies as are identified in the review relate to coverage and the suggestion that either new areas (institutions of the English Legal System; Company or Law of Business Organisations) be included in the Joint Statement; or that areas like Contract be given more prominence and that more detail be required for fundamental principles (Law Society 2001: 8–9).

Unusually for a review that purports to be based upon competencies, discussion of the undergraduate stage seems to concentrate upon knowledge (and its accompanying skill – legal research) as the only significant competence to be achieved. Benchmarking is largely ignored, other than in the aside that the Joint Statement states that students should 'be above the minimum level of performance that they [the benchmarks] might specify' (Law Society, 2001: 22).

The law school

Despite the fact that law has been studied at university since the 12th century, the law school as we know it today is generally accepted to be a post World War II phenomenon. All previous attempts to institutionalize the study of law had not been very successful. As Twining describes '[o]ne of the recurrent themes that runs through debates and histories of legal education... is the low prestige of law schools and the low status of academic lawyers, both within the university and in the eyes of the profession' (Twining, 1994: 25). Until the 19th century, law was seen primarily as a vocation, not a subject for academic study. No value was accorded to studying law divorced from its practice. Consequently, the professions dominated legal training with the emphasis on an apprenticeship approach to learning the law. Thus, academic lawyers have not taken their place by right in the academy; they have had to fight for it.

In the absence of a clear indigenous professional identity, law schools have looked elsewhere for role models. Most commonly, progressive law teachers look either towards other jurisdictions, notably the United States or Australia, or other disciplines, particularly medicine. Alternative role models provide useful insights into one's own character, but unsuitable prototypes for imitation. For example, US legal education differs fundamentally from the UK model – it is postgraduate and entirely vocationally oriented. For a jurisdiction whose law students are all embarked upon a legal career, the US system offers a less thorough foundation in the competencies of legal practices than do the two UK professional courses. On the other hand, the US experience has longer concentrated on both legal pedagogy and the characteristics of professional work. Langdell and the realists were concerned both about the methods by which legal knowledge was assimilated and the importance of a curriculum that went beyond the narrow study of appellate court decisions and statutory interpretation.

The clinical movement in the final quarter of the last century was an important development in legal education. The fusion of education objectives and legal services for the poor has initiated a rich vein of pedagogical legal scholarship as well as a significant volume of clients whose legal problems have been dealt with by a growing multitude of law students (see Chapter 2). The clinical movement was influenced in part by borrowing experiences from the education of the medical profession. The concept of doctors' hospital rounds accompanied by medical students learning from the live symptoms that patients presented, highlighted the poverty of a legal education that involved months or, in the United Kingdom, years of textual study before the theories and advice were related to a client. The medical model emphasises the need for considering the client or community as the recipient of legal service. In the United States, this has developed into a concept of therapeutic jurisprudence. Medical education also shares with law a pedagogical environment with untapped experiential and problem-based learning potential, performance assessment challenges and the need for a coherent programme for continuing professional development. Whilst there is much scope for interdisciplinary research and comparative review, law has its distinctive characteristics that defy too close a comparison. Again, the connections with professional competence are more marked in medical schools than law.

While these influences have played their part in the development of the law school in the United Kingdom, it is evident that their effects have not been general or consistent across all law schools, tending to be mediated by the particular enthusiasms and interests of individual law teachers. The continuing lack of consensus about the role and function of the law school is evidenced by periodic manifestations of the ongoing debate about 'what law schools are for' (see, for example, Birks, 1996). The following section suggests that while a consensus that leads to standardization and lack of innovation is not to be desired, it is nevertheless valuable to seek a response to changes being wrought in Higher Education that seeks to preserve certain core understandings of the value of legal education.

Section 2
Responding to change

Leaders of law schools could be forgiven for being preoccupied with the management of resources, implementation of education reforms and the sheer bulk of administrative tasks that are needed to maintain the teaching programme. These are responsibilities faced by all heads of department. However, in at least two respects, law schools have opportunities to take the initiative and shape their own distinctive futures. They may respond to the various appeals for curriculum reform by providing programmes that match the diverse interests of students, meet professional demands and provide an alternative vision of studying law at HE level and beyond. They may also recognise the benefits of the law degree as an opportunity to understand the essential elements of a system that purports to address major questions of governance and development. The law degree has arguably more claim than most other disciplines as a programme that seeks to explain and respond to the practical exercise of state authority and to provide a value system for the mediation of individual and collective interests.

Searching for purpose and designing a programme response

In the face of frequent and often unwarranted criticism from many quarters, law schools have not yet succeeded in articulating arguments capable of fulfilling their agenda and addressing the disparate needs of other interests. So contradictory are some of the criticisms that cogent response is difficult. Hence the oft-repeated charge that undergraduate programmes do not 'teach enough law' is accompanied by claims that students who have studied it for only 10 months on the Common Professional Examination or Post Graduate Diploma in Law are better equipped for practice. When this is pointed out, the preference for the conversion course students is justified by a notion of more recent learning of core concepts. As newer law schools produce more graduates with good degrees, so employers increasingly look to other programmes in the older universities for their recruits. As employers demand more rigour in legal research and problem-solving skills, so HE policy adopts mass learning approaches. As HE policy urges more interactive methods throughout universities, so the professions argue for more coverage, leaving even less time in the curriculum for experiential and problem-based approaches.

Law schools are responding to the increased demand for legal knowledge by providing more 'service' teaching for other disciplines as well as introducing more options to meet the increased number of professional specialisms and the creation of more law jobs. The burgeoning of global commerce and regulation and the consequent specialisation of legal and financial services has produced a new list of topics for undergraduate and postgraduate study – intellectual property, securities, pensions, mergers and takeovers, bankruptcy, as well as all the regulatory and service enterprises that are necessary to facilitate this global traffic, such as shipping, insurance and the management of communication systems. This has recently been fuelled by renewed interest in public law areas such as environment, refugee and asylum law and international interest in human rights. Postgraduate courses have also blossomed. However, diversity is not just reflected in the curriculum; in common with other university subjects, law must also now cater for an increasingly varied student body with a range of backgrounds and qualifications. For some law schools, international students constitute a significant number of those registered on the programme as well as contributing a substantial proportion of income.

Despite the variety reflected in both the expansion of the law curriculum and the student body, however, it is notable that the learning and teaching response appears to remain fairly standard. With the exception of the progress being made with new technologies, it seems from the Harris and Jones surveys that traditional teaching methods still dominate in law schools (see Harris and Jones, 1996 and the discussion of assessment methods in Chapter 3). Nevertheless, there have been a number of initiatives to encourage greater attention to the theory and practice of legal education in recent years. These enterprises have produced a succession of specialist or discipline-based projects, as well as a bewildering array of acronyms (see explanatory notes on page 22). Perhaps the most significant programme in recent HE development was the Computers in Teaching Initiative (CTI). For law, this led to the establishment of the Law Technology Centre and Law Courseware Consortium. As well as coordinating and promoting law school ICT activity, the LTC was instrumental in the successful development of the British and Irish Law, Education and Technology Association. Whilst 'computers have failed to deliver the kinds of changes to the law curriculum which were predicted by their most enthusiastic admirers' (Alldridge and Mumford, 1998: 117), the ICT revolution has massively changed the ways in which lawyers, legal academics and students communicate and the research methods that lawyers and scholars utilise.

Other programmes have sought to expand support for learning and teaching development whether or not based on the use of technological approaches. Launched in 1996, the Fund for the Development of Teaching and Learning (FDTL) sought to encourage discrete projects that addressed specific issues in HE, often relating to a single discipline or group of disciplines. One such project serving law and social work was the Self and Peer Assessment in Higher Education (Saphe) project at Bristol. In its three-year life span, Saphe drew the attention of law teachers to the potential of self- and peer assessment as tools for learning as much as evaluation and in doing so reminded law schools of the significance of assessment practices in general. FDTL funding also established the National Centre for Legal Education (NCLE), which between 1996 and 1999 coordinated learning and teaching events for law teachers, commissioned a series of generic and subject-based manuals and set up a Web site dedicated to promoting improvement in teaching practice. It also established, under the umbrella of the Learning in Law Initiative (LILI), a network of teaching enthusiasts and organised an annual conference for the deliberation and dissemination of new developments in law teaching. LILI, along with the Association of Law Teachers, the Society for Public Teachers of Law and the Socio Legal Studies Association, continues to support the development and analysis of legal education in the United Kingdom. Their efforts have been strengthened by the Learning and Teaching Support Network (LTSN), which is sustained by the funding bodies' Teaching Quality Enhancement Fund. Along with the Institute for Learning and Teaching (ILT), the LTSN directs its energies towards improving teaching in HE at institutional, discipline and individual levels. The UK Centre for Legal Education is one of 24 subject centres established by the LTSN. It provides a service to all UK law schools and promotes the development of teaching and learning in law through publications, events, a Web site (http://www.ukcle.ac.uk) and support for legal education research.

Thus there are local pockets of innovation, national support projects and, arising from both, nascent appreciation of the benefits of engaging with learning and teaching development as a basis for constructing an effective and educationally principled response to the changes that are demanded in Higher Education. The UK Centre for Legal Education is one, principal vehicle for all law teachers to contribute to an exchange of views, resources and experience. Other avenues are also available and, through dialogue and engagement with current issues and concerns, an informed perspective can be fostered and effective influence exercised to determine future directions. The ability to articulate and champion the existing and potential contribution of Higher Education, and specifically that of legal education, is essential to the development of a shared professional identity.

Serving society, the administration of justice and students

The appreciation or inculcation of values at its most basic rests in the notion that there is something inherently 'civilizing' in achieving understanding through knowledge and the elimination of ignorance. There is also widespread acceptance of a relationship between the methods by which learning occurs and the example that those methods pass on about the exercise of teacher power, the ownership of knowledge and the consideration of others who lack knowledge. Shils, for example, has argued that the recasting of the student as customer has had the effect of causing universities to respond to market forces and jeopardizing their proper role as institutions for the 'teaching of truths about serious and important things' (1984: 3). If this is so it represents a direct reversal of Dearing's aspirations for Higher Education reflected in his brief acknowledgement of the relationship between education and wider social values (Dearing, 1997). Others have explored these in greater detail, and the connections between learner autonomy, consultative democratic values, and non-authoritarian teaching styles are obvious (see Chapters 2 and 9). By contrast, however, the power of the university teacher over syllabus, method and assessment is often underplayed.

There is thus a sense in which 'massification' has more significance for the learning of law than other disciplines. The management of larger numbers of students with scarce resources may be inimical to some of the social objectives of law – the ideals of justice and empowerment. Autocratic and authoritarian tendencies are evident in the impersonal constraints of managing these large numbers. Values in legal education are explicit elsewhere in the law curriculum. Jurisprudence, legal philosophy and legal theory are subjects that invite enquiry and reflection into law's claims to prescribe just norms and provide a framework for the fair implementation of public and private force. Human rights discourse has brought a new impetus to our understanding of law's treatment of oppressive state behaviour and the adjudication of competing social interests (see Chapter 6).

A legal education that is student-centred should also be one that is concerned about the personal development of students. This is what Webb (1999) describes as '... the true liberal "outcome" of higher education: that it makes our students into better people... ' (1999: 253). The study of law, within a framework of Higher Education that itself values independence of mind, is ideally suited to the exploration of values and a critical examination of the way in which society is constructed and maintained. Nigel Duncan, in Chapter 5, describes how ethical dilemmas are presented to those on a BVC course. Undergraduate students, too, can be guided to consider the values that are being promulgated in the law that they study. An awareness of the law as a phenomenon that affects real people in real life is essential to a proper appreciation of law as a pervasive and determinant feature of our society. It is also a valuable mechanism for the development of students as critical and reflective participants in the learning process.

Since the 1990s in the United Kingdom there has been a burgeoning interest in legal ethics, in the sense of lawyer roles and behaviour and their regulation. (Economides, 1998; O'Dair, 2001; Webb, 1998a, b; Webb and Nicolson, 1999). Ethics is now required by the Bar to be taught pervasively as part of the BVC and the Law Society's review of training (Law Society, 2001) proposes ethics as a separate competency. The UK experience can be contrasted with the United States where lawyer ethics has long been a topic for scholarship. Its late arrival in UK legal education may have been prompted by a recent 'backlash against professional society' (Webb, 1998a: 134) but, as Webb also argues, the reforms 'were informed by a restricted model of competence, which emphasises substantive knowledge and only a limited range of skills... ' (1998b: 291).

Our thesis is that law schools are in the midst of significant reshaping of their legal, social, economic and institutional environment. These influences are unlikely to dissipate and the need is to adapt and control the future, rather than become subservient to it. Solutions at present are not being canvassed by either the law schools or the professions. In the past, development has been instigated by individual enthusiasm that attracts institutional support. There is the potential at large for creating a professional identity for law teachers and the adoption of an effective practice to accompany it. Fulfilment lies with the law teachers who draft the syllabus, organise the programmes, devise the learning methodologies, provide the opportunities and assess progress. The final section of this chapter therefore addresses the basis of such a professional identity, and the articulation of a practice and ethical foundation for law teachers.

Section 3
Promoting professional teachers

The preceding discussion has traced the many changes and tensions affecting the academic and vocational stages of legal education. Little attention has been paid so far to the implications for those who are charged with delivering change and dealing with the consequent pressures. Higher Education initiatives have engaged legal education at various points and the individual law teacher's role has changed perceptibly as a result of the various initiatives. Amongst the suspicions and beyond the additional administrative tasks are resources and opportunities for law teachers to improve both their own and their students' lot. The success of any search for a fresh identity is dependent upon law school staff being able to influence the changes that are being wrought upon them. To do so they need to fashion an image for their professional development that both represents the fulfilment of their collective aspirations and addresses the reasonable needs of their students, the professions and the ideals of justice education.

Some choices that law schools might make to facilitate a more focused and deliberate advance have been suggested in the many recent commentaries on legal education's future. Partington, at the beginning of the 1990s, pointed to the potential for law teachers but cautioned the need for vision and leadership:

> [T]here are substantial opportunities ahead for professional legal educators. It will, however, be for the leaders of this branch of the legal profession to offer a clear sense of vision as to what the future might be like, if they are to seize the opportunities that could lie ahead.
>
> (Partington, 1992: 174)

Partington's leaders have not so far emerged, although there have been a number of visions of the future offered (Alldridge and Mumford, 1998; Cownie, 1998; Twining, 1998; Webb, 1998a; Wilson, 1995; Paliwala, 2000). Part of the explanation of this lack of leadership has been the different experiences of older and newer universities extending to the make up of their professional associations (Partington, 1992; Leighton, 2001). The Committee of Heads of University Law Schools strives to provide a voice for law schools, but it has insufficient resources and support from its members to organise and articulate authoritative reports necessary to establish considered positions and produce a representative law school perspective (ignoring for the moment whether such a consensual position obtains for many issues).

The development of legal education in the United Kingdom is hindered by the absence of professional identity amongst law teachers and their ambivalence about whether they are a subset of the legal or HE teaching professions. Despite Partington's allusion above to professional legal educators as a 'branch of the legal profession', there is no contradiction in adopting a professional identity that reflects the teaching role as well as the discipline-defined one. Arguably, it is the failure to identify the key characteristics of the law teacher, the skills and knowledge that explain the expertise that they possess, that continues to undermine their position in the eyes of the professions, the funding councils and the Lord Chancellor's Department. At the heart of this lies their impotence as legal experts and their consequent marginalization. There are three aspects of professional identity that can provide the basis for collective and self-development and for promoting aspects of any job or occupation according to:

- the experiences, qualifications, knowledge, and skills it requires;
- the social functions it performs;
- the collective responsibilities that it bears.

We set out below the features that might comprise a professional identity for law teachers. It borrows aspects common to other occupations and the result is a composite character that nonetheless has a recognisable profile and could become a distinctive and distinguished variant of the reflective practitioner.

Characteristics of the professional law teacher

The salient features of the law teacher to be found in all sectors of their activity but particularly prominent in both undergraduate and vocational programmes are: core professional knowledge; specialist expert practices; legal scholarship.

Core professional knowledge

The knowledge that underpins law teaching combines both understanding of the contexts of law's influence and the processes of learning. The former is definitive of the branch of the legal education teaching profession and includes all that (often unarticulated) expert knowledge that most if not all law teachers display. This expertise arises from their past study, any resultant qualifications and the accumulated experience that has been the basis for their appointment. It is continuously built upon and expanded. It includes an understanding of law's methods, sources, systems, processes, institutions, hierarchies, boundaries, size, costs, history and social, economic and political context. In subject specialisms more detailed knowledge is expected – the application of legal rules to social realities, hard case appreciation, the direction of doctrinal development, research insights, internal dysfunctions, fitness for purpose, ineffectiveness and injustice as well as success and appreciation, and an evaluation of its social function and efficacy in broad terms. We would suggest this core knowledge exists at varying depths in law teachers already, irrespective of the sector in which they work.

At the outset of a legal career, knowledge in some areas may be only superficial but the relevance of such issues to an understanding of the discipline will inform future progress. We would also suggest that this underpinning knowledge of law's empire and territory should include familiarity with its workings, including its role in dispute processing, regulatory implementation and its utilisation in law jobs. The way law is practised and invoked is an integral context for appreciation and critique of its social function. It may need more emphasis in the under-graduate curriculum just as the vocational programmes, where the detailed proce-dures and practices of law are the main focus, may need more reflective and critical appreciation of the implications of those practices.

The second area of knowledge required by the professional law teacher is knowledge of pedagogical practice and theories of how students learn. Studies of the psychology of learning and theories of the most effective methods that teachers can adopt to present the best opportunity for learning and to evaluate any consequent improvement now fill many shelves (or should do) in all university libraries. Irrespective of the distorting propensities of the RAE to distract teachers in HE away from teaching practices as an object for reflection and development, for all but a few Research Fellows in a small minority of law schools, teaching remains a core activity of all academics.

This conceptualisation of core professional knowledge presents a break from previous attempts to prescribe the basis for the undergraduate or vocational programme. Whilst it suggests changes to the syllabus and teaching plans, it is more likely to be accomplished in the reform of teaching, learning and assessment than it is in content revision. Nor, as we hope to show below, does it represent as fundamental a shift as those content with present arrangements may argue.

Specialist expert practices

There is a large body of research in education that provides crucial insights for teachers into the way in which students learn. As professionals within Higher Education, law teachers need to acquaint themselves with this literature and work to integrate some of the key findings into their practice. For example, researchers have shown that learning is mediated by students' prior experiences of education. Therefore students learn best when teachers 1) recognise the importance of prior learning experiences and 2) enable students to build upon these prior experiences in the process of making sense of current learning tasks (see, for example, Marton and Säljö, 1997; Prosser and Trigwell, 1999). What this means in practice is that the educational process must be student-centred. It must recognise the individuality of each student and take account of the fact that each one will interpret the learning situation differently. A learning process that enables students to apply their knowledge, reflect upon the experience of applying it, adjust their understanding of the subject and then plan to retest their understanding is also supported by the work of writers such as Kolb (1984). Enabling students to take control of their learning and to process it in ways that are meaningful to them encourages a deep approach, which is more likely to produce learning that lasts. Essentially, the learner has not only understood the information but has taken ownership of it by applying their own knowledge and experience in order to create personal meaning for themselves.

The challenge for law teachers is clear. The pressures of massification described above appear to militate against this individualistic approach to Higher Education even where there is a willingness to engage in the pedagogical changes that a student-centred approach demands. Nevertheless, as described in Chapter 2, law teaching already encompasses several methods that tap into and recognise the importance of learning from experience. Indeed many law teachers would argue that law cannot be understood purely through the passive absorption of text but that law, like medicine and engineering, is a 'doing' discipline. To divorce theory from practice is to radically distort the nature and understanding of law. To recognise this is not, as some may infer, to succumb to an agenda that seeks to present law as a vocational discipline. Rather it is to be responsive to the findings of educational theory and also to promote a thorough engagement with law in the true spirit of academic enquiry.

The traditional practices of HE teachers have commonly concentrated on the staples of lecture and seminar, or tutorial in better-resourced institutions, which are assessed usually by examination and a small amount of assessed written work. This is as common in law as it is elsewhere. It is true for undergraduate and many postgraduate programmes. Law has a distinct advantage, however, in that in recent years the vocational programmes have adopted experiential-based classes, incorporating role-play and competence-based assessment (see Chapter 2). It has also witnessed a rich vein of innovation utilising technologies, especially interactive and communication-based courseware (see Chapter 4). Whilst valuable and in many ways representing the vanguard in international law teaching, all these innovatory approaches are not yet evident in the majority of law school programmes, and some law schools may not yet have adopted any of them. Individual institutions and support agencies such as LTSN and FDTL make a variety of efforts and provide specialist funding to widen participation and expand dissemination. It remains the responsibility of the individual law teacher to instigate such reforms.

Other expert practices relate to programme and modular planning and presentation. The provision of generic sessions on aspects of Higher Education teaching practice – teaching observation, diversity in assessment, teaching in large groups, problem-based learning, and other topics for development – need to be complemented and enhanced by subject-specific initiatives. In an age of increasing specialisation, law teachers need to ensure that the distinctive features of their subject are reflected in the materials, methods and assessment practices that underpin learning approaches.

The challenges to individual law teachers are now becoming those of spontaneity, creativity and critical reflection. The temptation to fall back on prepared-earlier teaching plans and off-the-computer seminar sheets is strong. Indeed, much of the purpose of outcome definition and student-centred learning has been to support consistency and ease preparation by a programmed approach. The danger would lie for most of us if the planning became no more than a once-for-all operation; if it became the immutable blueprint, defined in every moment and designed to produce a single identical product. When education managers demand rigid and uncritical adherence to programme objectives, module outcomes or seminar plans, they should be met with a collective response based upon our professional expertise as teachers that builds upon institutional and national policies rather than submits to them. Learning styles differ. Outcome-fixated programmes have their limitations. Kolb says so (and many others). Because learning styles differ, we need to ensure as teachers that we employ a variety of methods to meet different needs and to accomplish different tasks. Because laws change and social relations shift, the programme and syllabus must keep pace. Because knowledge is 'created through the transformation of experience' (Kolb, 1984: 38) and because experiences differ, teaching needs to respond. These issues are developed further in Chapter 2.

The emergence of legal education scholarship

Legal knowledge and teaching practice are useful descriptors of a law teacher's expertise. The discrete knowledge and practices of legal education undergo continuous adjustment. If either is to develop we need to know more about all aspects of the phenomena. Law's effectiveness, and learning's process needs to be investigated and theorized. The essence of an intellectual discipline derives from its ability to reflect, challenge, recreate itself and reform according to its own precepts and informed by its own practitioners. In the process it may borrow from other disciplines, conscript other practitioners, establish merged sub-disciplines with other interests and sectors, or fragment new specialisms to address fresh challenges.

Empirical and theoretical research are therefore integral to the development of the law teaching profession. In recent years, legal academics in the United Kingdom have added considerably to the body of legal education research. However, far too little is still known and much of the debate about reforming the law degree and other stages of legal education and training is conducted with little if any empirical appreciation of existing provision. We have argued above that the process and experience through which students learn about law and come to understand its principles and reasoning is associated with a wider appreciation of its ethical environment. If accurate, such a conclusion holds major implications for law teaching. Legal education scholars urgently need to join the small band of academics already exploring these and a multitude of other issues.

Implications of the professional teaching practitioner

The recognition of a professional identity for the law teacher carries with it a responsibility for learning how to teach and teaching how to learn. The box below highlights some of the practices necessary to discharge this reponsibility.

Responsibilities of the professional law teacher

- The onus of continually developing fresh programmes, objectives, modules etc. Law is a dynamic discipline. Legal practice is constantly changing and education theory and our own experiences of success or lack of it suggest change.
- The adoption of a reflective practice. The reflective practitioner is obliged to develop his/her expertise. This entails for the law teacher the constant reappraisal of the way students learn and their response to the syllabus.
- A more transparent relationship with students, employers and other stakeholders. In return for greater autonomy over the methods and purposes of the law degree, law schools can be expected to deliver and will be called to account if they fail.
- The obligation to develop robust and transparent systems of self- and peer evaluation.
- Professional status is accorded the privilege of a large element of self-regulation although modern quality assurance in the public sector increasingly favours greater involvement of external assessors. The law schools and the professions along with colleagues in other disciplines should provide a suitably trained cohort of assessors of legal education.
- The need for accreditation of expertise.

In return for specialist status the teaching practitioner would need to display expertise in the field. As the Institute for Learning and Teaching (ILT) has consistently argued, enhanced status is likely to incur demand for an evaluated performance of competence. Given similar demands upon other professions and the clamour for accountability, accreditation may be difficult to resist.

The development of these expert practices will be demanding and challenging but the emergence of a professional identity also carries with it many of the following benefits, highlighted in the box on page 21.

Benefits of a professional identity

- The identity establishes a clear and authoritative standpoint from which to respond to external demands and challenges.
- A practitioner profile based upon expert knowledge and practice, scholarship and critique provides many alternative ways to portray excellence and expands career opportunities. It promotes scholarship amongst law teachers and should facilitate more promotions on teaching grounds.
- It provides additional, transparent (more objective?) criteria for promotion.
- It is more responsive to market needs, which may enable law teachers to benefit from enhanced salaries.
- It will encourage the development of an international market for law teachers.

Conclusion

The chapters that follow expand upon the characteristics of a professional law teaching practitioner. We have tried in this chapter to explain why such a development is necessary at present and we have set out to present an outline of one such new vision for law teachers. It would be naïve to expect any startling reform immediately and such a project is likely to evolve rather than lurch forward, particularly since any readjustment is unlikely to be matched by any commensurate salary enhancement or the improvement of working conditions. The possibility of moving beyond the restatement of established positions or debilitating reaffirmation of past credos, deserves more attention and thought. The identity that is developed in the following pages essentially preserves the distinction between the academic and vocational study of law, but it envisages an undergraduate programme that involves the study of legal practices and the widespread adoption of experiential learning methods. At the same time it advocates a vocational stage that reflects upon the competences that the profession requires and reviews its practices for the social and economic purposes served.

Acronyms

ALT	Association of Law Teachers
CTI	Computers in Teaching Initiative
CPE	Common Professional Examination
FDTL	Fund for the Development of Teaching and Learning
HEFCE	Higher Education Funding Council (England)
ICT	Information and Communications Technology
ILT	Institute for Learning and Teaching
Iolis	Not an acronym – just looks like one
LCC	Law Courseware Consortium
LILI	Learning in Law Initiative
LTC	Law Technology Centre
LTSN	Learning and Teaching Support Network
NCLE	National Centre for Legal Education
PGDL	Post Graduate Diploma in Law
QAA	Quality Assurance Agency
SHEFC	Scottish Higher Education Funding Council
SLSA	Socio Legal Studies Association
SPTL	Society for Public Teachers of Law
UKCLE	United Kingdom Centre for Legal Education

References

ACLEC (1996) *First Report on Legal Education and Training*, ACLEC, London

Alldridge, P and Mumford, A (1998) Gazing into the future through a VDU: Communications, Information Technology and Law Teaching, *Journal of Law and Society*, **25** (1), pp 116–33

Bastin, N (2001) Unpublished letter to the Committee of Heads of University Law Schools

Birks, P (ed) (1996) *What Are Law Schools For?*, Oxford University Press, Oxford

Boon, A (1998) History is Past Politics: A Critique of the Legal Skills Movement in England and Wales, *Journal of Law and Society*, **25** (1), pp 151–69

Bradney, A (1992) Ivory Towers or Satanic Mills: choices for university law schools, *Studies in Higher Education*, **17**, p 5

Bradney, A (1995) They Teach You Nothing Useful… , *SPTL Reporter*, **11**, p 17

Bradney, A (2001) The Quality Assurance Agency and the Politics of Audit, *Journal of Law and Society*, **28** (3), pp 430–42

Cownie, F (1998) Women Legal Academics – A New Research Agenda?, *Journal of Law and Society*, **25** (1), pp 102–15

Cuthbert, M (2001), Law Student 2000 Plus One, *Directions in Legal Education*, UK Centre for Legal Education, **2001** (4), p 11

Dearing Report (1997) *Higher Education in the Learning Society*, DfEE, London

DfEE (2000) *The Excellence Challenge* http://www.dfes.gov.uk/excellencechallenge/ excecha2.pdf (last accessed on 4 December 2001)

Economides, K (ed) (1998) *Ethical Challenges to Legal Education and Conduct*, Hart, Oxford

Gold, N *et al* (1989) *Learning Legal Skills*, Butterworths, London

Harris, P and Jones, M (1996) *A Survey of Law Schools in the UK* http://www.lawteacher.ac.uk/1996report/index.html (last accessed 4 December 2001)

Hepple, B A (1996) The Renewal of the Liberal Law Degree, *Cambridge Law Journal*, **55** (3), pp 420–87

Hodgson, J and Bermingham, V (2001) What Lawyers Want From Their Recruits, *The Law Teacher*, **35** (1), pp 1–32

Kolb, D (1984) *Experiential Learning: experience as the source of learning and development*, Prentice Hall, New Jersey

Law Society (2001) *Training Framework Review Consultation Paper*, Law Society

Leighton, P (1998) New Wine in Old Bottles or New Wine in New Bottles?, *Journal of Law and Society*, **28** (1), pp 85–101

Leighton, P (2001) *Legal Education in the UK Today: why do we have so many enduring barriers and divides?* Keynote address to the Association of Law Teachers conference, University of Durham, April 2001 (unpublished)

Marton, F (1988) Describing and improving learning, *Learning Strategies and Learning Styles*, ed R R Schmeck, Plenum Press, New York

Marton, F and Säljö, R (1997) Approaches to learning, *The Experience of Learning: implications for teaching and learning in higher education*, eds F Marton, D Hounsell and N J Entwistle, Edinburgh, Scottish Academic Press

Nathanson, S (1996) The Culture of Design, *International Journal of the Legal Profession*, **3** (3), pp 301–13

O'Dair, R (1998) Recent Developments in the Teaching of Legal Ethics, *Ethical Challenges to Legal Education and Conduct*, ed K Economides, pp 151–68, Hart, Oxford

O'Dair, R (2001) *Legal Ethics: Text and Materials*, Butterworths, London

Ormrod Report (1971), *Report of the Committee on Legal Education*, Cmnd 4595, HMSO, London

Paliwala, A (2000) Leila's Working Day: one of the futures for legal education, *The Law Teacher*, **34** (1), pp 1–16

Partington, M (1992) Legal Education in the 1990s, *Journal of Law and Society*, **19** (1), pp 174–93

Prosser, M and Trigwell, K (1999) *Understanding Learning and Teaching*, SRHE/Open University Press, Buckingham

Quality Assurance Agency (2000) *Academic Standards – Law*, QAA, Gloucester

Shils, E (1984) *The Academic Ethic*, Chicago University Press, Chicago

Toddington, S (1995) The Emperor's New Skills: the academy, the profession and the idea of legal education, *What are Law Schools for?*, ed P Birks, pp 69–90, Oxford University Press, Oxford

Twining, W (1994) *Blackstone's Tower: The English Law School*, Sweet and Maxwell, London

Twining, W (1998) Thinking About Law Schools: Rutland Reviewed, *Journal of Law and Society*, **25** (1), pp 1–13

Webb, J (1996) Why theory matters, in *Teaching Lawyers' Skills*, eds J Webb and C Maughan, pp 23–51, Butterworths, London

Webb, J (1998a) Ethics for Lawyers or Ethics for Citizens? New Directions for Legal Education, *Journal of Law and Society*, **25** (1), pp 134–50

Webb, J (1998b) Conduct, Ethics and Experience in Vocational Legal Education: opportunities missed, *Ethical Challenges to Legal Education and Conduct*, ed K Economides, pp 271–97, Hart, Oxford

Webb, J (1999) Post-Fordism and the reformation of liberal legal education, *The Law School: global issues, local questions*, ed F Cownie, pp 228–60, Dartmouth, Aldershot

Webb, J and Nicolson, D (1999) *Legal Ethics: Critical Interrogations*, Oxford University Press, Oxford

Wilson, G (1995) *Frontiers of Legal Scholarship: twenty-five years of Warwick Law School*, Wiley, Chichester

2

Learning law and legal expertise by experience

Roger Burridge

The casual observer of the traditional educational process would undoubtedly conclude that learning was primarily a personal, internal process requiring only the limited environment of books, teacher and classroom. Indeed the wider 'real world' environment at times seems to be actively rejected by educational systems at all levels.

(Kolb, 1984: 34)

Introduction

In Chapter 1, the unique separation of UK legal education into an initial degree stage, signified by the study of the principles and texts of law, and a second vocational stage, characterised by instruction and the performance of key lawyer tasks was described. The division detracted from a holistic approach that seeks to understand the efficacy of law as a process for regulating human relationships and resolving disputes. This chapter addresses the implications that the separation holds for learning and teaching. It pursues the need to review the ways in which students and trainees are taught and the mechanisms by which they learn. It propounds the benefits of a more widespread use of experiential learning methods, the adoption of which have been constrained by the academic–vocational divide. This has allowed academic teachers to relinquish approaches that include considerations of legal practice to the 'trade schools', and has also produced a misleading and prejudicial distinction between skills and knowledge.

At the academic stage in particular, law teachers in many institutions seem eager, as Kolb observes, to reject the 'real world' environment of legal practice. The objective of the chapter is to expound a reflective professional practice that will achieve 'holism' both through the integration of the totality of a student's abilities, intellect and perceptions and through combining in all stages of legal education a concern for law's content with its practical context. The chapter advocates a more student-centred and resource-focused learning, the benefits of which would be more effective teaching practices and the strengthening of the law degree, both as a foundation for a wide variety of social roles as well as for the next stage of professional education.

In Section 1 the chapter reviews the key theoretical explanations underpinning student learning and provides examples of each from legal education in the United Kingdom. Section 2 illustrates the diversity of teaching methods that can be accomplished using a familiar topic in a tort law syllabus. In Section 3 principles and plans that might guide the development of more active experiences for students are suggested. Continuing a theme from Chapter 1 that a key objective for law teachers is the establishment of a more clearly defined professional identity, Section 4 considers some of the implications of an experiential learning approach for the development of a reflective practice of law teaching. Some of the characteristics that it might exhibit and steps to follow in adopting a reflective practice of law teaching are sketched out. Section 5 speculates on some of the potential that education theory and legal education scholarship has for the development of legal expertise and extends the focus of learning law into the vocational programmes, continuing professional development and beyond.

Section 1
Lessons from educational theory and law school practice

Before I explore the meaning and potential of active learning methods, the relevance and strengths of traditional approaches need acknowledgement. Much of the criticism levelled at traditional methods pillories the incomprehensible, inaudible, or seemingly interminable monologues in the lecture hall, which dominate many law student memories. There is of course the alternative image of the charismatic speaker who has the ability to entertain, inform and inspire an audience. The large group or lecture is destined to continue as an integral feature of the law school experience. The opportunity to consider collectively a law teacher's account of the subject is a distinctive and significant learning experience. Phil Thomas has provided useful guidance on how to organise and conduct large groups for law teachers (Thomas, 2000).

Successful and engaging seminars and tutorials that rely upon conventional tutor-led questions and conversations frequently take place in law schools around the country. Student activity of some kind – listening, note-taking, the application of knowledge to factual hypotheticals, Socratic reasoning, even critical awareness – occurs in all of these but it is of varying effectiveness and all too often is the staple, sometimes the only, student learning experience outside of the private study of texts. Such experiences are inevitably restricted in their capacity to convey an understanding of how law works and its effect upon those who work with it or invoke its practices. They are also, particularly when they dominate the curriculum, prone to boredom and failure.

In being critical of such practices or their excessive use, we do not need to rely on our own uncomfortable memories or sad anecdotes from contemporary students. Education research frequently confirms the negative value of much undergraduate teaching (Evans and Abbott, 1998). The known inadequacies of such teaching that predominate in Higher Education are sufficient justification for searching for alternatives. Education scholarship, learning increasingly from psychologists, cognitive scientists, neurologists, and sociologists, reveals more about how students learn and suggests more effective ways of organising teaching and learning opportunities. It is the education discipline that has devised the theory and terminology of learning.

Newcomers to educational theory are likely to be as bemused by the array of theoretical perspectives as they are to be challenged by the differing interpretations of the various approaches on offer. It would be impossible in a chapter such as this to summarise adequately the rich vein of work explaining the mechanisms, motivations and methods pertinent to human intellectual development. Those interested in developing their teaching abilities and in understanding how we all learn will have to read further, but a few signposts and a simple map of the current paths of education may help. Experiential learning, constructivism, problem-based learning, resource-based learning, clinical methods, and problem solving, are all examples of teaching methods requiring a more active role for the student, and hence, it is argued, a different and more effective learning experience for the student. Combined with a commitment to frequently monitor, review, rethink and readjust our teaching plans, they constitute the basis for a reflective practice of law teaching.

Active learning

Active or participatory learning connotes a process in which the student utilises an activity or role as an opportunity for discovery and reflection. It is a term of imprecise definition that is often employed to contrast the passivity of inactive learning (sitting, listening, reading, writing). It incorporates all situations where pupils or students debate, discuss, explain, argue, act, play games, role-play, observe or work as part of a programme of learning. The exercise in the box on page 29 could be used in a Legal System course that is exploring the nature of the adversarial process and the role of personal experience and cultural conditioning in the interpretation of evidence by a jury or judge.

Experiential learning

Experiential learning is variously referred to either as an example of, or synonymous with, active learning. Its foundation lies in the way humans develop and its essence is a focus upon the process by which through contemplating real or simulated experiences we discover what is effective, successful or rewarding and discover aspects that can be improved. It is dependent upon our own reflection, but benefits from the observation and critique of others. In recent years a rich body of analysis and advice has emerged for law teachers (Webb, 1995; Maughan, 1996). Its most influential exponent, David Kolb (1984), famously found common ground in the work of Lewin, Dewey and Piaget to describe the four stages in the now familiar cycle of experiential development of concrete experience, reflective observation, abstract conceptualisation and active experiment (Kolb, 1984: 25). The cycle requires learners to be actively involved in the process of learning. The concrete experiences may be prior work or study experiences or may be created or simulated in exercises for the pursuit of specific learning objectives.

This approach to learning is contrasted to the traditional lecture and seminar, where knowledge is delivered and explained, before students put this knowledge to use and practise their ability to apply it to factual hypotheses. As I point out below, the study of law is invariably retrospective. In the private law field one of the key tasks of the practitioner is to predict how the courts would resolve a dispute based upon decided cases and established law. It is in essence an applied

Examples of passive and active learning

Learning outcome: To appreciate the processes by which personal experience and cultural development can influence a juror's or magistrate's understanding of evidence in the adversarial trial.

Passive learning example
Through a reading or exposition, explain the following problems in the adversarial system and the more general phenomenon of the linguistics of courtroom discourse:

1. In the adversarial process the fact-finder (magistrate, judge, juror) is dissuaded or prevented from asking questions of a witness even if they do not understand the testimony.

2. The fact-finder will in any case hear the evidence in the context of his/her own experience of the world, which may inform/distort the understanding of a witness's evidence.

3. We all carry with us views of the world, folk tales and prejudices against which we rationalise and explain other people's accounts and descriptions from their experience.

Active learning example
1. Ask students to draw as detailed a diagram as they feel able to illustrate the following account of a car crash. Read the description twice and do not answer questions about it. 'One car, a red Nissan Micra, was making a right turn. Another car, a blue BMW sports car, was coming in the opposite direction. The driver tried to stop but the cars crashed into each other.'
2. When the students have completed the diagram ask them to share it with the colleagues on either side.
3. Some of the students (probably many of them) will have explained the crash by drawing a road system, and the position of impact. If they have included a road system, those students familiar with UK roads will have positioned the cars on the left-hand side of the road.
4. Use their diagram as a discussion point to explore the implications for justice in the adversarial process and the possibility of prejudice and cultural relativity influencing the way in which evidence is heard.

discipline. There is much scope for a more developmental approach to legal scholarship, as much postgraduate research proves.

Whilst new knowledge and significant originality from undergraduate students may be scarce in an age when there has been an explosion in information, there is plenty of opportunity to engage students in the discovery of knowledge that is new to them. Kolb's main thesis was that, 'Learning is the process whereby knowledge is created through the transformation of experience' (Kolb, 1984: 38). It is this element of self-improvement and personal adventure that is being sought by education developers and it is this process that experiential and constructivist methods seek to promote.

The benefits and practices of experiential learning feature often unwittingly in UK law schools where there are rich examples of utilising or creating situations for learning about law. Mooting, for example, conforms to many of the characteristics of experiential methodology, albeit in a form that is restricted to the replication of a somewhat specialised and esoteric instance of lawyer activity. A moment of legal process is simulated – a hypothetical scenario and a fictional lower court judgement – as a vehicle for exploring legal reasoning and argument. Its effectiveness as an educational tool is often overlooked as it is valued for its mimicry of a rite of practice. In order to don the behaviour of an appellate, advocate, however, the participants have to research and master the minutiae of judicial reasoning, and be prepared to orally present and argue their position. Feedback is usually directed towards the internal consistency of argument and the behaviour of participants as professional advocates. As a contest, the rules of mooting are fairly clearly defined. As a learning opportunity, the objectives are usually unspoken.

The experience would be even more valuable, for example, if participants were encouraged to reflect more upon their performance at the end of the exercise and identify for themselves and with other members of their team, aspects of both the argument and the performance that they felt could be improved. Indeed, the distinguishing characteristic of experiential learning is its insistence that learning will only occur when the experience is registered, analysed and reflected upon.

Experiential learning permeates most of the recent innovations in legal education as this book frequently illustrates. Role-plays and simulations are common in many law modules, and the various clinical approaches described below and in Chapter 6 depend upon students learning from the situations that they encounter or are created for them. Games can provide valuable learning (Bergman, Sherr and Burridge, 1987). Learning on the LPC and BVC is now predominantly experiential as students are presented with documents and scenarios that replicate the materials of professional work.

The utilisation of student experience as a learning opportunity can therefore extend far beyond the role-play of a barrister in appellate court argument. It encompasses games, exercises, role-plays, work placements, indeed any real or simulated situation, which affords an opportunity to understand and reflect upon the relevance and effectiveness of legal knowledge and its application in action or within an activity.

Problem-based learning

Problem–based learning is a variation of experiential learning where students are confronted with the materials and facts underlying a problem from which they have to figure out an appropriate solution, usually without prior instruction in the necessary knowledge to solve it. Again, the education literature is confusing, as proponents of problem-based learning (PBL) advocate a purist approach – where entire programmes or even institutions are required to adhere to PBL methods. It is sufficient here to restate the commonly acknowledged characteristics of problem–based learning, before reviewing their appropriateness for law:

- using stimulus material to help students discuss an important problem, question or issue;
- presenting the problem as a simulation of professional practice or real-life situation;
- appropriately guiding students' critical thinking and providing limited resources to help them learn from defining and attempting to resolve the given problem;
- having students work cooperatively as a group; exploring information in and out of class, with access to a tutor who knows the problem well to guide their learning;
- getting students to identify their own learning needs and the appropriate use of available resources;
- reapplying this knowledge to the original problem and evaluating their processes.

(Adapted from Boud and Feletti, 1997: 4)

Problem–based learning is widely practised in legal education, although more commonly as a discrete task within a module rather than as the basis for a complete syllabus (Tzannes, 1997). Others have used experiential learning theory to emphasise the construction of ideas and creation of knowledge that occurs when students pursue their own solutions and meanings in organised learning activities. These are designed so that students are free to explore alternative or even infinite outcomes in contrast to the application of prior knowledge to predetermined problems.

In some disciplines, like medicine and architecture, problem-based learning has been adopted as a holistic approach to a complete programme. Elsewhere it often forms the basis for a complete module or substantial project. Examples from legal education are becoming more common, and law clinics with their focus on learning from the messy and unpredictable facts of a 'live client' case (see below) observe a problem-based methodology.

Resource-based learning

A variant of problem-based learning is resource-based learning, which acknowledges the potential that ICT can bring into the learning environment via the encapsulation, simulation and reality of new technologies. Resource-based learning is discussed at length and illustrated in Chapter 4. The emphasis upon the selection of resources as the starting point for problem solving illustrated the extent to which much of our law teaching in the academic stage is designed to lead students to the answer that the tutor intends them to provide. The classic land law problem that begins, 'The freeholder of Blackacre... ', intends to discover whether the student can apply a learned rule to a familiar, or almost familiar, set of facts. The provision on a Web site or on paper of a bundle of witness statements, correspondence, deeds and copies of a Land Registry Certificate will test the same knowledge but will also require the student to demonstrate that they understand the concepts involved and can relate them to social reality, if necessary, and the personal implications for the individuals involved. As Maharg and Paliwala explain in Chapter 4, new communications technologies provide infinite opportunities to create effective learning opportunities.

Research-based learning

Research-based learning is a relative newcomer to the educational theory menu but has obvious implications for those institutions and law teachers espousing research-based development. The conduct of empirical or theoretical research is an activity that provides its own distinctive approach to learning. Studies of research-based learning are still in their infancy and the field seems to be in the process of being defined rather than refined. The practice is common to law teachers whose role already includes research. The development of a researched-based learning methodology ensures that research enthusiasm, empirical and theoretical skills of enquiry and data collection and analysis are incorporated into teaching. Research-based learning has been described as exhibiting most of the following characteristics:

- Research outcomes from law teachers and students can impact directly upon the syllabus or lead to new options.
- Research practice can inform student work by providing informative models and examples of a variety of successful research methods for use in their own work.
- Research experiences can demonstrate the significance and distinction between empirical and theoretical research approaches.
- Research practices can be used to demonstrate the discipline and rigour of investigation and the conventions and requirements of referencing, report writing and publication.
- A research approach to teaching and learning can incorporate research tasks into the syllabus as problem situations for solving or as tasks for assessment (eg design a research proposal to...).
- A research ethos can help to develop a research culture.

(Warwick, 2000)

The Warwick approach emphasises the law teacher's research experiences. Whilst these provide powerful learning opportunities for the teacher and useful illustrations and examples for students, research-based learning can be most effective when the research project itself provides the learning opportunity for the student. This is of course the model for much postgraduate scholarship, but it is also common for undergraduate projects to include an empirical element.

Since courtroom observation is frequently a feature of Legal System modules, a research-based approach can be introduced by asking students to identify an issue in the courtroom and its use as a suitable topic for research. The students should then be invited to construct a research proposal to investigate their chosen issue, and to justify their project against the broader purposes of the administration of justice. The task could be informed by examples in a reading list of the many previous studies of courtroom behaviour. The project could be assessed by reference to the identification of research issues, the construction of an appropriate methodology, the feasibility of its implementation and the quality of the justification.

Clinical education

Clinical education is derived from the education and training of doctors. Book-based study of anatomy and pathology is a limited introduction to the causes and treatment of illness and injury. Real patients display symptoms and experience pain and other indicators in individual ways that any textbook or even simulation is unable to authentically replicate. Patients present problems that force professionals as well as students to reach beyond the application of prior knowledge and seek answers to new situations. Clinical legal education has borrowed this approach to learning by supervised student involvement in dealing with the problems of live clients and other 'real-life' issues.

The underlying notion of clinical legal education is that students can learn best about law by studying it in action. The lay client is put in the place of the medical student's live patient as a 'problem' to be resolved. In the process of solving the client's problem the student undertakes factual enquiries, legal research and becomes involved in a variety of contacts and transactions. Significantly, this is an assessed activity, which takes place as part of the curriculum. Specialist clinics are now common in most US law schools but in the United Kingdom they have enjoyed important but much rarer successes. The clinical approach has much in common with the principles of problem-based learning, and it is also manifest in a variety of different programmes, modules, occasional class or extra-curricular activity.

The UK experience of clinical legal education is comprehensively explained by Brayne, Duncan and Grimes in *Clinical Legal Education: Active Learning in Your Law School* (1998). This book is refreshingly directed towards potential students of clinical methods. The authors broadly define clinical legal education as 'learning by doing the types of things that lawyers do' (Brayne, Duncan and Grimes, 1998: 13).

The definition introduces a wider range of learning programmes and activities. If a broad understanding of lawyers and their work is adopted (including advocating, consulting, teaching, transaction brokering, drafting, researching, lobbying, commentating), the definition may not be as restrictive or vocation-oriented as first appears. Moreover, as an educational concept (rather than a vocational training technique) there seems no good reason to restrict the learning experiences to 'what *lawyers* do'. The activities of the police, environmental health officers, probation officers, or parliamentary drafters also provide valuable examples for learning about law in action. The objective of the programme will define the extent of clinical involvement – whether it is to provide an understanding of the main concepts, methods and functions of law as a social force or whether it is to equip future practitioners with the knowledge and ability to perform specific roles. Most undergraduate programmes espouse both objectives, but most also reject an approach that is solely directed at the accomplishment of professional tasks and responsibilities.

Live client clinics

Live client clinics are provided in a number of UK law schools, such as Central England, Kent, Northumbria and Sheffield Hallam. Under supervision and as part of a regulated programme, students learn to distil from the raw materials and uncertainties of their clients' stories the facts that may afford a legal remedy. They begin their quest with no prior knowledge of the circumstances their clients have experienced and little appreciation or knowledge of the applicable law. Learning occurs in the process of confronting a novel and messy scenario and researching the evidential, procedural and substantive issues involved. The engagement with real clients also necessitates the consideration of the implications, cost, practicalities and feasibility for the client. It is variously applauded for its holistic approach and its propensity to develop an ethical awareness. The Clinical Legal Education Organisation has published guidelines and standards for the guidance of those contemplating establishing such a clinic.

Recently, the involvement of students in live client clinics has received considerable support from the establishment of the Solicitors' Pro Bono Group and the Bar Pro Bono Unit. Linking with the concerns of practising lawyers to organise and focus their pro bono activities, a number of LPC and BVC courses have established live client clinics and the Pro Bono Group is promoting them amongst undergraduate students.

The characteristics of live client clinics, whether generalist or specialist, accord well with the principles of problem-based learning. The cost of such programmes is often cited as the main obstacle to their adoption, but the advent of Community Legal Services may provide educational opportunities for live client work on behalf of local advice agencies. The entrenched opinions amongst academics about the inappropriateness of the practical context of law in the undergraduate curriculum and their lack of the necessary professional expertise are probably more significant obstacles to the widespread adoption of live client clinics in the undergraduate curriculum. Law firms, too, are sometimes said to be against the inclusion of practical elements in the undergraduate curriculum. Such caution or short-sightedness is unfortunate. The possibilities for learning more about law and its effectiveness, as well as the potential for developing competencies and confronting ethical challenges, can all be accomplished in live client work. From an educational point of view the benefits are almost unassailable, although the incidence of live client practitioners and enthusiasts, whilst increasing, is still low.

Street law and community development projects

The live client clinic emulates the professional lawyer client model of dealing with the personal plight of individuals. It thus presents only a limited and partial account of modern legal work. There is no reason why clinics should restrict themselves to this model and there are many examples of alternatives in Australia, the United States and the United Kingdom. Lundy and Duncan describe a legislative reform clinic some years ago at the Polytechnic of the South Bank (Lundy and Duncan, 1998: 163–66).

Clinical programmes often occur in response to a perceived local need for legal resources. In the United States and in South Africa in the final years of apartheid, a few law teachers recognised the opportunity for their students to learn by providing advice and support to particular sections of the community. There are now a large number of law schools around the world that engage students in community education and human rights promotion. The University of Natal Law School in Durban established a 'street law' programme where their law students went into the townships and schools to explain the laws affecting juveniles and the powers and responsibilities of the state to groups of young people at risk from oppressive police activities. The Natal programme became the model for a global network of street law projects.

Sheffield Hallam law department organises a street law project for sixth formers in a local school. The College of Law has recently introduced programmes involving students working with prisoners and others (Grimes, 2001). A similar project organised at Warwick University Law School is described in more detail in Chapter 6. In the United States, street law programmes are plentiful. *Street Law: A course in practical law* is a useful guide for anyone contemplating such a course and the Street Law organisation maintains an informative Web site including details of programmes around the world.

Placements and work experience

Occasions for law students to involve themselves in external legal experiences are plentiful and with the recognition throughout UK education of the role of shad-owing and work experience, the idea that a student may spend a portion of their studies outside the university is now commonplace. Law schools in the United States and some in the United Kingdom have made extensive use of placements in the curriculum. These extend from sandwich courses where a whole year or semester may be spent in the external agency, to part-time attendance, and vacation visits. The object of study or work experience is often a lawyer's office, judge's chambers, or regulatory agency. Lundy and Duncan have described a range of approaches in the United Kingdom and present valuable advice for those contemplating a course where students work in external agencies.

Much has been written about the pitfalls and potential of work-based learning (often confusingly referred to as 'internships' and 'externships') and different teachers advocate principles and practices that programmes should observe to be effective. These accounts are valuable and anyone planning a clinic that works with death row inmates, for example, should first read Boon and Hodgkinson's (1996) account of their University of Westminster initiative and visit the University of Central England Law School's Web site. Lessons and models from elsewhere will invariably be informative at some level.

From the perspective of the experiential learning enthusiast, all our experiences are activities from which we can learn and therefore the law teacher needs to match the experiences with the learning outcomes. The vast majority of our knowledge and understanding results from our learning from experience – our observations, responses, conclusions and feelings that we have amassed throughout our lives. Experiential learning differs from learning from experience in that it is a conscious process, which focuses on a subject with the purpose of deriving some meaning from the experience (Usher, 1993: 169). For the law teacher, therefore, the challenge is how to identify experiences for students from which meanings relevant to the course or subject will be derived, although an experience 'like a text does not have its own intrinsic meaning waiting to be discovered' (Usher, 1993: 170). Module objectives might begin, for example, with the recognition that one of the most significant may be 'to assist students to learn from their experiences'!

Some student experiences such as vacation placements in lawyers' offices are currently wasted as opportunities for experiential learning. They will invariably provide experiences from which students will learn about the firm's expectations of its recruits, the lore and practice of legal work and their own responses to such an environment, but the experience is usually lost as an opportunity for them to derive meanings pertinent to their undergraduate study. This could be achieved by their keeping a journal, completing a simple research project or submitting a reflective essay. Their combined experiences could be the focus for comparative study, or seminar discussion based upon tutor- or student-selected topics.

Work experience, observation and voluntary participation as learning opportu-nities are valuable alternatives to traditional teaching methods. They require harnessing in a framework that sets out their purpose and fits the needs of the degree. The knowledge, insight and meanings that can be discerned will be more effective, promote broader learning outcomes and generally be more appreciated than traditional methods. They also can often be delivered at less cost to the law school and university where staff and space are increasingly scarce resources.

Different learners

The various teaching and learning methods that have been discussed can be utilised to suit learning different module objectives, learning outcomes and resource constraints. They will also be differentially appreciated and effective according to students' individual learning styles. Kolb and others, as we saw in Chapter 1, have distinguished between the different approaches that individuals display. Kolb's Learning Styles Index (LSI) identifies four learning modes – affective, perceptual, symbolic and behavioural – and relates these to four learning orientations that he says are prevalent to differing degrees in all of us:

- *concrete experience* – personally involved in experiences and human situations;
- *reflective observation* – concerned with understanding the meaning of ideas and situations through observation and impartial reflection;
- *abstract conceptualisation* – focuses upon using logic and formulating concepts; emphasises thinking rather than feeling;
- *active experimentation* – seeks to actively influence situations and people; emphasizes practical applications.

(Kolb, 1984: 68)

Different active and more passive learning situations will be more suitable to some students' orientation than others, emphasising that to ensure that all learning styles are catered for, a suitable range of learning and teaching methods should be deployed. Kolb tells us that students learn by doing and active experimentation. In creating alternative learning approaches, diversity may be as important as purpose.

In all these experiential approaches – clinics, street law projects, and problem- and research-based methods – a distinction can be made between *surface learning*, which is accrued knowledge learnt and retained in the memory from instructional sources, and *deep learning* (or understanding the context and relevance of knowledge). The latter is more likely to occur when learners are forced to find knowledge and discover solutions by personal enquiry and experiment. It makes a deeper impression and is more likely to be retained longer than surface learning. Experiential learning is esteemed by educationalists for its propensity to promote deep learning.

Section 2
Diversity in teaching methods

A tort law example

Students' appetites for play-acting their images of lawyers and legal work can be utilised for educational advantage in the undergraduate curriculum as much as for professional development at the vocational stage. With only a little imagination on behalf of the teacher, the external world of lawyers, courts, legislation, regulation – any example of the role of law – can be harnessed to explore the basic skills of legal study. There are many ways, for example, by which students can approach the study of negligence, beginning with the analysis of the most celebrated case – *Donoghue* v *Stevenson* – and extending to a Consumer Advice Clinic. The case and its circumstances are used in the boxed example below to illustrate a range of learning opportunities that can be employed to pursue different learning outcomes. Any of the examples may find a place in a tort syllabus. The various approaches can be adapted for different topics and may be appropriate for a variety of levels.

Tort law example of *Donoghue* v *Stevenson*

Traditional case analysis
Instruction: Read the case of *D* v *S* and prepare to discuss answers to the following in your seminar:

1. Which judges are in the majority and what is the *ratio decidendi* in the case?
2. Who do you consider delivers the leading judgement?
3. Why was it necessary to establish that the drinks manufacturer owed Mrs Donoghue a duty of care?
4. Would it have made any difference if the bottle had been transparent and she had been able to see the snail?

Student experience: Independent research, assimilation of reasoning, and application of gained knowledge to alternative scenario. Making notes for reference later. Chance of being asked to present oral explanation amongst group of up to 20 colleagues and opportunity to contribute to discussion or ask questions.

Case method
Instruction: Read the case of *D* v *S* for discussion in class next week. You should be familiar with the facts of the case and be prepared to recite details

---

of the case to the rest of the class and then to answer hypothetical changes to facts of the case. For example, what if the bottle was made of clear plastic? What if there was a sign over the counter stating that the proprietor would not be liable for any damages suffered by customers on his premises? Or what if the ginger beer had been stolen by Mrs Donoghue? Implications for a variety of different situations.

Student experience: Independent research, assimilation of reasoning, memorising of details, and application of gained knowledge to alternative scenarios. Making notes for reference later. Random selection of students to engage in Socratic dialogue with tutor in front of 15–20 colleagues.

Applied problem solving
Instruction: Read *D* v *S* and then consider the following scenario. Prepare to discuss the liability of H and M to W, S and K in your seminar: 'H is a manufacturer of soft drinks. He supplies bottles of ginger beer to a café proprietor, M. M sells a bottle of the ginger beer to W whose bottle bursts, severely injuring her hand; S almost swallows a decayed snail in the bottle and K is allergic to ginger.'

Student experience: Independent research, assimilation of reasoning, and application of gained knowledge to alternative scenarios. Making notes for reference later. Chance of being asked to present oral explanation amongst group of up to 20 colleagues and opportunity to contribute to discussion or ask questions.

Active learning exercise
Instruction: You will be assigned the role of either Mr Stevenson's or Mrs Donoghue's lawyer. Read the case and write out the statement that you think the lawyers for S or D would have taken from his/her client at the time and the theory of the case that best favours that client.

In the seminar you will first be asked to compare your statement with that of a colleague who has the same role. You will then be paired with a colleague with the opposing role. S will read out her/his prepared statement as if they were the witness and D will ask questions designed to support the opposing theory of the case. The exercise will then be repeated with D reading her/his statement before questioning by S.

Student experience: Independent research, assimilation of reasoning, imagining the lawyer's role and drafting a statement based upon information from the report of the case. Every student present will be required to engage in the exercise and consider alternative arguments and compile relevant questions. The exchanges provide all students with an experience and viewpoint for discussion with other members of the seminar.

Problem-based learning exercise

Instruction: You and two colleagues are representing a Mrs Donoghue or a Mr Stevenson, whose initial witness statement is attached. Together with the other members of your team, you should consider what other information you think that you require in order to advise your client. You should consider whether your advice would include any legal action on behalf of your client. If it does you should consider what evidence is required and draft any correspondence and pleadings. If the circumstances warrant it you may pursue this matter to trial (or defend your client if sued/prosecuted).

Course leaders will supply any information that cannot be supplied by your opponent. It is your responsibility to research the law and procedure relating to this case, which will be discussed with course tutors every fortnight. You are referred to the course document for the criteria by which your performance on this project will be evaluated.

Student experience: As a member of a small team the student will investigate the facts of the case, conduct legal research, devise a plan for meeting the client's objectives and implement that plan in response to the action of the students advising the other side.

Clinical approach

Instruction: You will attend at the Georgetown Community Centre to participate in the Consumer Advice Clinic. (A consumer complainant may come through the door who has become ill as a result of drinking from a can or bottle of cola that was contaminated by a dead snail...)

Student experience: The breadth of possible learning outcomes in clinical teaching is explained fully in Brayne, Duncan and Grimes (1998). Amongst these are the involvement of students in coping with harm and illness, which may have a legal remedy, and all the attendant knowledge and skills required to support the consumer or commercial client.

These approaches to learning are further illustrated in a series of manuals featuring learning and teaching in different subjects that have been produced by the National Centre for Legal Education. The subjects include Family Law, Legal Systems, and Human Rights. They are available from the UKCLE and can also be downloaded from its Web site.

Section 3
Principles for facilitating experiential learning

Much of the effort involved in the construction of experiential learning opportunities involves their planning and construction. Once these are developed, however, they will only require updating and development and the bulk of the tutor's time can be devoted to mentoring and supporting students. The main considerations in the construction of a module using experiential methods include the five questions below.

1. Is the module adequately planned?

Experiential teaching methods require more thought and effort in their preparation than traditional lectures and seminars. In planning the module, the following components need attention:

- *Module objectives.* As in any module, teaching objectives are essential and the type of experience will be dictated by them.
- *Curriculum context.* The module may have clear objectives and a coherent teaching programme, but it should also relate to the overall curriculum. Whilst it may only be optional, some thought should be given to its relevance to other modules, as well as whether the benefits of the module should be available in some form to students not selecting the module. It will also be necessary to ensure that all internal regulations have been followed and any approvals obtained.
- *Experience delivery.* The nature and delivery of the student experiences is also time-consuming. The organisation and administration of a live client clinic, arrangements and briefing for external placement agencies, and simulations (whether virtual or otherwise) all make substantial demands on experiential law teachers before teaching begins. For paper-based simulations, real-life cases suitably adapted and anonymized can be useful. Scenarios for role-play by students need careful drafting to create and maintain plausibility.
- *Student materials.* Experiential methods require a lot of explanation. Students need clear instructions and time guidance since much of their work will not be directly supervised by the course tutor.
- *Assessment pattern.* The module objectives and learning outcomes will indicate areas in which student performance can be assessed. Clear assessment criteria must be identified and conveyed to students. Assessment methods (both formative and summative) that fit the learning experiences are crucial to the success of the module. Self- and peer assessment are a natural part of the experiential learning process. There are growing numbers of examples of performance assessment, especially on the vocational courses.

2. Is the module adequately resourced?

Experiential learning opportunities require different rather than extra resources. Staff–student contact may require both more intense and more small-group sessions but may also involve students in more individual research or observation and long periods of group learning. Teachers may need some additional training in practical legal situations and procedures, although local practitioners will often be willing to provide support through the local Law Society branch or local Circuit of the Bar. Different spaces may be required or the seating layout may need re-arranging. Courtroom simulations will benefit from dedicated rooms or special furniture. On the other hand, group work lends itself to students working in communal areas and using rooms outside normal working hours. Individual legal research is likely to be more intensive and hence access to adequate libraries and access to up-to-date and reliable legal databases needs to be adequate, but fewer legal sources and textbooks may be required of students than for conventionally taught modules and smaller payments to the Copyright Licensing Agency required.

3. Is the teaching programme pertinent and coherent?

The module should complement the rest of the curriculum and pursue the overall programme objectives. Law schools might usefully reflect, however, upon whether their current programme objectives would be enhanced by the additional fields of legal knowledge and extended insights that experiential learning can introduce. There is considerable research, for example, in both education and jurisprudence, indicating that experiential methods are more effective in the development of professional ethics and personal moral values (see Chapter 1). Course objectives need to be matched to learning outcomes and, as Chapter 3 emphasises, effective modules maintain alignment between learning outcomes, teaching methods and assessment.

4. What arrangements are there for reviewing the programme?

In addition to reflective pauses and contemplative checks that you and the students are 'following the plot', there needs to be (as in any course) more formal evaluation and review. Experiences of clinical teachers show that student appreci-ation of such courses is high, but more rigorous analysis of performance and achievement is required. Since the appreciation of experiential methods amongst law teachers is still very limited, teachers who introduce them may benefit from encouraging observation of their classes by colleagues and introducing an element of external review. University authorities usually welcome such initiatives and offer support or even additional funding, particularly if the module reinforces community links and can be held up as an exemplar of good teaching practice.

5. How will the benefits and challenges of the course be disseminated?

Because experiential methods in law teaching are still relatively underdeveloped, there is a pressing need to exchange experiences and contribute to the accounts of experiential learning in other disciplines. Legal education is generally under-researched and inadequately recorded. Our teaching can provide a ready source of data for analysis and students can become compliant respondents. Studies of experiential modules, student development and learning effectiveness provide a rich vein of research opportunity and such studies are likely to become important factors for promotion as legal education is increasingly regarded as an object of scholarship.

Section 4
Developing a reflective teaching practice

In Chapter 1 it was argued that one of the challenges for law teachers is the fashioning of a professional identity. Two of the characteristics of a professional practice were identified as a familiarity with the theoretical basis of learning and a commitment to experiential and reflective learning. A broad picture of experiential learning possibilities is explained above. It has been suggested that learning from experience is dependent upon the Lewinian cycle of:

concrete experience → observations and reflections → formation of abstract concepts and generalisations → testing implications in new situations →concrete experience → and so on

(quoted in Kolb, 1984: 21)

The cycle is now so familiar that it is followed by many law teachers and adopted by cohorts of students who keep learning journals, as recommended in Schon's depiction of the reflective practitioner (Schon, 1983). Their effectiveness as a learning tool is attested in accounts of effective learning in UK law schools (eg Burridge, 1998).

Learning journals have almost become an accepted (if minority) orthodoxy amongst law teachers, but their increasing use warrants fresh questions. Can students keep too many learning journals? Are all student learning experiences comparable with Schon's model of the practitioner reflecting-in-action? In complex situations or activities, which bit is selected for reflection? What proportion of the cycle is devoted to reflection rather than to the other stages of the cycle? Blasi suggests, for example, that in guiding students as to what they should be reflective about, a crucial role of the trainer (sic) may be to point out the most critical aspect of a situation or problem (Blasi, 1995: 390). The educationist, as opposed to the lawyer-problem-solver, might retort that such choices should be left to the student to discover *from experience*. The dilemma is a reminder that, as teachers, we are fulfilling objectives that require that we will, and probably should, intervene in our students' learning experiences. They in turn will learn from our guidance and are able to incorporate it in their learning cycle as the observation or reflection of another.

The promotion of a reflective practice for law teachers turns the focus of reflection upon the teacher's practices, not that of the lawyer practitioner or even student learner. It is *our* experiences of interaction with students or trainees that need self-evaluation. The following steps may assist in developing a framework for a reflective practice:

- *Identify personal targets*. Consider personal objectives or a checklist of teaching attributes for a class or module. (It may also be revealing at some stage to ask the same question about overall career choice.) The identification of personal objectives/characteristics could provide the basis for subsequently considering the extent to which personal goals have been achieved or teaching practices altered.
- *Research student needs*. It was pointed out in Chapter 1 that students have multiple learning styles, and that the range and incidence of these differs between students. Since the students will respond differently to different teaching methods, an occasional or even isolated survey of learning styles amongst the class can provide an illuminating profile as well as draw students' attention to the significance of their own personality to studying law. It may also be helpful to explore other aspirations of the students (career, final grade etc).
- *Utilise and adapt available support*. The large group, seminar or practical exercise are the concrete experiences from which law teachers will develop their capacity for reflection. Whether or not teachers keep learning journals of their experiences (unlikely), there are a number of sources of support and simple measures that can be utilised. These come mainly from the growing literature and experience of the reflective practices of others, and can be adapted appropriately to suit law teachers rather than architects or doctors.
- *Monitor performance*. Peer observation can be a source of external critique. The various models for self- and student evaluation that appear in staff development manuals or teaching guides provide a basis (see references, for example in Thomas, 2000). Occasional less formal enquiries into student perceptions of the course can focus their attention upon learning.

The following exercise, to be completed midway through module or year, can be used for feedback to the tutors or could be the focus for a debate involving students about the strengths and challenges of the course that they perceive.

Example of a feedback exercise

Student instruction: Divide a sheet of paper into two columns. On the left write down up to three things that you enjoy about this course and in the other column put down up to three things that you have not enjoyed. Form into groups of four and share your opinions with your colleagues. Hand in the piece of paper and your opinions (anonymous) will be analysed for the next class.

Rationale: It provides instant and unprompted feedback on student perceptions of the teaching methods, course organisation and learning experience. Obtaining feedback during a course enables you to calm anxieties or adapt practices. Focusing on enjoyment first will encourage positive feedback but still allow negative comment. Sharing feedback amongst students will ensure that any extremes on either side will be moderated by a larger group. The exercise is more effective if it is followed up at the next session with an analysis of student responses.

Section 5
Implications of learning theory for developing legal expertise

I have suggested that one of the objectives for the future development of legal education should be a holistic approach to the various stages, particularly if a significant proportion of undergraduate students intends to pursue a legal career. I have also argued that an understanding of law, its methods, role and efficacy, whether its students intend to practise or not, is more likely to occur if the curriculum includes enquiry into the practices of law, and expounds at least in part an experiential learning approach. In the last section, I advanced some of the characteristics that such a practice might observe. In this section, I consider the implications of experiential learning and a reflective practice for the future of legal education and in particular its potential for the development of legal expertise.

In Chapter 1 the emphasis upon competencies in the LPC and BVC was welcomed. Whilst the focus in recent years has increasingly been on the tasks that lawyers perform, most attention has been paid to equipping the vocational student to a level of being 'fit for' a training contract or pupillage. Both the Law Society and the Bar are concerned to ensure that development continues, both during the training contract or pupillage and beyond. Because this is left to the firms or chambers, the approach to learning and development is likely to be uneven and in many instances uninformed by a theoretical understanding of how trainees learn.

Imprecision in learning outcomes, training methods and the selection of appropriate experiences is not surprising because our knowledge of what constitutes legal expertise and the foundations of creative thinking are very much in their infancy. Significant questions, such as the roots of creativity and the nature of legal expertise can, however, be linked to the development of an experiential learning practice. A brief review of emerging scholarship indicates the potential that education theory and experiential methods have for the accomplishment of more complex tasks.

It is the essential messiness of real problems that has attracted the attention of educationalists to the importance that problem-based learning holds for the development of creative solutions. Gary Blasi has considered the nature of legal expertise in problem solving in the context of US legal education. His conclusions are therefore particularly pertinent in the UK context to the vocational stage and beyond. Utilising recent developments in cognitive science, he analyses aspects of legal expertise that are usually considered as 'simply unknowable or suitable only for speculation and bare assertion' (Blasi, 1995: 317).

Blasi identifies problem solving as a core activity of lawyering. He contends that this legal expertise 'consists mainly of the acquisition of a large repertoire of knowledge in schematic form' (1995: 345) and that this knowledge is accrued through successive experiences. It consists of the ability to 'match patterns in the problem-solving environment with stored schemas for problems, solutions or solution procedures'. He concludes that this 'structured knowledge' is made up of more than individual experience, and is 'mediated by the internalised effects… of the partially communicated experience of others, and of culture, theory, language, philosophy, ideology, situation, viewpoint, and desire' (1995: 355). Blasi acknowledges the use of reflective journals in the construction and memorialization of experience and advocates a more scholarly approach to the pedagogy of law.

I have dwelt upon Blasi's thesis for both its pertinence to legal problem solving and its implications for the development of legal education in the United Kingdom. It suggests a staged development of expertise that can be reflected in ever-increasing complexity of the problems set for the learner. It suggests a place for problem solving throughout the different stages of legal education and continuing professional development and commends a holistic approach that transcends current divisions into academic (knowledge) and vocational (skills). It also takes the reference point beyond the tasks that might be expected of a trainee, and reflects a world of complex transaction brokering, legislation design for policy ends and the critical analysis of the capabilities of legal mechanisms.

In Chapter 1, personal as well as professional development as an objective of undergraduate education was raised. The possibility was suggested that emotion as much as cognitive understanding played an important role in learning achievement. Legal education scholars have recently turned their attention to the importance of addressing this affective aspect of a student's personality: 'While the development of and assessment of cognitive abilities have become highly formalised, the affective domain remains the private business of the learner and of any tutors who care to engage with it' (Maughan, Maughan and Webb, 2001).

Personal choices and emotional responses are involved in the adoption of an ethical practice (see Chapter 1). The affective domain also plays its part in legal expertise or 'artistry' as Webb has called it (1995). Webb sees the need for a holism in legal education that links the different domains – affective, perceptual, symbolic and behavioural (Kolb, 1984: 141). He applauds those instances, particularly clinical experiences, which are provided in some law schools. Tutors on undergraduate programmes who employ other experiential methods also engage with the 'affective domain'. Role-playing a battered wife (or the battering husband) in a family law class on domestic violence and legal remedies for a victim will produce aspects of the issue (both social and legal) that may not be appreciated in a straightforward seminar discussion. The feelings of being a client or perpetrator may lead students to readjust their understanding of both the social problem and the legal solution. Role-play can challenge gender, power and cultural perceptions in ways that textual description and analysis are likely to miss. Such techniques encourage imagination and are pertinent in any stage of development.

Kolb, however, maintains a particular significance for experiential learning as a basis for professional development and maps out its pertinence to human maturation to which he ascribes three broad development stages:

- *acquisition* – extending from birth to adolescence and signifying 'the acquisition of basic learning abilities and cognitive structures';

- *specialisation* – extending through formal education and career training into early experiences of adulthood;
- *integration* – representing personal fulfilment in the confrontation and settlement of personal desires, ambitions, interests with society – work, family, friends etc.

(Kolb, 1984: 142–45).

Integrative development may not occur for all of us, but it is at the heart of lifelong learning according to Kolb (1984: 209). 'The challenge becomes to shape one's own experience rather than observing and accepting experiences as they happen' (1983: 145). It is a perspective that may have significance for the nature of legal expertise, redolent as it is with the notion of accumulated knowledge, internalised processes, and the accommodation of individual personality and professional practice. It is perhaps here that Blasi's concern for the nature of advanced problem solving and his identification of the insights of cognitive science engage Kolb's model of experiential learning development.

Conclusion

Global pressures on Higher Education and legal services will require radical developments that cannot be addressed by adjusting the content of the undergraduate curriculum or the topics to be included in the vocational programmes. The quality of lawyer competence and professional responsibility will demand more coherent and far-reaching focus and delivery if it is to be relevant to the needs of global commerce and local community development (Burridge, 2000).

I have sought to illustrate how experiential learning methods and problem-based approaches provide a dimension to understanding law and equipping lawyers and others with the intellectual abilities to tackle complex social and commercial issues. If law schools in the United Kingdom are to build upon their past success, law teachers will have to develop fresh strategies and approaches to developing their students' learning, which international experiences suggest may encounter either reluctance or outright resistance. Tzannes has identified many of the negative attitudes felt by law teachers in her analysis of the challenges to introducing problem-based learning in law schools in Australia (Tzannes, 2001). She suggests that such fears are largely born of ignorance, misinformation or reluctance to face unfamiliar working practices.

The champions of change – whether for more creative approaches to teach legal expertise (eg Blasi, 1995) or for an holistic, reflective teaching practice (eg Webb, 1995) to enhance the understanding of client, student and lawyer alike – would transform the law school. Their visions however are largely constructed upon a model of lawyering that resembles for the most part the conventional (if progressive) conception of the private practitioner.

Exponents of a more radical vision of legal practice inevitably raise additional, rather than alternative, paradigms for law schools to address. Studies of lawyers who deviate from the safe role of the objective, detached and dispassionate professional in favour of the commitment to a cause or community (Sarat and Scheingold, 1998, 2001; Cooper and Trubek, 1997; Trubek and Cooper, 1999) suggest that fresh competences and new knowledge will be needed to equip the modern lawyer adequately. In Chapter 8 of this work Macfarlane challenges the dominant model of the adversarial warrior and advocates a curriculum based upon conflict resolution, co-operation and teamwork.

All these perspectives are rich with opportunity. They also indicate that much of our current law teaching lacks the imagination, intellectual challenge, social relevance and professional value that legal services of the coming century will demand. Whilst legal education may be something of a patchwork of resources and provision, present experience indicates that there is considerable invention and energy to be found in UK legal education institutions. The coming decade will expose whether law schools will develop the strategies and foster the talent necessary to meet the needs of tomorrow's law students.

I am grateful to Caroline Maughan, of the University of the West of England, Mike Maughan of the University of Gloucestershire and Julian Webb of the University of Westminster for their suggestions.

References

Barnhizer, D (1995) 'Of Rat Time and Terminators', *Journal of Legal Education*, **45** (1), pp 49–59

Bergman, P, Sherr, A and Burridge, R (1987) Learning from Experience: Non Legally-Specific Role Plays, *Journal of Legal Education*, **37** (4), pp 535–53

Blasi, G (1995) What Lawyers Know: Lawyering expertise, cognitive science and the functions of theory, *Journal of Legal Education*, **45** (1), pp 313–97

Bone, A (1999) *Ensuring Successful Assessment*, National Centre for Legal Education, University of Warwick

Boon, A and Hodgkinson, P (1996) Life and Death in the Lawyer's Office: The internship in capital punishment studies, *Law Teacher*, **30** (2), pp 253–69

Boud, D, Keogh, R and Walker, D (eds) (1985) *Reflection: Turning Experience into Learning*, Kogan Page, London

Boud, D, Cohen, R and Walker, D (eds) (1993) *Using Experience for Learning*, SRHE and Open University Press, Buckingham

Boud, D and Feletti, G (eds) (1997) *The Challenge of Problem-based Learning*, Kogan Page, London

Brayne, H, Duncan, N and Grimes, R (1998) *Clinical Legal Education: Active Learning in Your Law School*, Blackstone, London

Burridge, R (1998) Role play and simulation in the clinic, *Clinical Legal Education: Active Learning in Your Law School,* ed H Brayne, N Duncan, and R Grimes, pp 173–208, Blackstone, London

Burridge R (2000) Legal education and development – false dawns, fresh breezes in *Government, Development and Globalisation*, ed J Faundez, M Footer and J Norton, Blackstone, London

Cooper J and Trubek L (eds) (1997) *Educating for Justice: Social Values and Legal Education,* Ashgate, Aldershot

Evans, L and Abbott, I (1998) *Teaching and Learning in Higher Education*, Cassell, London

Harris, P and Jones, M (1996) A Survey of Law Schools, *The Law Teacher*, **31** (1) pp 38–126, also available from the UKCLE [Online] http://www.ukcle.ac.uk/news/alt96_report.html

Grimes, R (2001) How was it for you?, *New Law Journal*, **15**, pp 87–88

Hattie, J and Marsh, H (1996) The relationship between research and teaching: a meta-analysis, *Review of Educational Research*, **66** (4), pp 507–42

Heron, J (1982) *Education of the Affect*, British Postgraduate Medical Foundation, London (quoted in Postle, 1993)

Jones, P (1994) *Competences, Learning Outcomes and Legal Education*, Institute for Advanced Legal Studies, London

Kauchak, D and Eggen, P (1998) *Learning and Teaching, Research-based Methods*, Allyn and Bacon, Boston

Kolb, D (1984) *Experiential Learning, Experience as the Source of Learning and Development*, Prentice Hall, New Jersey

Le Brun, M and Johnstone, R (1994) *The Quiet Revolution: Improving Student Learning in Law*, The Law Book Co, Sydney

Lundy, L and Duncan, N (1998) Working with other agencies, in *Clinical Legal Education: Active Learning in Your Law School*, ed H Brayne, N Duncan and R Grimes, pp 136–72, Blackstone, London

Maughan C (1996) Learning how to learn: the skill's developer's guide to experiential learning, *Teaching Lawyers' Skills*, ed J Webb and C Maughan, Butterworths, London

Maughan, C, Maughan, M and Webb, J (2001) How does it feel to think like a lawyer?, paper presented at the W G Hart Workshop June 26–28, Institute for Advanced Legal Studies, London

Postle, D (1993) Putting the heart back into learning, *Using Experience for Learning*, ed D Boud, R Cohen and D Walker, pp 33–45, SRHE and Open University Press, Buckingham

Sarat A and Scheingold S (1998) *Cause Lawyering: Political Commitment and Professional Responsibilities*, Oxford University Press, Oxford

Sarat A and Scheingold S (2001) *Cause Lawyering and the State in a Global Era*, Oxford University Press, Oxford

Schon, D (1983) *The Reflective Practitioner*, Basic Books, New York

Schon, D (1987) *Educating the Reflective Practitioner*, Jossey-Bass, San Francisco

Sherr, A (1998) Legal Education, Legal Competence and Little Bo Peep, *The Law Teacher*, **32** (1), pp 37–63

Thomas, P (2000) *Learning about Law Lecturing*, National Centre for Legal Education, Warwick

Trubek L and Cooper J (eds) (1999) *Educating for Justice Around the World: Legal education legal practice and the community*, Ashgate, Aldershot

Twining, W (1994) *Blackstone's Tower: The English Law School*, Sweet and Maxwell, London

Twining, W (1996) Rethinking Law Schools, *Law and Social Inquiry*, **21** (4), pp 1007–16

Tzannes, M (1997) Problem-based learning in legal education: intentionally overlooked or merely misunderstood?, *The Law Teacher*, **31** (1), pp 180–97

Usher, R (1993) Experiential Learning or Learning from Experience: Does it make a difference?, *Using Experience for Learning*, ed D Boud, R Cohen and D Walker, pp 169–80, SRHE and Open University Press, Buckingham

Warwick University (2000) internal discussion paper on Research-based Learning

Webb, J (1995) Where the action is: developing artistry in legal education, *International Journal of the Legal Profession*, **2** (2/3), pp 187–216

Williams, G (1984) Using Simulation Exercises for Negotiation and Other Dispute Resolution Courses, *Journal of Legal Education*, **33** (3), pp 307–14

Useful Web sites

Street Law at http://www.Streetlaw.org

UKCLE Web site at http://www.ukcle.ac.uk/news/alt96_report.html

University of Central England Law School Web site at http://www.uce.ac.uk/web2/Lawcour/index.html

3

Diversifying assessment and developing judgement in legal education

Karen Hinett and Alison Bone

Introduction

If you were to ask most law teachers what their main interests are you would expect them to cite their specialist area such as Obligations, Criminal law, Property or Human Rights. You would expect this because they are, by profession, teachers of different areas of law. Think then, of the amount of time spent in designing the curriculum, specifying learning outcomes and making judgements about the quality of work produced by students. Law teachers are not just experts in their field but also professional assessors. They help students to develop a sense of justice and what is considered a reasonable judgement based on the facts of the case. As teachers and facilitators they define and assess the qualities and knowledge expected of students. They also help students to understand what is meant by criteria and to begin to make evaluations for themselves.

This chapter takes as a starting point the tensions and challenges posed by the many functions of assessment. In doing so, it acknowledges the need to provide summative information required by stakeholders (Quality Assurance Agency, The Bar Council, The Law Society and recruiters of law graduates) as evidence of scholarly rigour. However, it is concerned more centrally with *students* as stakeholders and examines the provision of formative information by which students can improve their performance and begin to diagnose and remedy intellectual shortcomings. As comments have been received, the chapter has grown in length. As a result, readers may wish to dip into sections as appropriate, or alternatively refer to Bone's *Ensuring Successful Assessment* (1999) for further reading.

Programmes of law vary enormously and it would be both inappropriate and foolish to suggest that the many tensions and dilemmas of assessment can be addressed in any meaningful way in one chapter. More modestly, the chapter offers some support and structure for discussions about assessment to take place in law schools. The chapter begins with a brief examination of what is known about assessment and learning and relates this to the aims of law programmes. In the light of these findings, you are asked to reflect on the appropriateness and suitability of your own assessment systems.

Section 1 represents the first stage of a reflective process in which you are encouraged to 'take stock' of your own assessment activities and to examine how specific modules and areas of study contribute to the development of knowledge and legal and transferable skills. Section 2 examines the use of criteria and feedback mechanisms, exploring how they can contribute to a transparent and equitable system of assessment. It is here that the challenges of consistency of marking, standards and the problems of plagiarism are considered. The chapter further encourages law teachers to reflect on assessment practice, identifies gaps and goes some way to offering examples of practice, such that where appropriate these may be fed back into your own programmes. Section 3 draws on current work and innovations in information and communication technologies (ICT) and looks at ways in which assessment can be diversified and enhanced.

Section 1
Assessment and learning

Research informs us that assessment drives learning (Boud in Knight, 1995: 38). Students interpret the values of their programme and those of the profession through what is assessed. In students' eyes, anything that is assessed is important. The converse is also true and in increasingly competitive market-led times students can be forgiven for attributing less status to those activities that are not formally assessed.

To a large extent, the assessment task also dictates the intellectual approach taken. Where students are required to display knowledge and understanding alone they will do so in quite cursory terms. This is often referred to as a 'surface' approach. An assessment task that requires a student to discriminate between different approaches or theories and to extrapolate or evaluate from them is likely to induce a more focused analytic and 'deep' approach (Entwistle and Ramsden, 1983). Research has revealed that students employing a 'deep' approach take into account their own personal experience, relationships and meaning. Surface approaches are indicated by an emphasis on unrelatedness, memorisation, and unreflectiveness.

A third 'strategic' approach has been used to characterise those students who are driven by vocational aspirations and who see education as a means to an end. 'In each approach the main distinguishing feature is the intention – to understand ideas for yourself (deep), to cope with course requirements (surface), or to achieve the highest possible grades (strategic)' (Entwistle, 1996: 100).

Useful as these terms are for describing various approaches, considered alone they contribute little to the development of robust assessment systems. Such research findings need to be considered in tandem with our expectations and desires for law students. The important point is that assessment systems must be able to accommodate a variety of responses and interpretations. In serving a variety of stakeholders and purposes, assessment strategies must be both sturdy enough to gauge the extent of a student's achievement and flexible enough to offer the potential for future development. Paradoxically, assessment needs to both certificate and verify that learning has taken place and to provide the feedback to promote future learning. It is this tension between certifying competence and promoting further development that creates tension. Too often, assessment methods are used inappropriately and for the purposes of talent development and accountability. It is this lack of consideration to fitness that is problematic. Experience working with law staff reveals that failure to think through the purpose, function and audience (stakeholder) results in second-rate assessment.

Research on student learning also tells us that it is not enough simply to change the context and design of assessment; students must perceive it to be relevant (Entwistle and Ramsden, 1983). Students are more likely to adopt a 'deep' approach to an assessment task when they perceive it to be relevant to the aims of the course, when they believe it is similar to a 'real' legal problem and when fear of failure is minimized. This suggests that in order to be effective assessment has to be considered as part of the learning experience. The practical implication for law teachers is that we should seek to design assessment tasks that invoke an individual and committed response.

Before looking at what this may mean in terms of content and approach, it may be worthwhile to reflect on how many assessment tasks are to be set. One of the many criticisms of modular programmes is that students tend to be 'over-assessed'. Arguably it is possible to be taught too much, but can students ever learn too much? With many students paying fees and often working while studying, it is important to be realistic about the amount of time they can spend on general and specific reading for assessment purposes. A good assessment will encourage this by the way it is structured and timed. It will also enable students to take responsibility for their own learning and reflect on what they have achieved. Assessment tasks that achieve these goals are likely to be very different from those that attempt to measure content knowledge. Diversification of assessment is therefore central to the achievement of a coherent and challenging law curriculum.

Alignment: learning outcomes, teaching methods, assessment

In order to meet these challenges law teachers need to conceptualise assessment as a necessary and integral part of their remit. Assessment should not be something that is 'done to' students at the end of a period of study. It should be an integrated and largely indistinguishable part of the learning and teaching process. The whole experience of law should be one of gaining clarity, understanding, and confidence in legal concepts and procedures and, where appropriate, the acquisition of skills and application to legal practice. Assessment should be an ongoing process of demonstration, feedback and evaluation of progress in order that the student can move on.

The first step in considering effective assessment is therefore to reconsider the purpose that assessment serves. The second step is to be clear about what you are attempting to assess. What is it, in clear and uncomplicated language, that you want students to be able to do at the end of the learning experience? The law benchmark statement offers guidance on the minimum expectations and threshold standards of a law graduate but this needs to be used to develop learning outcomes for each individual programme. The benchmark statements can be used as a way of structuring discussion about the values, aims and expectations of the course. They may also be used as a catalyst for revising inappropriate assessment methods.

One of the most generic learning outcomes for legal education is for students to be 'active' or 'independent' learners. These terms are used interchangeably to refer to students taking more responsibility for their own learning. 'Active learners seek out the information they need, judge their own progress, and are self-motivated' (Entwistle, 1996: 98). This suggests that students are given opportunities to practise and demonstrate making judgements about what they study and the quality of the learning that they undertake. As Le Brun and Johnstone highlight:

> If, as we argue, genuine learning engages the individual in the making of meaning as an internal, self-appropriated process, we should teach law and respond to our students in such a way that they can learn how to learn law and, in so doing, become independent of traditional educational methods.
>
> (Le Brun and Johnstone, 1994: 182)

Developing active learners is just one of a number of likely learning outcomes. The box below reveals the learning outcomes and assessment areas identified during focused discussion. Working with staff in developing assessment strategies, it is clear that this kind of discussion between staff is essential if any coherent picture is to be achieved about the expectations of students.

Ensuring alignment between learning outcomes, teaching and assessment

Learning outcomes
When designing a programme of study it is useful to write the learning outcomes first. Decide what you want the students to learn, or be able to do at the end of the period of study, and then design the content and assessment around those areas. **When writing learning outcomes it is useful to think in terms of three stages. It may help if you think in terms of verb, object and condition. For example:

Examine critically (verb) theoretical frameworks and research (object) relevant to Contract law (context/condition).

Teaching
Having defined your learning outcomes, consider what you need to include in the programme or module. The list below is an example of the content that might inform a law course. Those marked with a star* might be more appropriate at the professional stage. Those without may be seen as important across the range of LLB/MA and professional programmes. Think about how these areas might be taught and then consider what constitutes appropriate assessment:

- communication skills;
- adequate subject knowledge (LLB);

- ★advanced subject knowledge (LPC/BVC);
- use of ICT including research;
- ★competency in a range of skills (eg advocacy, negotiation) (LPC/BVC);
- independent thinking;
- critical analysis;
- understand theoretical perspectives;
- writing skills;
- transferable skills (numeracy, risk assessment);
- application of fact;
- problem-solving.

Assessment areas

Skills: research, writing, analysis, communication – written and oral – understanding, evaluation, application, ICT.

Qualities: confidence, communication, social awareness, commercial awareness, creativity, critical reading, ★professional conduct, developing a legal mindset, independence, ★ethics.

Other: time management, personal organisation, prioritizing.

★★The authors are grateful to Mike Laycock at Education Development Services, University of East London, for allowing them to use this idea.

Perhaps the most important point to be made about assessment is that there must be an alignment between content, learning outcomes and assessment. The three are inextricably linked and cannot operate effectively without each other. They are, if you like, the holy trinity of good assessment practice. What is learnt must be congruent with what is assessed and the two must contribute towards the overall achievement of the learning outcomes of the programme. Not all modules or subject areas have to assess every area or skill but taken as a whole there must be a route that leads to the student demonstration of achievement of the overall outcomes.

The metaphor of 'mapping' works well here. In planning the 'best' route to a particular destination, the navigator/driver will take into consideration a number of factors both internal and external such as: volume of traffic, time of day, urgency to reach the chosen destination, a preference for a scenic route over motorways etc. The driver can then decide what route to take, perhaps making last-minute adjustments as a result of traffic information or unforeseen hold-ups.

In much the same way the student should be provided with a clear 'map' of the content and assessment strategies of each subject area or module. Acknowledging the need to develop key skills and legal knowledge, the student can identify the most appropriate and appealing route to success. Provided it is clear what skills and knowledge are developed in each discrete unit, the student should be able to determine the route taken depending on individual dispositions and propensity for certain types of assessment. If the student prefers to take modules or subject options that have an intrinsic (read 'scenic') interest for them, it should be possible. The only restriction is that students demonstrate they are able to navigate in certain specific conditions (assessment) to reach a particular destination (programme outcomes).

This is not to suggest that assessment is an 'obstacle' to be navigated around but a way of ensuring that the student can cope with unforeseen circumstances in different contexts. We can all appear competent on a virtual racetrack at the amusement arcades but it's not the same as manoeuvring a diesel engine up a steep icy hill!

In identifying and mapping the content, assessment and learning outcomes for the programme on which you teach, we suggest you develop a 'learning matrix'. This will help to ensure that all learning outcomes are being assessed and that students are exposed to a variety of assessment methods that enable them to

---

Assessment criteria: drafting a matrix

How are your learning outcomes defined? Do they use the new template as recommended by QAA? If necessary, redefine your learning outcomes to cover:

- subject knowledge;
- cognitive skills;
- subject-specific/professional skills;
- general intellectual transferable skills (including key skills).

Draft your assessment strategy for each module/unit. Be as specific as possible. Ideally samples should be used. Construct a matrix using learning outcomes across the programme as one axis and module/unit titles as the other. Using the assessment strategies, check off programme learning outcomes against the individual modules/units. Are your learning outcomes all assessed? Are you assessing some much more than others? Can this be justified?

Issues

- Must all learning outcomes be summatively assessed?
- Is it acceptable to have no formative assessment at all in some modules/units?
- What balance (if any) needs to be achieved between the different types of learning outcomes?
- Can a student fail a course because she cannot demonstrate she can write good English?

demonstrate their learning in different ways. See the box on drafting a matrix on page 58.

By way of example we offer two specimen tables that reveal the processes of assessment used in a Postgraduate Diploma in Law. Table 3.1 illustrates an assessment schedule indicating the learning outcomes against each module of the diploma. Table 3.2 takes this process one step further and delineates the type of assessment and weighting for each module. The matrix was then drawn up, which plotted the learning outcomes against the assessment proposals and the latter modified accordingly after discussion by the team.

This is a useful illustration of how the process of discussing and mapping assessment types allows course teams to see how modules fit together as a whole and identify whether certain elements or skills are over- or under-assessed and whether there is a predominant use of one form of assessment. Research by Harris *et al* (1993) indicates that 93 per cent of law schools use examinations as the main form of assessment. Allowing for error and coincidence, this is a significant number. The matrix is a pedagogic tool that allows adjustments to be made in the light of aims and outcomes. It is also a useful structuring tool that provides an explicit and clear picture of the assessment process, which can be used to illustrate teaching and learning activities for quality assurance procedures.

Learning matrices help to expose what is being assessed and the gaps in provision. It may be that certain skills such as written communication are being assessed in nearly every module whilst research skills feature in very few. Decisions need to be taken about dictating core modules or expanding the opportunities for students to develop skills. Another issue to be addressed is whether to assess multiple outcomes in one assessment task. This can help to reduce the amount of assessment but as Yorke highlights, the likely consequence of this; 'is that a generalised grade is awarded in which strength in one aspect is used to compensate for weakness in another' (Yorke, 2001: 7).

Table 3.1 Specimen assessment schedule

Module	Examination	Coursework	Weighting pass/fail
Legal System, Method and Skills I		100% a library exercise a ratio decidendi exercise a statutory interpretation exercise a five-minute individual presentation on a topical issue concerning the English Legal System	pass/fail
Contract Law	70% unseen three-hour paper section A would contain essay-style question section B would contain problem-style questions candidates would be required to answer four questions, two from each section	30% a mini case study	12.5%
Law of Torts	70% paper as Contract Law above	30% a mini case study	12.5%
Public Law	70% paper as Contract Law, but only required to answer one question from Section B	30% critical analysis	12.5%
European Union Law	70% paper as Contract Law above	30% critical analysis	12.5%
Legal System, Method and Skills II		100% a research skills exercise a 15-minute group presentation on an aspect of English Legal System	pass/fail
Criminal Law	70% paper as Contract Law above	30% a mini case study	12.5%
Equity and Trusts	70% paper as Contract Law above	30% a mini case study	12.5%
Land Law	70% paper as Contract Law above	30% critical analysis	12.5%
Project		100% an independent piece of research on 'Another area of Legal Study' (4,000–4,500 words)	12.5%
Total			100%

Table 3.2 Mapping specimen assessment schedule (Table 3.1) against course learning outcomes

	Legal System I coursework	Contract Law coursework	Contract Law exam	Law of Torts coursework	Law of Torts exam	Public Law coursework	Public Law exam	European Union Law coursework	European Union Law exam	Legal System II coursework	Criminal Law coursework	Criminal Law exam	Equity and Trusts coursework	Equity and Trusts exam	Land Law coursework	Land Law exam	Project
Demonstrate a knowledge and understanding of: substantive areas of law; legal system and process, interrelationship between different areas of law; pressures shaping development of law; and proposals for reform	X	X	X	X	X	X	X	X	X		X	X	X	X	X	X	X
Identify, find and use a range of sources of legal information	X	X		X	X	X	X	X			X	X	X	X	X	X	X
Analyse legal information and apply it to the solution of problems		X	X	X	X		X	X	X		X	X	X		X		
Critically evaluate law and proposals for reform					X	X	X	X	X		X	X	X	X	X	X	X
Communicate legal information orally efficiently and effectively	X									X							
Communicate legal information efficiently and effectively in writing	X	X	X	X	X	X	X	X	X		X	X	X	X	X	X	X

With grateful thanks to law group at the University of Brighton, especially James Macdonald.

Section 2
Appropriate and valid assessment

Taking stock of what and where we assess are vital steps to developing quality assessment strategies. How we assess is equally important. A multiple-choice questionnaire is a valid way of assessing basic knowledge, eg in what circumstances a duty of care may arise, but is not suitable for assessing problem-solving skills. The familiar 'advise John' problem question can be a useful way of assessing legal knowledge and application but it needs careful structuring if it is to take the student beyond basic processing and into the realm of evaluation and creativity.

In thinking about appropriate and relevant ways of assessing development many lecturers have turned to educational taxonomies such as those outlined by Bloom (1956), Perry (1970), and Biggs and Collis (1982). Each of these outlines a hierarchical structure of development beginning with a basic comprehension and leading to an ability to synthesise and evaluate information. In Perry's scale this means moving from a position of 'dualistic thinking', a crude state where everything is viewed as right or wrong to one of 'contextual relativism' where the student acknowledges and distinguishes between multiple possibilities. The transition for Biggs is characterised by a move from pre- or uni-structural thinking to one where parts are related, integrated and reconceptualised thereby creating an individual perspective. The common denominator between these hierarchies is the concept of the student gaining a critical and individual perspective. Inherent in the hierarchies is an assumption that the 'good student' will build on existing knowledge and come to appreciate the knowledge and skills of law as tools by which various interpretations can be made. This means that students need to have some idea of what is expected of them and given an opportunity to practise skills. The ability to appreciate the broad issues of a subject and then discriminate and manipulate information such that it supports a particular school of thought is quite complex. Students need to be able to explore their own values and to locate these within the canon of legal theory. They need to be able to make mistakes without fear of retribution and be given opportunities to critique the respected work of their subject discipline and their own contribution to the debate.

Fulfilling these requirements can appear daunting since it requires a more structured and transparent approach to learning, teaching and assessment than hitherto in legal education. Helping students to reach the peak of their potential requires both extensive scaffolding and the integrity of staff in order to let students determine their own path of investigation. Later in the chapter, we explore ways of achieving this through the use of feedback and peer and self-assessment. We return now to the use of taxonomical objectives.

Designing criteria

In designing criteria it is common to use Bloom (1956) or Biggs and Collis (1982) as a structure for grading. For example, a student who displays an ability to relate, integrate and evaluate material might receive 65 per cent and above compared with the less able student who has simply described material and thus receives 40 per cent. What is often unclear is whether the criteria reflect a development in *each* of these areas. Do all criteria have to be met in order to gain a high mark or is it possible to shortcut on one and compensate in another? For example, is it possible for the student receiving 65 per cent to have displayed a basic level of description but to have provided a sophisticated analysis and application of theory, therefore boosting the overall grade?

Criteria can be hierarchical without necessarily being developmental. Criteria may help to illustrate what a student has achieved without adequately revealing the value-added progression. It is possible for a student to achieve 65 per cent in an assessment having met all the criteria but this does not necessarily illustrate the development of the student's skills of evaluation compared with the previous assessment. Neither does it reveal the differences in processing and application between two assessments both receiving the same grade.

Law teachers have yet to deconstruct the assessment systems used in traditional three-year courses to the purposes of modern, modularized law programmes. In traditional linear programmes it may (and this is questionable) have been acceptable to assess individual undergraduate law subjects using an essay and a final examination at the end of each year because the students were unified. Each student was exposed to a similar teaching programme. Comparisons of grades were made on the assumption that each student had equal opportunity to develop. Transfer and application of knowledge were not considered because of the holistic nature of the programme. However, in a modular programme in which students choose their own route, some provision must be made for the transfer of knowledge. Grades that indicate what a student can do against a set of criteria do not reveal the process by which skills were developed, nor do they accommodate the various contexts in which the law student may work.

By definition, modular programmes are incremental and lead to an aggregate of grades. The grade represents the acquisition of knowledge and skills and this determines the overall degree classification. The problem with this is that it denies any acknowledgement of progression or development. The challenge to law teachers is how to build this into the programme design.

One way to ensure that development is recognised in the structure is for law teachers to reflect on the nature of the outcomes to be achieved. Law schools that offer CPE programmes will be aware of the recent problem posed by the QAA framework debate. Are such students truly studying at postgraduate level or are they merely approaching new material almost by way of a second undergraduate programme? Graduates by definition have (or should have) better communication skills, better analytical skills and higher thinking skills. How do we assess students on such programmes?

Another approach is via curriculum design. Which subjects are studied in the second year of a three-year programme? Which in the first or third? Would an external examiner be able to identify the different levels of the programme because of the different nature of the assessment tasks? This takes us back to Bloom's taxonomy. If it is not easily transparent to those looking for evidence of progress it is unlikely that a student has picked up any implicit, subtle nuances about progression.

Some law schools have tried to develop a generic set of criteria and marking sheets to cover all subject areas. Whilst this may appear to provide comparable statistics, in effect it is meaningless to students and stakeholders unless each criterion is broken down and explained in terms of each assessment task. The use made of legal knowledge in an oral presentation may be the same as in a written assignment but the application will differ depending on purpose. The student has to make a judgement about the appropriateness and suitability of knowledge to purpose.

In developing criteria that can be tweaked to fit various forms of assessment, we suggest you ask yourself the following questions:

● Are the criteria meant to be hierarchical?
● Are the criteria developmental?
● Do the criteria reflect the entire marking range (1–100 per cent) or only part of it (30–70 per cent)?
● Are the criteria specific to one level or can they be used throughout the duration of the programme?
● What mechanisms are put in place to ensure that the students understand what is required of them?

Consistency and standards

A common staff development technique is to go through a blind-marking technique with law teachers. This never fails to illustrate the subjectivity and difficulty in producing consistency amongst a group of markers. Even when criteria are defined, the various interpretations made of them lead to wide variations in grade allocation and discrepancies about what is of importance. The reality is that law teachers hold implicit concepts of what is quality work and this affects any meaningful evaluation of student work. Inevitably comparisons are made between scripts and performances and it is easy for this, albeit unconscious, norm-referencing to affect the standard of the cohort of work. As Elton points out:

The traditional type of examination… in which a student answers in two to three hours some few questions… usually by choosing them from a larger number of questions offered, is worryingly unreliable. Not only do different examiners give different marks to the same candidate but they rank them in different order, and this is equally true if the same examiner re-marks a set of scripts after an interval of time.

(Elton, 1987: 88)

The Legal Education Research Project undertaken by Harris and Bellerby (1993) revealed that depending on the institution, students can take anything between 18 and 30 modules to complete a law degree. As each module invokes its own discrete assessment, that can mean an enormous amount of assessment and a correspondingly large margin for inconsistency. Current research by Mitchell *et al* (2001) aims to investigate the reliability and consistency of marking undergraduate law assignments. Faculties of law at three universities are using identical criteria to mark work. The preliminary findings have revealed huge discrepancies in the grades awarded. So much so, that in terms of degree classification the student could receive a third or upper second class.

Yorke, Bridges and Woolf (2000) quoting from HESA (1999) show that there were fewer first class law degrees awarded than in any other discipline surveyed and that across other disciplines the range of marks used varies considerably. In addressing these problems there are several obvious steps that can be taken:

- *Triangulation of evidence*. Increase the number of people involved in the assessment. This can include faculty staff, external examiners, professional practitioners (eg solicitors brought in to the university, those responsible for the student on vacation placement). Peers and the students themselves can also offer a useful formative role, which can be used as an additional source of corroborative information.
- *Repeat observation*. If, as suggested earlier, students are offered at least two opportunities to demonstrate a particular skill or knowledge development this allows a picture of competency to be built up over time. Judgements are therefore based on a number of assessors evaluating different instances of the same skill (eg negotiation). Performances can be compared and demonstrated by video, script or report documentation.
- Alignment between learning outcomes, teaching and assessment task. Ensure that assessment questions are concise and measure that which students are required to learn.
- *Reduce ambiguity*. Keep assessment tasks simple and related directly to the subject. If you are attempting to assess multiple outcomes in one assessment make sure it is 'fit' for purpose.
- *Negotiated criteria*. Allocate sufficient time and resources to the design of assessment criteria. Ensure there is some agreement about the hierarchy of criteria amongst subject specialists. If self- and peer assessment are to be used, consider involving students in the negotiation process.
- Use a range of assessment methods so that all students are challenged and aggregation reflects a more realistic picture of students' abilities.

The work by Mitchell *et al* (2001) may be discouraging but what it does illustrate is the need for law teachers to discuss assessment and what is valued in their teaching. It may be difficult to show inter-reliability (across communities) but intra-reliability within one faculty is achievable with planning.

The *QAA Code of Practice: Assessment of Students* (2000) has induced a number of discussions in law schools. It outlines 18 precepts that must be adhered to. Consistency and standards are addressed throughout the document, eg under precept 2 (page 5) institutions are asked to consider 'how to make information and guidance on assessment clear, accurate, consistent and accessible to all staff, students, placement or practice assessors and external examiners'. Within the law school it is obviously very important that all teachers are aware of the different range of assessments students are exposed to on any given course, and that expectations as to what, for example, a first year undergraduate may realistically produce in the early weeks of a course are identified and agreed.

On the topic of grading and marking, the *QAA Code* on assessment states that, '[i]nstitutions should publish, and implement consistently, clear criteria for the marking and grading of assessments... [and] ensure that there are robust mechanisms for marking and for the moderation of marks' (2001: 8). 'Robust mechanisms' include examination boards, meetings with external examiners and appeal procedures, most of which will be dealt with at institutional or faculty/school level. Meetings between internal examiners within and across subject areas (especially in mixed degrees) to discuss marking criteria are also essential and yet not always to be found.

However good the intentions of quality mechanisms, the increased responsibility of law teachers to define, align and monitor assessment methods has resource and staff development implications. As the other chapters in this book indicate, legal education is concerned not only with downloading case law but with developing ethically responsible, reflective individuals. Law teachers need to be concerned that students come to appreciate justice and values for themselves. One neat way of introducing this topic is to discuss issues of moral integrity within the framework of assessment. In considering this we turn to the increasing challenge presented by plagiarism.

Plagiarism

According to the literature (Carroll and Appleton, 2001; Franklyn-Stokes and Newstead, 1995; Ashworth, Bannister and Thorne, 1997; Evans, 2001) plagiarism in the United Kingdom is increasing. Plagiarism constitutes a variety of forms of academic inappropriateness. The term 'literary theft' is used but this is inaccurate since it focuses on the written word. The more common definition of 'passing off work as one's own' is more illuminating since 'work' can mean anything that is written, spoken, produced or articulated through the medium of film or photograph. Defining what we mean by plagiarism is not just a semantic issue but is central to the prevention of such activities.

Stefani offers a useful distinction between what she calls 'problem activities' (1999). These include:

- copying – reproducing or imitating a specimen answer;
- plagiarism – to steal the thoughts or writing of others and pass is off as your own;
- collusion – an agreement to deceive.

If viewed as a taxonomy, copying and plagiarism indicate slightly less serious 'problem activities' than collusion, which involves a conscious intention to deceive and to sabotage the work of others. All can be loosely described as 'cheating' but it is important that students understand the often subtle dividing line between collaborative work and collusion.

Defining terms is the first step to combating plagiarism. The second is to be aware of plagiarism and alert to the systems that support it. The Internet is blamed for much of the uprise in plagiarism, whereby simple 'cut and paste' essays can be created in minimal time. Web sites also provide online order and delivery services of law essays on a number of topics. Students with the available funds (£30 is the minimum rate for an essay) and the inclination to sacrifice their own learning can submit an essay that they have had no part in producing. The enterprise is acceptable since an explicit statement is offered about the use of materials. Finchley Law Tutors maintain that; 'As a professional body we do not support plagiarism, materials may only be used for individuals' sole purposes as revision study aids only. Under no circumstances should anyone attempt to pass the work off as their own' (www.knowledge.co.uk/lawessays/order.htm).

Whatever opportunities the Internet provides for the facilitation of plagiarism it also offers a number of deterrents. Research at Sheffield Hallam University (MacDonald, 2001) indicates that most students are aware of the poor quality of the essays for sale. As part of an experiment to deter plagiarism, students were encouraged to search and use the materials available online and were trained to reference appropriately. Interviews with the students revealed that the training was a much stronger deterrent than sanctions. Detection tools such as http://plagiarism.org allow teachers to check submitted assignments against other work on the Web, whilst 'CopyCatch' detects collusion by comparing essays in a shared student cohort and looking for shared material (other electronic tools are listed at the end of the chapter). Each has limitations but offer a quick way of scanning a number of texts, which may be advantageous given the large student numbers commonly found in law schools.

Being aware is one of the key ways to combat plagiarism. As teachers and regulators of quality in legal education, it pays to be vigilant to warning signs. These include URLs and dates on pages, Americanisms (where the student is not from the United States), above average use of vocabulary, out-of-date references and reference to work that has not been covered on the course. Institutions that permit handwritten work may be less aware of the problem since obvious 'cut and paste' plagiarism is more difficult to detect; the student has at least had to rewrite the information but this does not mean it should go undetected or unpunished.

Knowing how students cheat is one way of policing the problem but understanding why students cheat is more helpful in prevention. There are very few empirical studies into plagiarism in the United Kingdom but those undertaken indicate three main reasons for cheating. In rank order these are:

- 'stress and pressure for good grades' (Franklyn-Stokes and Newstead, 1995: 160; Norton *et al*, 2001);
- inadequate assessment that 'encourages students to cheat' (Franklyn-Stokes and Newstead, 1995: 170);
- a genuine confusion about what constitutes cheating (Ashworth, Bannister and Thorne, 1997: 196).

Interviews with students at Sheffield Hallam University also indicated laziness, over-assessment or bunching of assignments and poor management skills as motivations for cheating. Looking briefly at each of these reasons for cheating it is clear that steps can be taken to help students. Assessment is a powerful incentive to learning but it is also a powerful prompt to plagiarism. Faced with failure some students do adopt desperate measures. In supporting students, law teachers have a responsibility to design valid and appropriate assessment. It is rare for induction to address issues of assessment or plagiarism in any detail and easy for law teachers setting early assignments to assume that issues relating to referencing have been dealt with by someone else.

The research indicates that students perceive some forms of assessment as 'inviting cheating' (Ashworth, Bannister and Thorne, 1997: 202). Examinations are given much more kudos than coursework. Only 6 per cent of students reported that they had been involved in premeditated collusion to communicate answers to each other during an examination. This compares with 54 per cent who admit to plagiarizing from a text, and a worrying 72 per cent who 'paraphrased without acknowledgment' (Franklyn-Stokes and Newstead, 1995: 169). Students appear to feel less responsible for plagiarizing coursework. There is agreement in the research that the concept of plagiarism is simply less meaningful for students than it is for staff who value intellectual property and the concept of a scholarly community. As indicated earlier, one of the ways to address the problem may be to integrate training in referencing and citation within the context of teaching on ethics.

It is assumed by many law teachers that students know the difference between collusion and collaboration but the line of distinction is thin. In interviews with students, Ashworth and colleagues attempted to find out reasons why students might not cheat. All the reasons given by students related to a sense of integrity and moral obligation either to themselves, their peers or tutors. The third point about confusion over what constitutes plagiarism is clearly one that can be addressed through learning and teaching and the engagement of students in group work where they can learn for themselves the difference between supporting colleagues and supplying a ready-made assignment. Clearly there is much that can be done by individual law teachers and institutions to clarify the procedures and regulations around plagiarism. The QAA *Code of Practice* on assessment addresses this too under precept 3 (page 6):

> ... Additionally, institutions will wish to consider how students are provided with information and guidance on their responsibilities within the assessment process including for example: definitions of academic misconduct in respect of assessment, such as plagiarism, collusion, cheating, impersonation and the use of inadmissible material (including material downloaded from electronic sources such as the Internet); accepted and acceptable forms of academic referencing and citation.

In *Plagiarism: A Good Practice Guide* (www.jisc.ac.uk/pub01/brookes.pdf), Carroll and Appleton make several recommendations for dealing with plagiarism. Individual law teachers are urged to design out cheating options by changing essay titles and rethinking assessment tasks. It is suggested that institutions and professional bodies:

- define terms, give examples, reach consensus;
- train and use skilled academic misconduct officers;
- monitor compliance;
- develop shared tariffs for punishment;
- create a culture of 'no tolerance' for cheating.

In addition to this generic list, law teachers may wish to consider the following recommendations for assessment and legal education:

- Write or reinterpret regulations surrounding plagiarism specifically for the law school and particular programme being studied. Plagiarism is not just an offence at undergraduate level; it applies equally to professional programmes.
- Provide a supportive environment where students feel comfortable to discuss issues surrounding work and plagiarism. This could be achieved by engaging them in a problem question or simulation that deals with the ethical dilemma of intellectual theft.
- Endeavour to inculcate a sense of community of students as both legal scholars and professional practitioners. Evidence suggests that assessment through clinic, Virtual Learning Environments (VLEs) and problem-based learning help students to view themselves as responsible people who uphold values and justice.
- Follow up written assignment with oral defence (like a PhD viva) where the student has to explain the issues and confirm knowledge of sources.
- Use self- and peer assessment to identify obvious cases of plagiarism. This will need to be supported by a negotiated group commitment to fair play and a thorough understanding and appreciation of assessment criteria.

- Discuss the merits and shortcomings of an essay on a Web site such as Finchley Law Tutors as a way of helping students to understand what constitutes quality.
- Use reflective statements to accompany written work including questions such as, 'What problems did you face and how did you overcome them?', which forces the students to account for the process of learning as well as the product.
- Reduce the amount of assessments required and be aware of other deadlines, especially for joint honours students. Desperation can lead to underhand tactics even for the most committed student.
- Ensure that offenders are punished. Students need to see that penal systems are put into effect; this may be particularly pertinent to students of law.

Like all complex problems, plagiarism can only be effectively dealt with by a number of strategies. A comprehensive review of curriculum design and assessment is more likely to be successful in combating plagiarism than the threat of policing.

Use and application of feedback

Quality of feedback is an important issue for quality assessors, external examiners and, of course, students. As discussed in the introduction, the tension between audiences is part of the problem in providing feedback both for accountability and the development of student learning.

Knight (2001) makes a distinction between 'Feedback' for the purposes of development and the 'Feedout' of statistical information for external stakeholders. Feedback should identify the strengths and weaknesses of the work or performance such that students can reflect on the comments and move forward. To be useful to students it needs to be given at a time when it can be used for development purposes (ie not at the end of a module where the assessment is never to be repeated). It also needs to be detailed and specific enough to be of use and written in a way that promotes the transfer and application of skills and knowledge to other contexts.

Feedback is often written in negative and 'final' language (Boud, 1995) that suggests that little can be done to improve performance. If students are to embrace the challenges of critical analysis and evaluation they need honest guidelines about how to move forward.

The *QAA Code of Practice* on assessment (2000) also addresses feedback issues. Precept 12 (page 9) states:

'Institutions should ensure that appropriate feedback is provided to students on assessed work in a way that promotes learning and facilitates improvement. In meeting the needs of students for feedback on their progress and attainment, institutions will need to consider: the timeliness of feedback;

specifying the nature and extent of feedback that students can expect in relation to particular types and units of assessment, and whether this is to be accompanied by the return of the assessed work… '

A quick review of different practices within one's own law school can be quite illuminating and those with experience of external examining will be aware again of how students often receive very different amounts of feedback, at very different times and for apparently different purposes. Coursework that is summative in nature is less likely to contain extensive comment than that which is formative, ie there is still a tendency for teachers to assume that summative assessment 'signs off' a piece of work and that there is no point looking back. Developing reflective practice in our students, however, requires us to encourage them to revisit completed work and we need to be specific about how it could be improved. Even such positive comments as 'good!' in the margin of the work, do not help if the student is entirely unaware what was good or, more importantly, why it was thought to be good!

It is common practice to provide feedback via an assessment proforma. Some institutions adopt a centralized system of statement banks where teachers can select from a list of adjectives accompanied by individual comments. This provides a consistency of terms between markers and means that the student can judge improvement from one assignment to the next.

By contrast, examination scripts are rarely written on except for informing fellow markers, or the external examiner, of the marker's thoughts at the time of marking. There has been discussion about returning 'A' level examination scripts to students so that they may learn from the examiners' reports, which are published with their own scripts to hand (and undoubtedly to encourage transparency of marking in the first place). Consider how the law teachers at your institution would react if they were told that examination scripts had to be returned. What would be the likely impact on marking practices?

First year students in particular gain great benefit from looking again at the work they have done under stress in an examination. If they are referred and need to do an examination again surely there is every good pedagogic reason for allowing them to see where errors occurred and areas could be improved? If handing over examination scripts seems too radical a step, then there is a good argument for allowing students to see a comprehensive report on a previous examination, with a breakdown of questions attempted, mark spread and guidance on what was done well and what less well.

Section 3
Diversifying assessment

At the beginning of the chapter, we identified 'active' or flexible learning as one of the main aims of legal education. Entwistle claims this may involve:

- providing structured resource materials;
- offering negotiation of tasks and topics;
- encouraging self- and peer assessment;
- devising 'real-life' projects for collaborative group work.

(Entwistle, 1996: 109)

In seeking to fulfil these requirements, law teachers need to relinquish some of their power as the 'keepers' of knowledge and adopt a more facilitative role such that students are motivated to seek out information for themselves. This new role may not automatically fit the traditional, arguably narrow image of the legal educator as the fount of legal knowledge but it is certainly no less demanding. Supporting students such that they gain confidence in their own abilities and capacity to make judgements is a skill executed only by the very best law teachers. A dogmatic resistance to the diversification of assessment and to the modern demands of society, professional bodies and students is arguably borne out of fear and ignorance rather than a commitment to professional values.

In exploring how this diversification can be achieved, we examine the increasing use of self- and peer assessment, oral assessment, reflective journals and the use of information and communication technologies (ICT). There is not space here to elucidate on the many other forms of assessment that can be used in legal education; however, we highly recommend Le Brun and Johnstone (1994), who provide an excellent overview of assessment practices.

Self- and peer assessment

Despite common belief there has been considerable work conducted on the use of self- and peer assessment in law (Boud and Tyree, 1980; Tribe and Tribe, 1989; Hinett and Thomas, 1999; Hinett *et al*, 1999). Almost certainly these practices are being used, but not documented, in many law schools. Distinctions have been made between self- and peer assessment and self- and peer evaluation. The 'Self Assessment in Professional and Higher Education (Saphe) project involving law staff at three institutions found that the term 'evaluation' had more resonance with formative, qualitative statements. By contrast, 'assessment' was perceived as the act of attributing grades. There has been much debate about the distinctions between the two but for the purposes of this chapter Klenowski's definition is neat. She maintains that self-evaluation is broader than the attribution of grades because 'it refers to ascribing value to a learning experience: first in the identification of criteria used; second by what it considered meritorious: and third, by outlining the implications for future action' (Klenowski, 1995: 151).

The aim of both self- and peer assessment is to bring the learner into the territory of making judgements. It elevates the student from the position of 'assessee', about whom judgements are made, to that of 'assessor'. This ensures that students are required to take responsibility for their own development and to acknowledge what is expected of them. In order to self-evaluate, students have to understand the criteria that define quality in legal education. Some law teachers choose to involve students in the negotiation of criteria (Tribe, 1996). This process enables students to understand and communicate ideas that they consider important, with the lecturer and their peers, about what should be assessed, and what weighting should be given to each specific criterion. As Le Brun and Johnstone state: 'The ability to assess oneself lies at the heart of legal practice' (1994: 190).

As well as being a pedagogically sound assessment tool, self- and peer evaluation can also serve a practical function. Faced with hundreds of examination scripts, even the best law teacher is likely to suffer from assessment fatigue. The danger is that staff fall back on norm referencing, ie comparing the work of one student with that of another. Feedback becomes shorter and less individualised and therefore less useful for learning. However, 'If students mark their own work, either with respect to specified standards or their self-established criteria, they not only release staff for more educationally worthwhile activities, but they are encouraged to reflect on their own work and the standards which can be applied to it' (Boud, 1995: 169).

Peer assessment can also be attractive to the busy law lecturer. Students produce draft scripts or rehearse oral performances and their peers, fully aware of the criteria and learning outcomes, offer preliminary feedback. The experience of the Saphe project is that so long as students 'contract' (verbally or in some cases in writing) to the ethos of supportive learning, the feedback they offer is clear, relevant, concise and produced in a much quicker time than the law tutor can provide. Peer learning and evaluation also aids teamwork. Practical experience in clinics confirms that student learning is 'deeper' in a cooperative setting than in traditional competitive settings.

However, self- and peer evaluation are not without their problems. Providing evidence of validity (that what is being taught is actually what is being assessed) is relatively straightforward but offering evidence of reliability in a system where learners not only define their own criteria but also assess their own work by that criteria is problematic. Boud and Falchikov (1989) conducted a major review of the literature on self-evaluation including 48 studies. They concluded that they could find no overall consistent tendency for students to either under- or over-rate performances. Studies have also shown that when criteria are negotiated with students the rate of agreement between student and tutor increases. Given the problems of reliability and consistency in traditional forms of assessment, self- and peer evaluation are no less problematic. Safeguards such as tutor marking can be put in place. The University of Hertfordshire operates a moderating policy whereby both student and tutor allocate a grade to a piece of assessment. If the staff and tutor grades are within 5 per cent of each other it is accepted; if it is larger than 5 per cent more discussion based around the criteria takes place (Tribe, 1996). Presumably in cases of real discrepancy a third opinion could be sought.

Inevitably there will be some resistance to the use of self- and peer evaluation. However, the educational value of such practices far outweighs the reservations held on the grounds of tradition. Students come to value their own learning, they begin to understand what reflecting on practice means for their own development and learn how to work effectively with others. Both the Law Society and Bar Council have expressed their support for the integration of such practices.

Oral assessment and performance

Oral work is not given much currency in the literature on legal education. Examples of advocacy and interviewing skills are more common in professional legal education but there is a dearth of accessible examples of assessed presentations or assessed discussion work at undergraduate level. Law schools are using discussions, presentations and student-led seminars as learning tools but there are very few examples describing how such activities are assessed. This is likely to change with the introduction of benchmarking. The documentation clearly values oral communication as a key skill:

> Law students are expected to be good at both written and oral communication. Whereas written communication is assessed heavily by formal examinations, oral communication is demonstrated by a variety of compulsory and voluntary activities, eg tutorial performance or mooting.
>
> (QAA, 2000: 7)

Most law teachers agree that oral communication is a key skill; what is not made clear is how oral communication should be assessed. Again we return to issues of function and purpose of assessment. Are we assessing content knowledge or the ability to articulate an argument in front of an audience? Research into student learning suggests that there are a number of pedagogic reasons for using oral communication as a way of enhancing learning (Hinett 1997; Joughin 1999; Hounsell and McCune, 2001).

Research carried out with students from a range of disciplines explored how students know when they have 'learnt or understood an aspect of the programme' (Hinett, 1997). Anticipated responses included 'when I get a good grade'. However, the most common answer was 'when I can talk about it'. It seems students evaluate their understanding by their ability to talk about the subject or explain it to someone else. As educators we are well aware of the steep learning curve that takes place when we try to structure information in a way that can be taught. We should not be surprised to learn that students also use oral articulation as a benchmark for understanding. There appears to be a connection between speech and understanding. In one instance, a student was reminded that she had performed an oral presentation as part of her assessment and she replied, 'yes, but that didn't feel like it was being assessed. Somehow it had a different feel to it. To me work signifies exams and writing things down' (Hinett, 1997).

Joughin hypothesises that oral assessment is more likely to lead to a deep approach to learning since it requires a personal commitment and engagement with subject matter. Oral assessment is not perceived as an easy option; indeed studies reveal that students find oral assessment and presentations difficult. Students allocate additional time to the preparation of a presentation and express feelings of apprehension about their ability to express themselves coherently. This is partly due to inexperience in oral assessment but has more to do with the perception of an 'audience'. Learning involves interaction between a number of 'agents'. Agents might be tutors, placement teachers, professional practitioners, or peers, all of whom influence the learning potential of an individual. Students perform in the knowledge that their work is being judged by these agents and if the form of assessment is oral and face to face then the pressure to perform well is greater. Ignoring the problems of self-confidence, several factors emerge about students' perception of oral assessment that may explain the adoption of a deep approach:

- Students do not wish to make fools of themselves in front of those passing judgement, which prompts a responsibility towards work.
- Speech is transparent to waffle and padding.
- In order to answer questions on a subject the student has to understand for him or herself (reducing the opportunity for plagiarism).
- Speaking inevitably means that you are heard (eradicating any possibility of confused areas being overlooked by those making judgements).
- Oral assessment involves body language conveying more about the level of comprehension than can be expressed in written form.
- There is a personal involvement and ownership of the spoken word.

In written assessment it is possible for students to submit and deny responsibility for their work. The power differential between 'learner' and 'assessor' ironically enables the student to disengage from the learning process. One student remarked: 'you only have to hand it in and you don't have to be there when it's actually marked. You're separated from your piece of work because you're not there'. (Hinett, 1997). The physical distance created between the student's production of written work and the assessor's judgement appears to promote an intellectual separation in the mind of the student. Improving student learning therefore necessitates a closure of the perceived gap between feedback and action.

ICT in assessment

Information and communication technologies (ICT) can assist with the process of assessment by providing new forms of assessment as well as supporting existing forms. A major problem in assessment during a period of massification of legal education is the amount of resources required for both formative and summative assessment. ICT can provide some amelioration for this problem. For example, in interactive courseware such as Iolis, students carry out a variety of exercises for which they are given formative feedback as they go along (see Chapter 4). Of course the electronic feedback is not geared to the individual needs of the student. Nevertheless because the feedback is provided progressively and immediately on undertaking a particular exercise, students have the opportunity to improve by learning from their mistakes as they progress through a workbook.

A development of significant potential is the use of multiple-choice questions for summative assessment. Multiple-choice exercises are not new, and in the past have been delivered on paper. However, computerised multiple-choice assessment systems such as QuestionMark enable the instant and secure delivery within the examination context of questions where the student is given a mark for their performance immediately on completion as well as feedback on the questions answered correctly and incorrectly. The examiners are saved a great deal of effort because they obtain an instantly tabulated markset as well as detailed analysis of student performance. The problem, of course, is that multiple-choice has a tendency to be associated with the quiz as only a test of surface knowledge. It is possible to devise multiple-choice tests that assess deeper conceptual knowledge. Nevertheless, for the foreseeable future, this type of test can only be used as part of an overall assessment strategy.

The impossible search for the Holy Grail of assessment is for a system that would automatically assess and provide feedback to written answers to problem questions and essays. Systems are being developed that will assess the quality of work on the basis of similarity to sample answers. Thus the program developed by Erasmus University Department of Computers and Law compares all answers and sorts them according to similarity to a sample set of answers marked by the examiner (Combrink-Kuiters et al, 1999). The system will also identify answers that do not fit the pattern. These are marked personally and fed back into the system to enhance the sample. A further advantage is that the system can detect through the analysis of language answers that may have been plagiarized.

ICT can provide support for traditional and new assessment systems in other ways. Spreadsheet-based systems can assist with the recording and tabulation of marks. The development of Virtual Learning Environments (VLEs) promises the automation of the administrative processes involved in learning and assessment such as registration, enrolment in modules and recording of marks and feedback. On-screen presentation of marks has been used in examination board meetings, because it is easier to provide a variety of views of mark profiles of individual students and compare them with the cohort being examined compared with traditional paper data.

Such VLEs can also assist the assessment process in new learning methodologies such as problem-based learning and experiential learning (see Chapters 2 and 4). For example, a virtue of the electronic PBL projects at Lancaster and Strathclyde described in Chapter 4 is that an electronic audit trail is provided of the interaction between the student teams. This can be an important record for the purpose of assessment. As the use of ICT becomes ubiquitous in clinical and experiential learning, it can provide effective audit trails to assist the process of assessment. VLEs can also assist in formative assessment of dissertations and projects. Much dissertation supervision now takes place through electronic mail or VLEs. The groupwork capacity of VLEs provides an excellent management facility for peer assessment. For example, in an experiment in Warwick Law School, students are encouraged to place the outlines of their essays and dissertations on the Web-based VLE and to comment on each other's work. This enables students to use examples of other people's outlines as well as their own to improve the quality of their own work.

Conclusion

Biggs suggests that assessment is such a controversial topic precisely because it serves both institutional maintenance and because it 'taps into belief systems about what learning is and what education is for' (Biggs, 1996: 5). What we assess says a lot about what we value. Our assessment systems indicate to students and to the outside world what constitutes a quality learning experience. The research into student learning has revealed to us that assessment drives learning and that what we assess affects what students find important. Students 'learn' the assessment culture and 'cue seek' what is to be assessed at the expense of true understanding (Becker *et al* 1968; Snyder, 1970). There is some evidence that students cheat on assessment to avoid looking a failure. The pressure to succeed is enormous and designing 'final' assessments such as examinations and product-oriented tests exacerbates the problem. Using a variety of assessment techniques gives each student an opportunity to shine and to gain confidence in their ability.

Commitment to student-centred learning requires a diversification of assessment and a reappraisal of the skills, qualities and dispositions required of law students. Where possible, students should be given opportunities to develop evaluative skills and to make judgements for themselves. However, the way in which such practices are implemented is crucial to the development of critical and truly independent learners. Self- and peer assessment must be integrated into current practices in ways that are relevant and appropriate to the goals of the programme. Furthermore, there must be a genuine commitment to the development of evaluative skills. It is unfair to imply through a peer assessment task that students have some part in the assessment process and then to negate their comments by exerting assessor authority and allocating a grade to the work.

A fairly radical proposal such as the dissolution of the classification system would help to ease the transfer of assessor power. The QAA and Universities have set up a Progress Files Implementation Working Group, which is working towards a means of recording achievement by the use of such files (see references for details).

Certainly institutions such as Maastricht Law School in the Netherlands, which adopts a completely problem-based approach to legal education, has fewer problems validating courses that involve self- and peer assessment (Moust, 1998). Whether we succeed in developing the autonomous learners and lawyers we hope for depends on the extent to which we are willing to relinquish power as assessors and to help students to develop their own conceptualisations of quality.

The authors are grateful to Jude Carroll, Oxford Brookes University for providing resources on plagiarism and to Abdul Paliwala for his input on ICT.

References

Ashworth, P, Bannister, P and Thorne, P (1997) University Students' Perceptions of Cheating and Plagiarism in Academic Work, *Studies in Higher Education*, **22** (2), pp 187–203

Becker, H, Geer, B and Hughes, E (1968) *Making the Grade: The Academic Side of College Life*, John Wiley and Sons, New York

Biggs, J and Collis, K (1982) *Evaluating the Quality of Learning*, Academic Press, New York and Sydney

Biggs, J (1996) Assessing Learning Quality: Reconciling institutional, staff and educational demands, *Assessment and Evaluation in Higher Education*, **21** (1) pp 5–15

Bloom, H (1956) *Taxonomy of Educational Objectives: the classification of educational goals. Handbook One: Cognitive Domain*, Longman Group, London

Bone, A (1999) *Ensuring Successful Assessment*, National Centre for Legal Education, University of Warwick

Boud, D and Tyree, A (1980) Self and Peer Assessment in Professional Education: a preliminary study in law, *Journal of the Society of the Public Teachers of Law*, **15** (1) pp 65–74

Boud, D and Falchikov, N (1989) Quantitative Studies of Student Self Assessment in Higher Education: A critical analysis of findings, *Higher Education*, **18** (5), pp 529–49

Boud, D (1995) Assessment and Learning: Contradictory or Complementary?, *Assessment for Learning in Higher Education*, ed P Knight, pp 35–48, Kogan Page and SEDA, London

Carroll, J and Appleton, J *Plagiarism: A Good Practice Guide*, JISC, Bristol [Online] http://www.jisc.ac.uk/pub01/brookes.pdf [last accessed November 26 2001]

Combrink-Kuiters, *et al* (1999) *Comparing Student Assignments by Computer*, paper presented at the 14th BILETA Conference, York [Online] http://www.bileta.ac.uk/99papers/mulder.html

Elton, L (1987) *Teaching in Higher Education: Appraisal and Training*, Kogan Page, London

Entwistle, N and Ramsden, P (1983) *Understanding Student Learning*, Croom Helm, London

Entwistle, N (1996) Recent Research on Student Learning, *The Management of Independent Learning*, ed J Tait and P Knight, pp 97–112, Kogan Page, London

Evans, J, The New Plagiarism in Higher Education: From Selection to Reflection [Online] http://www.warwick.ac.uk/ETS/interactions/vol4no2/evans.htm [last accessed November 26 2001]

Franklyn-Stokes, A and Newstead, S (1995) Undergraduate Teaching: Who Does What and Why? *Studies in Higher Education,* **20** (2), pp 159–72

Fransson, A (1977) On Qualitative Differences in Learning. IV – Effects of Motivation and Test Anxiety on Process and Outcome, *British Journal of Educational Psychology*, **47** (1), pp 244–57

Harris, P *et al* (1993) *A Survey of Law Teaching,* Sweet and Maxwell/Association of Law Teachers, London

HESA (1999) *Students in Higher Education Institutions 1997/98,* Higher Education Statistics Agency, Cheltenham

Heywood, J (2000) *Assessment in Higher Education: Student learning, teaching, programmes and institutions,* Jessica Kingsley, London

Hinett, K (1997) *Towards Meaningful Learning: A theory of improved assessment for higher education,* unpublished PhD thesis, University of Central Lancashire

Hinett, K and Thomas, J (1999) *Staff Guide to Self and Peer Assessment,* The Oxford Centre for Staff and Learning Development, Oxford

Hinett, K *et al* (1999) Managing Change in Assessment and Learning in Legal Education: A tale of two cities, *The Law Teacher*, **33** (2), pp 135–58

Hounsell, D and McCune, V (2001) *Making the Most of Oral Presentations by Undergraduates,* paper presented at the ILT Annual Conference, York

Joughin, G (1999) Dimensions of Oral Assessment and Student Approaches to Learning, in *Assessment Matters in Higher Education,* ed S Brown and A Glasner, pp 146–57, Open University Press and SRHE, London

Klenowski, V (1995) Student Self-Evaluation Processes in Student-Centred Teaching and Learning Contexts of Australia and England, *Assessment in Education: Principles, Policy and Practice,* **2** (2), pp 145–64

Knight, P (2001) Complexity and Curriculum: a process approach to curriculum-making, *Teaching in Higher Education*, **6** (3)

Le Brun, M and Johnstone, R (1994) *The Quiet Revolution: Improving student learning in Law,* The Law Book Company Limited, NSW, Australia

MacDonald, R (2000) Why Don't We Turn the Tide of Plagiarism to the Learner's Advantage?, *Times Higher Education* 24/11/00

Marton, F, Hounsell, D and Entwistle, D (1996) *The Experience of Learning: Implications for Teaching and Studying in Higher Education,* 2nd edn, Scottish Academic Press, Edinburgh

McDowell, L and Mowl, G (1995) Innovative assessment: its impact on students, *Improving Student Learning through Assessment and Evaluation,* ed G Gibbs, pp 131–47, The Oxford Centre for Staff Development, Oxford

Mitchell, B *et al* (2001) *Comparative Marking Standards,* paper presented at the Association of Law Teachers' Conference, Durham

Moust, J (1998) The Problem Based Education Approach at the Maastricht Law School, *The Law Teacher*, **32** (1), pp 5–37

Norton, L *et al* (2001) The Pressure of Assessment in Undergraduate Courses and Their Effect on Student Behaviours, *Assessment and Evaluation in Higher Education,* **26** (3), pp 269–84

Perry, W (1970) *Forms of Intellectual and Ethical Development,* Open University Press, Bletchley

Quality Assurance Agency for Higher Education (2000) *Code of Practice for the assurance of academic quality and standards in higher education. Section 6: Assessment of students*, QAA, London

Snyder, B (1970) *The Hidden Curriculum*, The MIT Press, Cambridge, MA and London

Stefani, L (1999) Paper given at an ILT Inaugural Assessment Event, University of the West of England

Tribe, D (1996) DIY Learning – Self and Peer Assessment, *Teaching Lawyer's Skills*, ed J Webb and C Maughan, pp 353–68, Butterworths, London

Tribe, D and Tribe, A (1986) Assessing Law Students, *The Law Teacher*, **20** (3), pp 160–68

Yorke, M, Bridges, P and Woolf, H (July 2000) Mark distributions and marking practices in UK higher education, *Active learning in higher education*, **1** (1), pp 7–27

Yorke, M (2001) *Assessment for Senior Managers*, LTSN Generic Centre, Briefing Paper, York

Useful Web sites
Electronic detection tools for plagiarism
The Joint Information Systems Committee (JISC) commissioned a technical study on the software available on plagiarism. The findings were reported in July 2001. http://www.jisc.ac.uk/mle/plagiarism/

http://www.google.com
Use as a first port of call. Will search and extract text and the advanced search facility allows exact matches of text to be identified.

http://Plagiarism.org
Tested by five HE institutions, it allows you to check work against other similar work on the Web.

http://www.plagiarism.com
Offers a self-teaching package that removes words from documents and times how long it takes students to put them back. Claims to reduce plagiarism but would need to be tested.

http://www.turnitin.com

Progress files
http://qaa.ac.uk/crntwork/progfileHE/guidelines/progfile2001.pdf

http://www.ltsn.ac.uk/genericcentre/projects.asp

http://www.recordingachievement.org/

4

Negotiating the learning process with electronic resources

Paul Maharg and Abdul Paliwala

Introduction

There is a growing and significant interest in pedagogy in legal education.
Increasing external surveillance of Higher Education from bodies such as Funding
Councils in the United Kingdom, the need to adapt to changes that are occurring
in the legal professions, global competitive pressures, declining resources and
increase in the consumer power of students have all led law teachers to develop
theory from and around their practice (see Chapter 9). Information and communications technology (ICT) is integral to many aspects of the changes in legal
education: it provides the pressures promoting changes as well as pathways, tools
and techniques for implementing them. Castells (1996) best describes the impact
of technology on social networks.

The objective of this chapter, which is aimed at both undergraduate and postgraduate law teachers, is to consider the relationship between electronic learning
resources and the pedagogy of legal education. In the process, we suggest that
while educational theory can be used to guide ways in which ICT can enrich legal
education, the competing paradigms in instructional design and educational
theory should warn us against finding exact pedagogical fits. Therefore, while we
have organised this chapter around the conceptual framework of resource-based
learning (RBL) we do so in order to explore how it might be adapted to the new
technologies of ICT.

Students learn by using resources. If this were all, of course, then almost every form of education could be called *resource-based*. But what distinguishes RBL from other learning approaches is the emphasis put on the resources themselves, and the importance of the resources for student learning. As Lisewski and Settle (1996: 109) suggest, 'resource-based learning is underlain by the philosophical assumption that allowing the learner to achieve learning outcomes in a more flexible and independent manner is inherently better than the traditional learning method'.

Resource-based learning is not a new concept in either secondary or Higher Education. It has many precursors in the forms of learning and tuition based around a corpus of texts. Large-scale examples of these in secondary-level education would include the Ford Teaching Project, the National Science Foundation's *Man: A Course of Study* (with which Jerome Bruner was associated) and, in the United Kingdom, the *Humanities Curriculum Project*, in which the educationalist Lawrence Stenhouse was heavily involved (Elliott and Adelman, 1973; Stenhouse, 1983).

In all of these initiatives, there is a move away from a transmission model of education (Ramsden, 1992) to one where tutors take on new roles, becoming facilitators or, in the case of the *Humanities Project*, 'neutral chairpersons'. The result of this is more focus not just upon the resource but, to a greater or lesser extent, upon student learning. Taylor (1971), quoted by Clarke, put it very well: 'I am "taught" by a teacher; but "I learn" from a book... Herein lies the essential difference between teacher-based and resource-based learning systems' (Clarke, 1982: 29).

As an undifferentiated learning resource, books have in recent years developed into new specialised learning forms such as open learning materials, study guides, textbook guides, and workbooks (Brown and Smith, 1996: 1). And in the 1970s RBL began to feature other media. Audio-cassettes, then television and later videotapes and teleconferencing were all used to enhance and supplement textual materials and small-group learning. Each of these had an effect on the structure of student learning, but it is interesting to note that to begin with, most were based on a textual model of delivery. Early television programmes for the Open University, for example, were often scripted around pieces to camera, interspersed with charts and pictures, which closely mimicked the forms of lecture and didactic texts available to students. In addition, the TV programmes could not be recorded and replayed on a VCR with the functions of review, forward, stop and pause that we now take for granted. Their overall effect in the resource base could therefore only be to enhance or to reinforce the content of the main course texts.

When we consider RBL in the context of ICT, it becomes clear that the context of the new media has a marked effect on the content and structure of RBL materials. Nowhere is this more apparent than in hypermedia and Web-based RBL, as we shall see below. Many commentators have pointed this out. Diana Laurillard, summarising much of the research in 1993, comprehensively demonstrated how different forms of educational technology can contribute to student learning. For example, she discusses how television is a poor informational medium, not merely because there was lack of user control over the TV programmes, but that where it did succeed in supporting learning, it was where there was 'image-argument synergy' (Laurillard, 1993: 115, quoting Laurillard, 1991).

By contrast, ICT techniques can be used to support learning in more flexible ways: text, graphics, stills, videos and sound can be used to interact upon each other in many different ways and to different purposes. Images can be digitised and text overlays added or juxtaposed to them; a full text of a video session can be made available, and a commentary can be run simultaneously, too (Maharg, 2001; Paliwala, 2001). Note-taking and other learning support applications can be added to toolbars. The result of this type of media is much more connection between texts and images, and user manipulation of and interaction with the visual images. Viewers thus enter a learning space that is rich with tools to help them dialogue with the materials of their discipline. Typically, these involve:

- multimedia courseware;
- electronic datasets;
- specialised communication devices such as electronic, audio and videoconferencing.

These media are distributed either through CDs or Internets and intranets. A fundamental problem in the delivery of computer-based RBL in the past was the lack of integration between different tools and items of courseware. However, this is being overcome recently by the development of increasingly sophisticated Virtual Learning Environments (VLEs) for managing delivery of learning systems. Blackboard, Web-CT and Lotus Notes are typical examples of such environments. Figure 4.1 is an example of a Web learning environment for law students developed by Hannah Jamieson and John Dale.

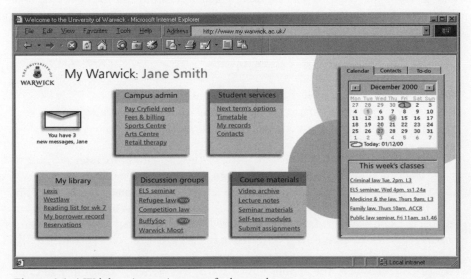

Figure 4.1 A Web learning environment for law students

When RBL works successfully in a course, students often:

- take responsibility for learning and peer-teaching;
- study at their own time, pace and place;
- undertake formative assessment at various points in the course;
- adopt reflective learning attitudes;
- work effectively in teams and groups.

Nevertheless, the achievement of success in the production and implementation of RBL requires project planning from the start. We combine here the helpful suggestions of Laurillard (1993) and Brown and Smith (1996) to suggest the main ingredients:

- a careful attention to pedagogy, including learning outcomes to be achieved by students from the project and methods of feedback;
- institutional commitment and effective resourcing for both development and implementation;
- integration of development, implementation and evaluation of RBL.

Learning via conversations in cyberspace

Laurillard's book, though published in 1993, is still essential reading for anyone teaching in HE because she applies educational theory and research regarding how students learn using educational media. Using the research of phenomenologists such as Entwistle, Säljö, and particularly Ference Marton, and the conversational theories of Gordon Pask, she develops what she calls a 'conversational framework' for describing the learning process (Hasselgren 2002; Pangaro 2002; Marton *et al*, 1997). Laurillard's approach bridges the gap in perception between students and lecturers. This is done by a process that:

- reveals the students' and lecturers' conceptions to each other;
- provides space for negotiation and adaptation of topic and task goals;
- provides opportunity for feedback, reflection and action upon feedback.

Laurillard's conversational framework outlines 'the conscious processes available to the learner to consider and modify'. The engine of this model is the movement between two actions: 'action on the world... [and]... talk about those interactions with the world' (1993: 105). Feedback is an essential element of both actions; but feedback, like the other of the dialogue, need not be that from a lecturer or tutor only. As Laurillard points out, '[f]or learning to take place, the core structure of the conversational framework must remain intact in some form: the dialogue must take place somewhere, the actions must happen somewhere, even if it is all done inside the student's head' (1993: 105).

On the basis of this theory, Laurillard then goes on to develop a sophisticated and effective framework for using educational technology, including many aspects of design, implementation and integration. The conversational framework as Laurillard defines it is an important one for describing how learning can be supported and mediated by educational media.

Typical examples of conversational learning in the context of traditional legal education are a Socratic session and the interactive problem-solving seminar/tutorial. The Langdellian Socratic session normally involves arriving at the main principles of law through question and answer-based study of decided cases. The problem-solving tutorial involves exploring a hypothetical legal problem to arrive at a solution. Hawkins-Leon (1998) provides an interesting comparison of the two methods. Problem-based learning (PBL) is a differently structured variation of the latter method (Boud and Feletti, 1997; Cruickshank, 1996).

In both these forms, students use 'resources' such as prescribed textbooks, cases, legislation, and law review articles to prepare for the class interaction. For the 'conversation' to be effective, a considerable amount depends on effective description of resources, a clear statement of learning methods and outcomes and the definition of learning tasks, for example in the form of hypothetical problems to be resolved or issues to be discussed.

In both Pask's and Laurillard's terms, the conversation is already taking place because students may be addressing learning needs before they come to the classroom. What takes place in the classroom is, however, another conversation. It may involve feedback from students on assigned learning outcomes and tasks, so that the tutor can adapt the tasks in the classroom. It may involve solving the problem interactively, with students being challenged and challenging their tutor or one another and the tutor contextualizing the problem both in terms of student learning needs, situating it within students' real world experience and providing space for reflection from specific experience to the theoretical and conceptual framework of law.

The post-class experience also provides space for reflection for both students and tutors, enabling room for relating what went on in class to the expected outcomes, learning tasks and resources and further extra class discussions among students and with tutors.

Unfortunately, the absence of this ideal type in the real world is becoming more marked. The classroom learning experience may be too short to carry out all the tasks expected of it and is becoming less frequent because of pressure on resources in a period of growing class sizes. One response to this is to move towards wholesale electronic RBL. The other is to develop RBL as supplement to traditional learning. We first discuss three experiments including a virtual law school, the teaching of courses online within an on-site university and the use of RBL to supplement traditional learning and teaching. After critical consideration of these, we propose a new model for thinking about the role in legal education of RBL using electronic resources.

Virtual law schools: Semple Piggott Rochez

Semple Piggott Rochez (Web site accessed in 2001) lay claim to being the first virtual law school in the world. Concord Law School in the US (Web site accessed in 2001) became a virtual campus in 1998. Unlike the Open University Law Degree, SPR and Concord rely almost entirely on electronic RBL delivered on their intranet Web sites. Students enrol electronically on to the intranet. On such enrolment, students are provided with restricted access through password to courses and materials on which they are enrolled.

The well-designed SPR site includes course notes for all subjects, which can be read on-screen or downloaded by the student. Textbooks and other supplementary reading for the student are also clearly identified in relation to each topic. In addition, the student has access to a digital library, including texts of public lectures and articles, law reports and public documents. There is also a small library of sound and video materials although at present these are too small to make a significant impact on student learning.

Students also have access from the Web site to a variety of commercial law datasets including LEXIS, WESTLAW, CONTEXT and LAWTEL as well as other free material on the Web. The conversational element in teaching and learning is developed through three devices. The course document provides clear instructions on approach to learning and a 'help desk' provides students with access to course tutors and to university administrators with a free phone line directly from a PC. An intranet 'chat room' provides real-time opportunity for student study groups for each subject and also includes a contact tutor.

In addition, there is access from the site for more structured learning through timetabled virtual learning seminars run by course tutors. Apart from a specific role for the tutor, the virtual tutorial provides for a structured engagement by means of a problem or discussion topic.

The system is therefore impressive in its attempts to replace the traditional learning environment with an electronic one. Surprisingly, it does not offer a consistent set of electronic lectures, although this technology is increasingly available (see, for example, the Boxmind Web site [Web site accessed in 2001]). It does, however, offer a set of electronic tutorials.

The SPR Law School, in attempting to reproduce the classroom experience on screen, may be missing the opportunity of using the full potential of ICT to produce new approaches to learning. For example, Sir John Daniel of the Open University has suggested that there are advantages to such asynchronous electronic conferencing in preference to the audio, video, or text lecture mode (Daniel, 1996). It provides students with more time and space to discuss issues. In addition, the SPR system does not have the benefit of interactive multimedia, which would provide generalised feedback to the student.

A more significant problem of the system is the lack of integration between student study groups and virtual tutorials. Neither provides room for the type of negotiated and focused dialogue which is possible with appropriate use of conferencing facilities. At present, the systems such as SPR, Concord and the St Thomas Law School lack the full richness of a traditional on-site law degree, but as the method becomes more sophisticated and the programmes become grounded, they may offer competition to traditional law schools (Byrnes, 2001).

Wolverhampton: an experiment in virtual learning

Unlike the full virtual environment of SPR, the Wolverhampton experiment attempted to use exclusively electronic RBL for only two course units in negligence and medical law in a university system, which relied otherwise on personal contact teaching for both full- and part-time students. The authors believed, '[o]ur courseware with its combination of full case reports, synopses and commentaries, text, articles and hypertexted study plans dramatically improves the quality of such tools' (Migdal and Cartwright, 1997). Furthermore, the incorporation in the courseware of video reproductions of key legal developments, for example a role play between judges discussing the decision in *Donoghue* v *Stevenson,* provided a new imaginative element to the course. Students also received feedback to questions. However, there were no virtual tutorials as at SPR. Instead, reliance was placed on asynchronous but free electronic discussion. The students liked many of the electronic aspects. However:

> An obvious and predictable finding was that however well designed the study materials are, students still place a very high value on personal contact with tutors and other students. One comment was that 'It is a good idea but... at best it can be described as a resource like a miniature library [but] in no way a teacher'.
>
> (Migdal and Cartwright, 1997)

Since then a very different approach has been taken to multimedia learning with the Wolverhampton Online Learning Facility (WOLF) (Web site accessed in 2001). This system provides a similar range of multimedia elements to the previous experiment. However, there is now a greater emphasis on providing structured resources for the students supplemented by personal and electronic communication. One lesson of the Wolverhampton experience is that multimedia courseware is a learning resource and not a learning system. It needs to be integrated into the overall learning experience – 'technology supported learning'.

Iolis courseware: integration into traditional learning

In principle, Iolis courseware (a CD ROM produced by the Law Courseware Consortium in six-monthly editions) is intended to provide such integration.

Unlike other projects described here, Iolis developed as a national project involving the contribution of over 100 academics to the broad range of courses in the LLB curriculum. A Scottish sister project developed courseware for Scotland using different approaches.

Iolis was developed not as a learning system but as a learning resource. Unlike other courseware, Iolis workbooks do not distinguish between lecture notes, full text of cases, statutes and periodicals, multimedia illustrations and exercises, but weave them into a hypertext and integrated learning conversation between the courseware and student. Within this framework, authors may develop their own approach to teaching by selecting from a wide range of interactions based on hypertext, multiple-choice, and image manipulation. Furthermore, the courseware offers opportunities to course teachers to customise and integrate Iolis within their own learning/teaching objectives by the use of a 'comment' facility or by links to their Web site (Grantham, 1999, 2000). Figure 4.2 shows an example of an illustration from the Iolis courseware extracted from the Iolis Workbook on Express and Implied Terms.

The key conversational element is feedback in response to choice of particular options or answers. Thus in Hugh Collins' workbook on Judicial Remedies in Contract law, the student is presented with a series of hypothetical problems. As each

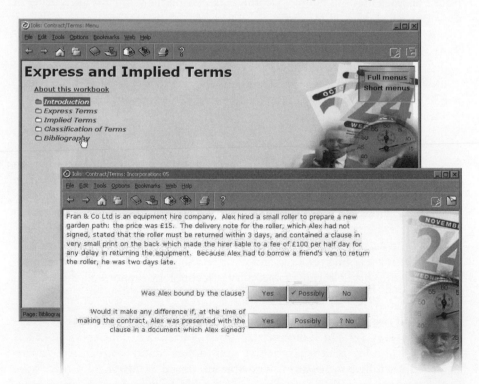

Figure 4.2 Example of an illustration from Iolis

problem is solved, a new problem is presented requiring a greater degree of sophistication. At each stage, the student is provided with feedback and invited to explore other issues, ideas, and resources. The conversation lacks the spontaneity of the typical face-to-face tutorial or seminar. The student cannot, subject to what we say below, ask an awkward question and get an answer. However, the system has the advantage of being one-on-one, with the pace and choice of navigation being controlled by the student.

Nevertheless, Iolis is not without limitations. In principle, it is a closed learning system, whereas a conversational RBL needs to allow dialogue between learner and teacher so that each can adapt to the other's needs. In addition, the pedagogical approach of the author of a particular workbook might not meet the approach or needs of the tutor. However, both issues are only a problem if Iolis is considered as an entirely stand-alone virtual learning system. Much depends on how it is adapted to the learning systems used by course tutors and students. Course tutors can decide not to use particular workbooks or parts of workbooks. Or they can adapt workbooks to their own needs through the use of comment and Web links facilities (Grantham, 1999, 2000). Unfortunately, many course tutors are not aware of these possibilities (Hall, 2001).

Beyond the conversational metaphor

Until now, we have stayed within the conversational metaphor. There are, though, a number of problems with it. Real conversations tend to be very loosely structured over time. They often take place in short bursts that we carry with us to a greater or lesser extent over a period of time, with episodic chunks being recalled some time after the event (Mercer, 1998: 70–71). And as Laurillard herself points out, teaching is a rhetorical activity, highly structured and planned (Laurillard, 1993: 29). Conversation is rarely that strategic, though, and learning is not just a process of conversation and feedback.

One approach to overcoming the weaknesses of traditional approaches is to adopt a version of problem-based learning (PBL) (Cruickshank, 1996). Learning by problem-solving has been a key feature of the legal educational process in many countries. However, PBL uses a highly structured methodology derived from medical education in problem-solving, with great emphasis on the empowerment of the student. Typically, the course teacher provides the problem, but the performance is student-led. Students determine the learning tasks in group sessions, assign research tasks, carry out the research, and report to the group, which discusses the problem and solution. Various academic interveners such as the course developer, the tutor and the resources librarian operate mainly as facilitators in this exercise. There is a shift in emphasis away from a conversational metaphor in which the key relationship is between teacher and student, towards structured student group work within parameters established by the group facilitator.

The derivation of PBL in medicine misses out the element of negotiation, which plays such a key role in legal work. In medical PBL, the underlying issue is diagnosis or problem solution, which can be communally performed with or without interaction with the patient. There are elements of legal learning in which this may be appropriate. However, law is a terrain of contested meanings and negotiated solutions. In a different and broader sense, learning itself is also a process of negotiation, and a number of educationalists, from traditions other than phenomenography, have recognised this for some time. The recent rhetoric, composition and literacies literature, for example, emphasises this element of the educational experience.

Linda Flower, in her study of student literacies, points out that conversational theory 'fails to capture some important social and psychological realities', which have been debated in anthropology and cognitive psychology for some time now (eg the ethnography of communication; schema theorists). As Flower expresses it, conversation is '*a* process, not *the* process' of how we construct meaning (Flower, 1994: 64).

Flower makes a convincing case for the place of negotiation to be considered in education. For her, the process of constructing negotiated meaning comes into play where there is pressure to change or unease; where there are 'multiple voices or kinds of knowledge that would shape action'; and where the meaning so constructed is 'a provisional resolution and a response to these voices' (1994: 68). Flower downplays the adversarial connotations of the negotiation metaphor, instead emphasising how students and writers navigate or arbitrate meaning in the contexts within which they need to learn, and often as 'a response to a perceived exigency' (1994: 72). Learners negotiate with their prior knowledge, with teachers' expectations, with texts, between the variant readings of different texts, with multiple readers, concepts of examiners, and so forth.

In any given context there are many complex moves that are made in the process: 'appropriation, co-option, cooperation... resistance' and so forth (1994: 106). Where Laurillard tends to focus on individual learning moments, Flower reminds us of the wider picture, particularly from a student perspective. In place of conversation theory, she proposes a tentative 'framework for enquiry' based upon a cycle of acts of interpretation, negotiation and reflection (1994: 75, 98).

This has direct relevance to legal education. Negotiation is of course inherently a skill practised by lawyers; and most jurisdictions include it in their professional educational skill set at some point or other. But in a deeper sense, students need to interpret, negotiate, and reflect upon the structure of law as they learn it. In a sense, this is true of any discipline in the university; but it is particularly true of law, where uncertainty and conflicts of value require to be negotiated by both law teachers and practitioners. Electronic RBL can play a role here by giving students the opportunity to construct and reconstruct their knowledge and skills in case studies, simulations and role-plays. Students become more engaged with the knowledge base of the tasks and, as a result, it is much more likely that in this type of environment, deep learning will take place.

RBL: negotiations in cyberspace

The process of negotiation is particularly relevant to RBL for two reasons. First, as we noted above, students tend to be responsible for much more of their learning in RBL than in other forms of teaching. Second, the highly structured nature of RBL means that students are required to navigate the learning process for themselves, and to cycle through the activities of interpretation, negotiation and reflection that Flower outlines.

If this is true of more traditional forms of RBL, it is even more applicable to hypermedia and Web-based learning. We can see it occurring in one aspect of computer-mediated communications, namely the discussion forum. Students can use the forum to communicate with each other, bring problems to light, or to discuss substantive law or learning processes. But as Laurillard rightly points out with regard to other channels of communication, the medium itself is not interactive *per se*: much depends on how the knowledge and information within it is used.

Much also depends on other factors, to be negotiated by students. What is the purpose of the forum, and who has access to the postings? Who will moderate the discussions, and what will be the tone of the moderating voice? Will the moderator be an active contributor, a mere provider of information, a teacher, facilitator or Stenhouse's 'neutral chairperson'? How complex ought the resulting discussions to be?

Whether or not teachers are aware of these factors that influence the forum when they set it up, students are aware of them, and need to negotiate them. These factors have a powerful effect on student contributions to a forum. In one legal educational project, for example, students were required to make at least one contribution to the forum during the span of the project. The resulting discussion was wide-ranging and practical (Barton *et al*, 2000).

Thus, legal education can make a distinctive contribution to both RBL and PBL techniques by integrating the processes of negotiation and electronic learning environments. To illustrate this in more detail, and to suggest ways in which Web-based RBL may be constructed and implemented, we take two detailed examples of RBL in an electronic context: a personal injury project in Scottish postgraduate professional legal education, and a postgraduate Anglo-French negotiation exercise to come to an agreement on an Internet contract.

Both projects take the issue beyond the conversation-based approach to RBL suggested by Laurillard and promote a negotiation-based strategy.

The Personal Injury Project

RBL is nearly always planned as a system of resources presented to students to use. But it is possible to create a resource-base online, which is not given to students overtly, and which they require to discover for themselves. RBL thus becomes a form of discovery learning. Materials are created, but they remain hidden or scattered. This is particularly useful if we want to simulate a legal trans-action in which students learn by doing and where, as in legal practice, they need to construct the problem before they can begin to solve it.

This is what was designed in the Personal Injury Project, which is one of a number of online projects carried out in the Diploma in Legal Practice at the Glasgow Graduate School of Law (GGSL). In this project in 2000–2001, students were divided into 'firms' of four students (46 firms in all), each with a virtual office. The office interface was constructed using MS Outlook, so that students had the functionality of the Outlook tools at their disposal: they could e-mail each other, use task organisers or to-do lists, consult project resource pages or their own document directories, calendars, Frequently Asked Questions lists and discussion forums, tutors, the other side in the transaction, and fictional characters. These characters – in reality teaching assistants who provide information via e-mail and attachments – inhabit a fictional town, called Ardcalloch, sited on the south bank of the Clyde. The town is represented by a zoomable map, photographs, a business directory giving access to firm and institution Web sites and it has a history stretching back to the thirteenth century. Figures 4.3, 4.4 and 4.5 are all extracts from the Ardcalloch online Personal Injury Project at the GGSL.

Figure 4.3 Map of Ardcalloch, overview, showing thumbnail illustration of town, top left, and zoomable map, right. Directory, Introduction and History buttons are top right

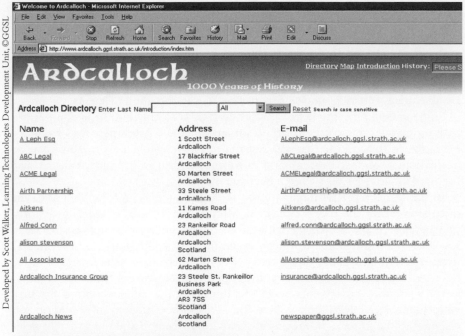

Figure 4.4 Extract from postal and email directory

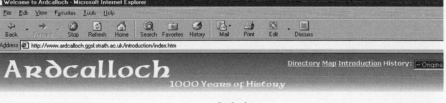

Figure 4.5 History of Ardcalloch – extract of section on town origins to early medieval period

In the project, half the student firms represented the claimant (an employee injured at work), while the other half were the insurer's solicitors. Twenty-three different scenarios were used, all based on a similar set of facts, but with important variables (eg injuries to fingers or thumbs, to dominant or non-dominant hand, etc). Each scenario had a different document set for claimant and insurer. The project began when initial memos were sent to the claimant firms, and Accident Book extracts and an insurance report were sent to the insurer's agents.

Students could meet to negotiate face-to-face once only, but the encounter had to be video- or audio-taped for assessment purposes. Assessment was based on evidence of five criteria: factual research, legal research, negotiation strategy, performance of that strategy and collaborative learning. Students were also required to write a 1,000-word reflective report.

In this project, the resources are the initial documents and the Web sites, the discussion forum and the virtual town. More resources, such as specialist reports, photographs of the workplace where the accident took place and the machines involved, were distributed throughout the fictional community, and available to firms that requested them appropriately from the personae in the town. An introductory lecture and a feedback lecture supported the process. But since collaborative work was actively encouraged within firms, the students within the firm were themselves a learning resource for one another. Indeed, collaboration was essential to the process of learning in firms, for we emphasised not merely delegation of work but peer feedback and group reporting as best practice. Studies indicate that when students are actively involved in collaborative learning online, the outcomes can be equal to or better than those for traditional classes. If, however, individuals in an online environment simply work on posted materials and return individual work, the results tend to be poorer than in traditional classrooms (Hiltz *et al*, 2000).

The project is thus built around the concept of collaborative learning: what the facts of the case are, how the different narratives interlock or contradict each other, which facts are more significant than others, which questions to ask. In the domain of legal research, they needed to determine which facts were legally significant, issues of liability, quantum and contributory negligence. In practice terms, they needed to separate out issues of Tax, Welfare Law and other areas of law, and deal with these.

Some practice issues were too complicated for them at this stage – for example, those of payment and fees – and these were deliberately left out of the project. Nevertheless, one of the key aims of the project's pedagogic design was to give students the opportunity to negotiate the key elements of the process for themselves, which they did by working within a set of resources. In this respect, conversations (via discussion forums, firm discussions, notes to file, etc) were subordinate to task negotiation, to the process of constructing the problem.

Throughout the stages of problem-construction and legal research, students were encouraged to begin the process of forming legal negotiation strategies. The process, which took place over 10 weeks, allowed students to develop a 'feel' for a complex process. The process of simulation within the electronic environment allowed them to learn by discovery (in the legal as well as the ordinary sense of the word), and to learn how to develop a professional voice in legal communications. It gave them the opportunity to practise the critical capacities and skills necessary to professional life as lawyers.

This time to explore is even more important in the domain of ICT resource-based learning than it is in other media. It is a valuable form of 'bricolage', discovery learning within a bounded domain (Turkle, 1994). In this instance, students undoubtedly needed the time to develop the problem and its solutions. The result, though, was that students learnt so much more of the process of pursuing or defending a claim than they would have in any other way. These findings are supported by theory and research (Schank and Cleary, 1994) and in student feedback, some of which is quoted below:

It was not so much a difficult question that I had to answer, so much as a difficult situation that the firm placed themselves in. We had recommended a figure to our clients and had later realised that our calculations had been wrong. How should we respond? Do we simply gloss over the mistake or do we apologize for our error, in which case we draw attention to the fact we were wrong? Would our client continue to trust our judgement after we had made a mistake of that nature? The fact that the mistake would have worked out as costing him only £2,000 was not the issue. We ended up deciding to tactfully apologize. We acknowledged that an error might have been made and explained how it came about without going into unnecessary detail. In the real world, it has to be questioned whether an action for Inadequate Professional Services might be brought.

The negotiation project certainly helped focus attention on letter writing skills and general IT skills. There were functions such as note to file and attachments to e-mails that I was not familiar with at the beginning of the project, but now using them is second nature. Furthermore, most projects/essays in the undergraduate degree have concentrated on testing your legal research skills; the negotiation project was probably the first assignment that I have done that has highlighted the importance of fact-gathering. Finally, the negotiation project gave you the opportunity to participate in the whole transaction from start to finish and take pride in the final settlement that you helped to achieve.

I found the whole experience to be extremely worthwhile. I believe it was as close as students will get to experiencing the 'real thing' before we commence our traineeships. It certainly taught us the importance of fact-gathering before jumping in and trying to find a solution.

We were unsure how to deal with the question of medical consultant's fees, given that we did not realise at first that there would be a fee and therefore did not seek the permission of the client to obtain a medical report and did not inform him in advance that he would be liable to pay the fee. When subsequently told by our client that he could not afford to pay a consultant's fee, we had to take responsibility for the fees ourselves until insurance paid for it. This was one of the questions that we posed to the discussion forum, as we were initially unsure how to deal with the situation.

The support mechanisms were designed to enrich student explorations, and to make these easier. The discussion forum, for instance, far from exemplifying long, sophisticated threads of argument, consisted of a series of 'how-to' and 'what-if' questions posed by students to a Visiting Professor who was an experienced Personal Injury practitioner, regarding the form, conventions and practice of actual legal negotiation in the PI field. From the students' point of view, this was exactly what they needed. Just as there are many types of tutorials, each with advantages and disadvantages, so there are different types of discussion forums (Salmon, 2000).

The important issue from the perspective of students is that the forum's purpose is clear, and that it enhances learning and motivation. Very often, this will involve a discussion about the process of how a task is to be carried out. As Stenning *et al* (2000: 346) point out, educational dialogue is more specialised than typical everyday conversations: it is 'very likely that much of the dialogue in computer-supported cooperative learning systems will also involve a need for… negotiation of acceptable mutual understanding, whether the dialogue is between the human and a computer, or between two humans mediated by technology'.

The EDHEC–Warwick electronic negotiations

The significance of the Glasgow Graduate School of Law's Virtual Learning Environment is its structured nature. It creates a flexible but structured virtual community that can be used for a variety of educational purposes and approaches. The postgraduate students are independent learners but within an environment that is structured but not enclosed, and that allows them to (as Flower has it above), cycle through acts of interpretation, negotiation and reflection. In this respect it is similar to the original Maastricht experiment into problem-based learning in law, in that it encouraged students to find out the information for themselves in relation to legal problems posed to them. Students were provided with general resources, instruction on how to use the environment and access to information supplied by the fictitious sources. They had to identify the problem and develop their own learning tasks (Cruickshank, 1996).

Our second and somewhat different example of this form of online learning is the electronic negotiation exercise that took place in the Spring Term of 2001 between the students of EDHEC Business School in France and the International Economic Law LLM Class at Warwick. The negotiation involved teams of lawyers (in similar fashion to the Strathclyde system). The French team represented a prominent French fragrance company, which was interested in securing a contract to sell its fragrances on an Internet site whose owners were represented by the Warwick team. The teams defined the learning/negotiation issues for themselves with the supervisors on each side providing learning assistance where relevant.

While students were provided with tasks, timetables and expected outcomes, they were not directed to specific learning resources. Intra-team communications mainly used electronic conferencing and face-to-face meetings. Inter-team negotiation took place via e-mail (although alternative conferencing systems could have been made available, these were not necessary) and ended with a final face-to-face session involving a two-hour video-conference. The intra-team context involved identification of learning objectives, research, and negotiation strategies, which are key features of PBL. Inter-team work involved processes of negotiation, which are specially relevant to legal learning. In particular, the process allowed for flexibility in the identification of issues, learning, research, negotiation, and writing tasks in accordance with the actual development of the project over time. This contrasts with more structured developments in medically derived PBL.

Both the above examples involved postgraduate students who might be considered more capable of independent learning than undergraduates. It may also appear that the type of clinical exercise involved in Glasgow's Ardcalloch is more suitable to professional legal studies than to academic studies at undergraduate level. However, negotiation exercises in a simulated electronic law clinic are a valuable way of learning law, as has been proved by Lancaster Law School's adventurous common law teaching programme. Teams of students are organised into law firms and electronically litigate cases involving Contract or Tort. The aim in each case is for parties to arrive at a negotiated settlement. The aim of the exercise is not so much to teach practical legal skills (although this is a by-product), but to encourage the students to learn law by problem solving, including doing their own legal research and using that knowledge in the negotiation process (Bloxham and Jones, 2001).

Issues and guidelines to good practice

There are a number of important issues in RBL projects that use electronic media. In common with RBL generally, the emphasis is shifted from teaching to learning where the role of the teacher becomes that of a facilitative guide. Much depends on the pedagogic context of the use of RBL. The conversational metaphor is relevant, but is ultimately limited in its dynamism and location in real-world situations. More significantly, the usefulness of various types of courseware depends on their integration into learning/teaching systems used by the course teachers. In these circumstances, learning systems, which provide room for structured group work as well as negotiation, provide exciting potential for student learning.

Production of RBL

RBL requires careful planning and resources, including:

- substantial initial start-up funding (Bacsich *et al*, 2000);
- skilled writing and production and project management;
- construction of interactive activities within materials and feedback mechanisms;
- peer review and piloting of materials with students;
- integration with assessment;
- support systems to be built into the structure of the learning experience;
- staff development to make the process effective.

A good example of this is the support system for student learning in RBL. Whereas a traditional teaching structure might consist of tutorials based around activities within materials, or small-group sessions devoted to acquiring skills or exploring topics within a particular aspect of the materials, the support systems in RBL do need to be carefully structured round materials. The model of 'surgeries', where students come with their own questions and interests to discuss with staff and each other, can be a useful discussion space in this form of learning. As a result, RBL can often be a more student-centred form of learning than a tutorial programme that has been designed around what staff think students ought to discuss.

Above all, RBL is a system. It requires detailed planning if it is to work well, and more organisation and forethought than is generally given to more traditional forms of teaching. This has two consequences. First, the possibility for something going wrong in such a structure means that students will find it difficult to turn to another learning resource, should the structure be lacking in some way or other. Second, the structure and its success is more highly dependent than is traditional teaching and learning on the effects of the media that are used to convey it.

Integration of media

Electronic learning materials can be text-based, video, still photograph, sound file, PowerPoint files linked to video, and so on. The environment is rich in potential, but requires management and integration. The development of commercially available Virtual Learning Environment software provides opportunities for such integrated delivery. Nevertheless it is important that the internal links in the materials are carefully planned, ie between the concepts to be understood, and the activities to be undertaken. It is often important to leave deliberate gaps or absences in the materials, and allow students to fill these in for themselves, via activities. Also important are the links between the Web-based RBL and other aspects of a course. Again, it is useful to keep the links between the various resources as flexible as possible, so that users can move between media.

Part of the planning of the materials must be timing and access. Students need to know where in a timetable they are expected to consult the materials, and how much time, in broad terms, they might be expected to spend on them (Boyd and Mitchell, 1992). Similarly, planning must take into account how students will access the materials. What hardware is available to them? And do they know or *should* they know, about the existence of all the materials, and the links between them?

Staff development

Staff development is key to both effective development and implementation. Unlike the production processing of traditional teaching materials, the process for RBL may involve a team with different competencies – the production of legal texts, the design of multimedia presentation, videotaping, product evaluation, technical post-production processes, and many similar tasks.

As far as teaching is concerned, the shift to RBL may create for staff a variety of disjunctures compared with traditional teaching. The RBL developer may not necessarily be the course teacher. In the case of negotiation-based independent learning techniques, the teaching team consists of the course director (who was in fact the key law academic in the course development process) and course 'facilitators'. In addition, the full team is made up of the IT support staff who manage the system and provide essential advice to students and staff in the use of the system. They also frequently complement the law librarians, who are the gatekeepers to complex electronic resources.

In this context, the staff development tasks are many and varied. The RBL developers have to instruct themselves not merely in the technical development issues, but in successful multidisciplinary teamwork. Technical staff do not always understand the needs of law academics and law academics often make the mistake of assuming that by learning to use some design tools they can be good independent courseware developers. Perhaps the most important task is the pedagogical one of transferring from a teaching-based to a learning-based approach.

Different issues arise for staff development in the teaching context. Course managers have to understand the technical tasks involved in managing the course, and especially in effective implementation. Compared with what might be termed a talk-and-chalk class, where the hardware (classroom, blackboard, chalk) and the software (texts) are alluringly simple, ICT course managers have to be involved in complex hardware and software management and a large number of extra classroom transactions. Even more important is the development, instruction and management of the other members of the team.

The Glasgow Diploma in Legal Practice is taught by over 100 part-time tutor practitioners. An advantage of this is that tutors bring to classes the immediacy and experience of their office practice, but there is a need for staff development in ICT applications. The Diploma has a rolling programme of tutor training via the European Computing Driving Licence, and for tutors who are involved in IT projects the School holds staff seminars in using the online tools. This is essential because the roles of online tutor or facilitator are quite different to those that tutors usually have in face-to-face classes with students. Roles can range from being mere providers of information when it is requested, to giving formative feedback online on student work, to dealing with formal assessment online.

In the Personal Injury project, for example, trained teaching assistants answered student queries for information. Occasionally they would comment on student work, or give assistance. Where appropriate, the teaching assistants would give feedback on poorly written letters, advising on points of style. If they felt that students had misunderstood a key element of the transaction, they would also point students in the direction of the discussion forum where a practitioner was online to help students. The assistants were familiar with the communications tools (Outlook, virtual community, discussion forum), and were given a CD with the different document sets on it for each firm. Thereafter they answered e-mail inquiries in different characters by using multiple mailbox functions. Each assistant answered inquiries from specific firms, and all mail from these firms to fictional characters would be routed to that assistant.

Such a system required the teaching assistants to become online facilitators, and the assistants needed training in order to fulfil this role effectively. It also required procedures to ensure that the assistants were responding to or withholding approximately the same levels of information across the firms – regular meetings, logs of e-mails and key points in the transaction, and other administration tools to enable the process of information exchange to be carried out efficiently. In addition, the assistants needed access to computing staff so that if anything went wrong with the information process this could be resolved speedily.

Project structures

It is important to structure RBL around tasks. These can take many forms. In this regard, the Personal Injury project presents a contrast to others in the GGSL such as online conveyancing or executry (probate) projects, where a firm will wind up a deceased client's estate. In the latter two, the transactions are fairly strictly constrained by the nature of the legal process, the 'milestone' documents, and the exchange of letters between legal agents and third parties. In the Personal Injury project, however, there are fewer milestones, and the project is much more open-field. After the initial intimation of claim, there are many different moves that a firm can make on behalf of its client. At an introductory lecture, students were given an outline of the typical communication pattern in a Personal Injury transaction, but they were not given a model transaction. The outline served to scaffold their learning, but they were asked to construct the learning, research and negotiation tasks for themselves, before they jumped to legal conclusions about liability, quantum and the like. The EDHEC–Warwick project involved similar flexible structuring of the negotiation exercise in a way that emulates the real world.

What are the advantages of carrying out electronic negotiation projects online over any other medium? While initial development time and resource costs may be high, a well-organised learning environment enables management of resources in ways that would not be possible within other contexts. The volume, structuring, and access to resources can be much richer than available in the traditional textbook and library context. Students do not have to compete for scarce library of resources when they can locate all they want at any time on Iolis (CD ROM) or the Internet. The electronic resources are navigable through a variety of navigation strategies including full text and index searches as well as through hypertext links. Much more significantly, virtual learning environments enable management of complex transactions from registration for courses and options to division into teams as well as effective communications in ways that go well beyond the capacity of traditional forms of teaching and learning. This is why the GGSL and Lancaster can manage large numbers of negotiations and Warwick and EDHEC can communicate with each other.

There are other gains as well, of course, including the ability to simulate different roles online, to practise working within a simulated environment, and the opportunity for students to practise professional communications and attitudes. Most significantly, the learners not only work in groups, but the group discourse itself becomes a transparent learning resource, which encourages reflective learning.

Conclusion

There are many different types of electronic RBL in law, and we have described only a few examples here. Nevertheless there are some brief general guidelines that can be stated for those thinking of constructing their own. These have been drawn from our own experience, and from the experience of others (for example Graham *et al*, 2001).

Don't:

- use IT unless there is a perceived need for it;
- develop RBL as an isolated strategy in your subject: integrate it as far as possible with other teaching and learning events;
- define benefits in terms of costs alone;
- design without practical project plans that take account of resource implications;
- plan without considering whether student and staff training is required;
- underestimate time, cost, energy in creating the resources.

Do:

- keep your development plan as flexible as possible;
- structure resource-based learning in ICT around collaborative learning activities;
- integrate learning technology with the rest of your teaching and learning interventions;
- try to anticipate the operational or day-to-day needs of students and staff, as well as the higher-level learning outcomes;
- make the resources part of the culture of your teaching and learning;
- use the resources as an agent of change as well as part of the change strategy;
- share vision and objectives – with everyone who will listen!

References

Bacsich, P *et al* (2000) *The Costs of Networked Learning,* Telematics in Education Research Group, Sheffield Hallam University [Online] http://www.shu.ac.uk/virtual_campus/cnl/report1.html [accessed 21st November 2001]

Barton, K, McKellar, P and Maharg, P (2000) Situated Learning and the Management of Learning: A Case Study, *The Law Teacher*, **34** (2), pp 141–63

Bloxham, S and Jones, C (2001) Networked Legal Learning: An Evaluation of the Student Learning Experience, *International Review of Law Computers and Technology*, special issue edited by P Maharg, **15** (3), pp 317–31

Boud, F and Feletti, G (eds) (1997) *The challenge of problem-based learning*, Kogan Page, London

Boxmind Web site [accessed on 4 June 2001] [Online] www.boxmind.com

Boyd, G and Mitchell, P (1992) How Can Intelligent CAL Better Adapt to Learners?, *Computers and Education*, **18**, pp 23–28

Brown, S and Smith, B (1996) *Resource-based learning*, SEDA, Kogan Page, London

Byrnes, W (2001) A Review of the Development of an Internet Delivered LLM Program in the United States, *The Journal of Information, Law and Technology (JILT)*, (3) [Online] [accessed 21 November 2001] http://elj.warwick.ac.uk/jilt/01–3/byrnes.html/

Castells, M (1996) *The Rise of the Network Society*, Blackwell Publishers, Malden Mass and Oxford UK

Clarke, J (1982) *Resource-based Learning for Higher and Continuing Education*, Croom Helm, London

Concord University Law School (last accessed on 4 June 2001), Web site of the Concord University Law School [Online] http://www.concord.kaplan.edu/

Cruickshank, D (1996) Problem-based learning in legal education in *Teaching Lawyers' Skills*, ed J Webb and C Maughan, pp 187–240, Butterworths, London

Daniel, Sir J (1996) *Mega-Universities and Knowledge Media: Technology Strategies for Higher Education*, Kogan Page, London

Elliott, J and Adelman, C (1973) Reflecting where the action is: The design of the Ford Teaching Project, *Education for Teaching*, 92, pp 8–20

Flower, L (1994) *The Construction of Negotiated Meaning: A Social Cognitive Theory of Writing*, Southern Illinois University Press, Carbondale

Graham, C *et al* (2001) Seven principles of effective teaching: A practical lens for evaluating online courses, *The Technology Source*, 2001 [Online] [accessed 21 November 2001] http://horizon.unc.edu/TS/default.asp?show=article&id=839

Grantham, D (1999) Iolisplus – Extending the Electronic Learning Environment, *The Journal of Information, Law and Technology (JILT)*, **99** (1) [Online] [accessed 21 November 2001] http://elj.warwick.ac.uk/jilt/99–1/grantham.html

Grantham, D (2000) Iolisplus – The Second Chapter, *The Journal of Information, Law and Technology (JILT)*, **2000** (1) [Online] [accessed 21st November 2001] http://elj.warwick.ac.uk/jilt/00–1/grantham.html

Hall, C (2001) Implementing Iolis, *16th BILETA Conference*, Edinburgh University [Online] [accessed 21 November 2001] http://www.bileta.ac.uk

Hasselgren, B (2001) Phenomenography Crossroads [Online] [accessed 4 January 2002] http://www.ped.gu.se/biorn/phgraph/home.html

Hawkins-Leon, C (1998) The Socratic Method-Problem Method Dichotomy: The Debate over Teaching Method Continues, *Brigham Young University Education and Law Journal*, 1998, pp 1–18 [Online] [accessed 1 December 2001] http://www.law2.byu.edu/jel/

Hiltz, S *et al* (2000) Measuring the Importance of Collaborative Learning for the Effectiveness of ALN: A multi-measure, multi-method approach, *Journal of Asynchronous Learning Networks*, **4** (2) [Online] accessed 21 November 2001] http://www.aln.org/alnWeb/journal/Vol4_issue2/le/Hiltz/le-hiltz.htm

Iolis (2001) *Iolis*, Autumn 2001 Edition [CD ROM] Law Courseware Consortium, University of Warwick

Laurillard, D (1991) Mediating the Message: Television programme design and students' understanding, *Instructional Science*, **20** (3), pp 3–23

Laurillard, D (1993) *Rethinking University Teaching: A Framework for the Effective Use of Educational Technology*, Routledge, London

Lisewski, B and Settle, C (1996) Integrating multimedia resource-based learning into the curriculum, *Resource-based learning*, ed S Brown and B Smith, pp 10919, SEDA and Kogan Page, London

Maharg, P (2001) Legal Skills and Multimedia: Enhancing student learning, *3rd Annual LILI Conference, University of Warwick* [Online] accessed 21 November 2001] http://www.ukcle.ac.uk/lili/2001/workprogress.html#maharg

Marton, F *et al* (1997) The experience of learning, Edinburgh, Scottish Academic Press

Mercer, N (1998) *The Guided Construction of Knowledge: Talk among teachers and learners*, Multilingual Matters, London

Migdal, S and Cartwright, M (1997) Pure Electronic Delivery of Law Modules – Dream or Reality? *The Journal of Information, Law and Technology (JILT)*, (2) [Online] [accessed 21 November 2001] http://elj.warwick.ac.uk/jilt/cal/97_2migd/

Paliwala, A (2001) Learning in Cyberspace, *The Journal of Information, Law and Technology (JILT)*, 2001 (1) [Online] [last accessed 21 November 2001] http://elj.warwick.ac.uk/jilt/01–1/paliwala.html

Pangaro, P (2002) Pask Archive at Pangaro Incorporated [Online] [accessed 4 January 2002] http://www.pangaro.com/Pask-Archive/Pask-Archive.html

Ramsden, P (1992) *Learning to teach in higher education*, Routledge, London

Salmon, G (2000) *E-Moderating: The Key to Teaching and Learning Online*, Kogan Page, London

Schank, R and Cleary, C (1994) *Engines for Education* [Online] [accessed 21 November 2001] http://www.ils.nwu.edu/ e_for_e/

Semple Piggott Rochez [accessed on 3 June 2001] Web site of Semple Piggott Rochez School of Law [Online] http://www.spn-law.com/site/master.html

Starr, R *et al* (2001) Measuring the importance of collaborative learning for the effectiveness of ALN: a multi-measure, multi-method approach, *Journal of Asynchronous Learning Networks*, **4** (2) [Online] [accessed 21 November 2001] http://www.aln.org/alnWeb/journal/jaln-vol4issue2.htm

Stenhouse, L (1983) *Authority, Education and Emancipation*, Heinemann, London

Stenning, K *et al* (2000) *Vicarious Learning from Educational Dialogue*, in *Proceedings of the Computer Support for Collaborative Learning (CSCL) 1999 Conference*, ed C M Hoadley and J Roschelle, pp 341–47, Stanford University, Palo Alto [Online] accessed 21 November 2001] http://www.hcrc.ed.ac.uk/Site/MCKENDJE.html

Taylor, L (1971) *Resources for Learning*, Penguin, Harmondsworth

Turkle, S (1994) Paradoxical Reactions and Powerful Ideas: Educational Computing in a Department of Physics, in *Sociomedia: Multimedia, Hypermedia, and the Social Construction of Knowledge*, ed E Barrett, MIT Press, Cambridge, MA

Wolverhampton Online Learning Facility [accessed on 4 June 2001] Web site of the University of Wolverhampton Online Learning Facility – WOLF [Online] http://wolf-nt.wlv.ac.uk/

5

Responsibility and ethics in professional legal education

Nigel Duncan

Introduction

In England and Wales those aspiring to join the main legal professions of solicitor and barrister must complete undergraduate education before taking a one-year professional course. At each stage, the individual has alternatives. The under graduate or 'initial' stage (ACLEC, 1996) may be completed either by taking a qualifying law degree or by taking a degree in another subject and then the one-year Common Professional Examination (CPE) course, which provides students with the foundations of legal knowledge identified by the two professions (Law Society/Bar Council, 1999).

The professional stage for those aspiring to become solicitors is the Legal Practice Course (LPC); that for aspirant barristers is the Bar Vocational Course (BVC). Both are one-year full-time courses available also on a part-time basis over two years. Both are designed to prepare students for the apprenticeship stage of their training as lawyers (the training contract for solicitors and pupillage for barristers) and for practice thereafter. Both are validated by their respective professional bodies.

What differentiates the professional courses from undergraduate legal education? Their content is clearly different. Students must learn the rules under which litigation is conducted and the requirements of lawyers' transactional work. They must acquire the necessary skills (drafting, research, advocacy and inter-viewing for the LPC; legal research, advocacy, drafting, opinion writing, conference skills and negotiation for the BVC). They must know and work within the letter and spirit of the professional Codes.

These differences have an impact on the pedagogical approach adopted, whereby more time is spent learning by doing the type of things lawyers do. Thus a major distinction between undergraduate and professional legal education is that the latter is designed to help students to encounter real-life problems, process them, then apply their developing knowledge and skills in order to produce a tangible result. The skills involved are those of evaluation, reflection and critical judgement. These are amongst the highest levels identified in Bloom's taxonomy of the cognitive domain of educational objectives (Bloom, 1956: 201–7) and facilitating the development of these skills is not easy. The risk is that only a low order of skill is developed, recognising only flagrant breaches of standards and responding mechanically. To overcome this risk considerable attention needs to be paid to ensuring that students learn in a reflective and critical manner.

Less easy still is to develop these skills while also socializing students into the values of the legal profession. These operate on many levels. Expectations are raised of:

- personal responsibility, initially for one's own learning and later for one's practice;
- using lawyers' language and understanding why;
- thinking like a lawyer (a phrase often used but rarely defined);
- complying with the letter and spirit of the professional Codes.

It is not enough to achieve mere compliance with existing legal cultures. In an age when the professional conduct of lawyers is subject to severe criticism, it is also necessary for students to develop a robust critical approach to current practice if they are to contribute to the maintenance of high professional values.

This chapter will explore methods of addressing these needs and will consider how the approach to classroom activities might be developed as well as how these might be enhanced by other activities. Drawing on examples from the Bar Vocational Course provided at the Inns of Court School of Law it will first consider what values need to be addressed on the professional course and explore the reasons for doing so.

Values

The educational process carries values of its own. We all hope to encourage independence and reflection in our students and this value should underlie all we do in our curriculum design and implementation. Education should encourage students to think deeply rather than superficially about the topic of their study. It should encourage a challenge to preconceptions and a questioning of what is presented as given.

Legal study introduces values of its own. The scope for disagreement about these values (of justice, liberty, democracy, equality) and their practical underpinning (procedural propriety, access to advice and representation) gives law as a field of study enormous potential from both an academic and an educational perspective. Professional legal ethics introduce yet another series of values, which involve rules to be learnt at the vocational stage but which are a fascinating source of critical study for undergraduates who wish to know about how law affects people rather than study it in ignorance of this important context.

Professional ethics underpin the work of solicitors and barristers. Contained in Codes (Bar Council, 2001a; Law Society, 2001) it is easy for these to be seen as the embodiment of professional conduct. Stick to the rules and you will act ethically. However, this narrow deontological approach has dangers of at least two sorts.

Firstly, the rules themselves may be subject to criticism. Although criticizing the legal profession has become something of a spectator sport in the United States there has been serious academic discussion of the principles underlying the rules (Pepper, 1986, 1986a; Luban, 1986, 1988; Kaufman, 1986). Similar criticism has been more muted in the United Kingdom, but recently critical debate has been growing. Boon and Levin (1999) criticize the ethical standards of both professions. Their analysis explores a number of underlying tensions (for example that between loyalty to the client and honesty, where they tend to favour a degree of shift from the former to the latter) and concludes not only with criticisms of the behaviour of many practitioners but also of the Codes themselves. This in turn focuses attention on the values of an adversarial approach to litigation and the changes occurring in practice. Other criticisms extend challenges to legal education itself, exploring the foundations of legal ethics and the ways in which it might be introduced into the curriculum (Economides, 1998).

Secondly, even with an ideal set of rules to guide the practitioner there will always be grey areas, areas where conflicts arise between principles or situations where the context forces a rethink of whether the rules should apply in *this* situation. When lawyers' training is borne in mind, it is apparent that lawyers are past masters at justifying different interpretations of rules. This can result in very dubious behaviour where ambivalent or conflict-laden situations arise. It is therefore important to explore the values that underlie the rules, so that students can develop the intellectual resources to apply the rules critically and to question them when they appear to lead to dubious outcomes.

This perspective has received considerable attention recently. The American Association of Law Schools organised a conference in May 1998, the core theme of which was values. The report of that conference concluded: '[t]he importance of teaching values with our students is to help them to understand how their values affect their lawyering... ' (Koh–Peters, 1998: 2). Evans goes further to suggest, 'that "values" are important here rather than "ethics" as such. The latter it would appear are now confused in the minds of many lawyers with the proscriptive rules of conduct and that association tends to kill off (in the minds of practitioners at least) any active exploration of the roots of ethics' (Evans, 1998: 277). Hutchinson is more pithy: 'Reliance on codes atrophies the moral intelligence and leaves lawyers adrift without a moral compass when the professional rules run out or give conflicting advice' (1998: 187). This goes some way to explaining the reason why the study of professional ethics in legal education should explore the underlying values, rather than simply concentrating on a rule-oriented approach to ethics.

Developing ethical appreciation on the professional courses

The LPC and BVC are introduced above. Both require the acquisition of prescribed knowledge and the development of certain skills with specific attention to professional ethics. Both are validated by the appropriate professional body, which establishes the curriculum and influences pedagogical methods. Beyond that they differ considerably, the LPC being more dominated by subject-specific content, the BVC more by its skills core. Nevertheless, similar approaches using a variety of pedagogical methods are adopted by the many providers and it is hoped that the examples offered below will be useful in many different contexts.

The whole process of legal education is regularly referred to as having stages (academic, vocational, apprenticeship). While this is true (and students can leave at any stage with a qualification of inherent value) it is important that it also be perceived as a continuum of development for those who intend to practise as lawyers (ACLEC, 1996: 22–25). Vocational courses should therefore offer a challenging shift from undergraduate study towards developing professionalism. Course design should emphasise that the vocational year is not their last year as a student but their first year as a professional. Indeed the standards required by the professional bodies lay significant emphasis on developing professionalism during the vocational year. Bar Council requirements include:

- Students will be expected to display and to develop a professional and responsible approach to the course and to their obligations to staff and other students.
- Students will be expected to demonstrate a sound working knowledge of the Code of Conduct for the Bar of England and Wales.
- Teaching and learning must be designed to enable students to appreciate the core principles that underpin the Code.
- Providers must demonstrate that professional ethics pervade all aspects of their course.
- Students must be assessed and judged competent in professional ethics and conduct.

(Bar Council, 2001b: S. 3: 25–27, 30, 31)

The 'core principles' referred to above include:

- the principle of professional independence;
- the principle of integrity;
- the principle of loyalty to the lay client;
- the principle of non-discrimination on grounds of gender, race, ethnicity or sexual orientation;
- commitment to maintaining the highest professional standards of work, to the proper and efficient administration of justice and to the Rule of Law.

(Bar Council, 2001b: S. 3, 32)

Further, ACLEC (1996: 18) argues: 'From the earliest stages of education and training, intending lawyers should be imbued not only with the standards and codes of professional conduct, but also more generally with the obligations of lawyers to help protect individuals and groups from the abuse of public and private power'.

This requires students' attention to be drawn to the need for fair treatment beyond the Codes. It involves more than the transfer of information and seems to raise expectations of students that they will not only know and apply prescribed rules (the Code) but also that they will behave professionally in their approach to their studies and those they encounter. How might vocational course providers approach this task of professional development? It will require the provision of information, opportunities to apply that information and assessment of the skill with which the underlying principles are applied. To ensure, however, that this approach is truly pervasive requires more. It requires attention to overall course design and to the design of individual sets of learning materials, whether providing information or providing scenarios within which students must display their growing professionalism. Even more, it requires the modelling of professional behaviour by teaching staff and others whom students will encounter. The practice described below makes a serious attempt to address all of these.

Access to the professional Codes themselves is essential and many providers have library copies, make them available electronically or provide students with their own copy. BVC students are able to use a manual (ICSL, 2001a), which introduces students to the issues of professional conduct (addressing all the 'core principles' referred to above) and includes a copy of the Bar's Code of Conduct. Students then receive discrete classes in professional conduct, which are based on a series of problem situations. These are generally taken by practitioners to bring in their current experience. Both professional bodies are keen for course providers to make active use of current practitioners in their course delivery. The classes are designed to explore not only areas where there is a right or a wrong answer, but also those where grey areas abound or different interpretations of the rules might legitimately lead to different responses. It is, however, important that students recognise ethical dilemmas for themselves without having them flagged up by staff. Moreover, talking about a problem is not the same thing as responding to it. To respond to both concerns students encounter role-plays, which are value-laden and which fit into the main subject and skill streams of the course.

Developing skills: negotiation and interviewing

Both LPC and BVC address the skill of client interviewing ('conference skills' on the BVC). Much of the development of this skill is taught through role-play activities, students taking on the role of lawyer and client. All students receive the brief that contains the lawyer's instructions. In addition, those playing the client receive 'secret' instructions providing them with the information as to the facts behind their problem and their particular concerns. It is possible to use these instructions to plant an ethical dilemma for the students playing the lawyer.

Thus in a Criminal case involving alleged shoplifting the student playing the client could be given an instruction such as: 'At a relatively early point in the conference find an opportunity to ask your counsel whether you would be guilty if your little boy picked the items up and you did not notice them until you were stopped outside the store by the detective.' To respond to such a hypothetical question would risk assisting the client to construct a false defence with the consequence of misleading the court.

In a civil case the student playing the client could receive this amongst the instructions: 'Your counsel has been warned that you want to discuss disclosure of documents. If he or she does not raise the matter, you should inform him of an internal memo, which is embarrassing because it suggests that you were not taking the matter as seriously as you in fact were. Explain that your colleague has suggested that you destroy this document and ask your counsel whether that is the best thing to do.' To recommend destruction of evidence that goes against your case would breach the Code. These dilemmas are all answered to degrees by paragraphs 301a and 302 of the Code:

301. A barrister... must not:
(a)   engage in conduct whether in pursuit of his profession or otherwise which is:
(i)   dishonest or otherwise discreditable to a barrister;
(ii)   prejudicial to the administration of justice; or
(iii) likely to diminish public confidence in the legal profession or the administration of justice or otherwise bring the legal profession into disrepute.

302. A barrister has an overriding duty to the Court to act with independence in the interests of justice: he must assist the Court in the administration of justice and must not deceive or knowingly or recklessly mislead the Court.

With the first problem, students should also be directed to paragraph 705 and the Written Standards for the Conduct of Professional Work paragraph 5.8:

705. A barrister must not:
(a)   rehearse, practise or coach a witness in relation to his evidence or the way in which he should give it;
5.8 A barrister must... not devise facts which will assist in advancing his lay client's case...

In respect of the second problem, students should also be directed to paragraph 608:

A barrister must cease to act and if he is a barrister in independent practice must return any instructions:

(d) if the client refuses to authorise him to make some disclosure to the Court which his duty to the Court requires him to make;

(e) if having become aware during the course of a case of the existence of a document which should have been but has not been disclosed on discovery the client fails forthwith to disclose it.

These are examples of embedded ethical problems, which have relatively clear answers in the Codes. It is important, however, that embedded ethical problems of this sort do not merely raise difficulties that have clear answers. To restrict activities in this way would be to encourage the view that problems can simply be answered by reference to a set of rules, which is often not the case. It is important, therefore, to include cases that not only force students to know their Code well but also identify areas where there are different arguably legitimate responses.

An example – Criminal Practice

Here, the accused, seeking advice as to plea, has been caught passing a forged note and then found to have a supply of such notes at home. He claims he was not aware of the fact that the note was forged when he passed it. The instructions to the student playing the client include the following:

> You think you may have used four other notes successfully. You certainly used two at your local butcher – he didn't look twice at them…

> In reality this is the second time you have bought dodgy notes. The first consignment…were under the floorboards at [home] when it was searched – they were not found. You still have a large number of these and you would like to know what you should do about this. You want your barrister to advise you as to whether you should mention this in court or stay quiet about it all.

The 'correct' answer is different in each case because of the distinction that in respect of the notes passed to the butcher the offence was in the past, whilst to continue to retain the notes under the floorboards would involve committing a continuing crime and no barrister could advise a client to commit a crime. Thus in respect of the butcher incident, counsel should explain to the client the advantages and disadvantages of asking for the offence to be taken into consideration while leaving the final decision for the client.

In respect of the retained notes, however, to advise that he should continue to retain them is not an option. To do so would be a clear breach of the Code under paragraphs 301 and 302 (above). What, however, should the advice be?

It is important to ensure that all tutors are informed of crucial perspectives. Teaching guides should be produced to provide the necessary guidance and practical experience so that students' experience is not dependent upon their tutor having recently encountered such a problem. The teaching guide in this case includes the following:

[t]he client may mention the box of other counterfeit notes he has at home and ask for advice. This is again a complex area and even senior practitioners have different views on it. The safest, and I suggest, the preferable approach, is to say: 'Counsel should tell him that he ought to hand them over to the police and that although as counsel he could not assist or report him to the police (duty of confidentiality), it would preclude him in mitigation telling the judge that those counterfeit notes before the court were the limits of his criminality. He could not tell the court that there was a box of money at the defendant's home. The Bar Council's adviser on Professional Conduct issues supports this view. On the other hand, one of our practitioner assessors wrote: 'the suggestion that the client should hand over the box of other counterfeit notes to the police and thus incriminate himself is highly disputable'. My own view, shared by one eminent Criminal silk and a number of senior juniors who discussed the point over a cup of coffee in the Southwark Bar Mess, is to advise the client to destroy the counterfeit notes immediately.

If it should come out in conference that he has already successfully passed some other notes in the course of the past few weeks, eg at the butcher's shop, a similar choice arises. One view is that it would be proper for counsel to advise [your client] to 'make a clean breast of the whole thing' and ask for any other offences to be taken into consideration at the same time, especially if he is going to plead guilty to all three charges. The serial numbers on all the notes are the same and a failure to admit any other usage could leave him open to fresh charges being preferred – charges where the court would not be minded to take as lenient a view as they might in this case. If he were to decide to plead guilty to the offences on the indictment, I do not think the prosecution would have much difficulty in being persuaded that this would be an appropriate course of action. The other view, of course, is that he should simply keep quiet (counsel being under a duty of confidentiality). Again, the safest view would seem to be the first.

Thus there may be more than one legitimate approach to a problem and students must recognise the need to apply the rules critically.

Characteristic of the advice in this teaching guide is an interplay of pragmatism and principle. For example, the risk of not confessing to other offences is greater if the notes all have the same serial number. The lawyer should not merely say what *should* be done but also provide the information necessary for the client to make an informed decision. This reflects a fundamental value: that of client autonomy. It is crucial that the lawyer leaves the final decision to the client.

What is more, confidentiality is equally crucial here. Some students find it difficult to believe that, knowing a client is planning to commit an offence (such as retaining forged notes) they must not tell the authorities. These are values that underpin the client/counsel relationship and lie at the heart of the Conference Skills course. Indeed they feature in the assessment criteria and it is made clear to students at an early stage that their task is to enable the client to make an informed decision. Students who bully clients or who offer only one alternative without explaining the strengths and weaknesses of that and other courses of action will lose significant credit and may fail their assessment.

Examples from students' Conference Skills Manual explaining the assessment criteria

Criterion 3: Effective client communication

There are many aspects of behaviour that contribute towards creating an effective interchange between you and your client. Much of what is required is born of basic common sense and an application of plain ordinary courtesy. It is useful to remind yourself that your client is, after all, a human being, just like you. To work well, and to ensure that the client responds in the most appropriate and cooperative way during the conference, you need to be sensitive to your client's fears, anxieties and likely needs as well as being aware of the legal predicament in which they find themselves. In seeking to communicate effectively with your client, try to ensure that you do the following:

- Make every effort to see that your client feels as comfortable as possible, whatever the circumstances of the conference or the location in which it is held.
- Use language that is appropriate and that your client can readily understand.
- Listen to what your client is trying to tell you even if you do not think it is necessarily of relevance to the case.
- Allow time and space to answer any questions that the client might have or to raise any anxieties with you.

- Demonstrate in a non-patronising way, a suitable degree of empathy/sympathy.

Where possible, and/or appropriate, attempting to satisfy these aims will, in large measure, reassure the client and consequently ensure that you can communicate effectively. However, perhaps the best overall reassurance that you can give a client (in addition to the above), is to remember that at all times you must appear to be completely non-judgemental in your manner and remain entirely objective about the case.
(ICSL, 2001b: 12.3.3.)

Criterion 5: Advising
You should ensure that you do the following:

- Provide the client with a full evaluation of the strengths and weaknesses of the case.
- Set out what realistic options are available to the client.
- Explain the legal and procedural issues in clear and unambiguous language.
- Check that the client fully understands the implications of the advice you have given.

To advise properly really does mean that: a client expects you to provide full and clear advice on his or her problem. You are the expert and you are being paid to exercise your professional judgement on behalf of the client. The final decision on what to do is always up to the client, but remember, the client cannot make any such decision(s) without you providing a clear and full evaluation of the merits of his or her case, and a summary of the available options…
(ICSL, 2001b: 12.3.5.)

Criterion 6: Professional conduct
Be familiar with the Code and ensure that you observe the rules of professional conduct at all times. You must, of course, act within your instructions at all times and not, for example:

- invent facts;
- agree to mislead the court in any way;
- mislead your client;
- provide answers or invent defences for your client;
- in any way coach your client.

(ICSL, 2001b: 12.3.6)

The aim in designing these learning outcomes is to integrate the underlying values into students' developing skill. It is only their behaviour that can be observed, not any underlying values they may hold. If, however, an interview can be observed that explores client concerns, uses appropriate language, explains the strengths and weaknesses of a case and proposes alternative routes with their likely outcomes before giving the client the opportunity to make an informed decision, there can be real hope that the underlying value of client autonomy has been learnt.

Client autonomy and the duty of confidentiality in criminal matters may give rise to a classic conflict: where the client admits to the crime but asks his lawyer to defend him. Here students have limited options and these are explained clearly. Withdrawal from the case is appropriate but may not lead to the ethically most desirable result. The intelligent client may simply respond by lying to another lawyer. Testing the prosecution case is also permissible (doing all possible to argue inadmissibility of prosecution evidence in the hope that insufficient will remain to establish some essential element of the offence while carefully avoiding challenging that evidence's veracity). A submission of no case to answer might then succeed. If this fails, the defence may offer no evidence and this needs to be explained to the client. The practical consequences of these alternatives provide powerful scope for exploring underlying values. Here these would include that of loyalty to the client (with the underlying value of client autonomy) and the duty not to mislead the court (stressing the values of an adversarial system).

It is important to distinguish between the situation described above and one where the lawyer simply *believes* that the client is guilty (for example by being presented with an unbelievable defence story). This may provide a starting point for a wide-ranging discussion of the role of the lawyer (representative not judge), the importance of access to justice and the limited circumstances where the lawyer is professionally embarrassed.

Assessing ethical issues

It is well-recognised that assessment is a powerful motivator to learning. On the BVC, students undertake a total of 10 skills assessments. Five of these will have specific ethical dilemmas embedded in them on a pass/fail basis. An example is provided in the box below. Students who fail must sit a multiple-choice test, which explores their ability to apply the provisions of the Code.

Example of a drafting assessment

In a drafting assessment, students are asked to draft the particulars of claim in a case arising out of an accident, which took place on scaffolding. Instructions include the following:

> However, it seems to Instructing Solicitors that, in addition to a possible cause of action under the above Regulations, liability under the Employers Liability (Defective Equipment) Act 1969 should be explored. If considered properly arguable on the evidence, Counsel is instructed to include a claim under that Act, as well as in negligence.
>
> S. 1 (1) provides that this liability only arises where the injury was caused by a defect in equipment provided by the employer, which is attributable wholly or in part to the fault of a third party. The evidence shows that the equipment was not defective, but inappropriate. Indeed an expert witness's evidence says: 'As domestic stepladders they were perfectly adequate, and no manufacturing defects were apparent'.
>
> There is therefore no evidential basis for asserting a claim based on the 1969 Act. If such a claim were to be included counsel would be in breach of paragraph 704 of the Code of Conduct: A barrister must not devise facts that will assist in advancing the lay client's case and must not draft any statement of case, witness statement, affidavit, notice of appeal or other document containing:
>
> (a) any statement of fact or contention that is not supported by the lay client or by his instructions;
>
> (b) any contention that he does not consider to be properly arguable...

A student who does not take the care to conduct this analysis properly and to decline to assert such a claim would fail the professional conduct element of this assessment.

It must be admitted, however, that a one-year vocational course is not always the best vehicle for a wide-ranging discussion of the values underlying the provisions of the Code. A Conference Skills class has as its main focus the development of the skills of effective client interviewing. A negotiation or advocacy class is equally focused on those skills, as are classes in the written skills of drafting and opinion writing, although all can provide opportunities for exploring ethical issues. Thus, the amount of time available for such discussions is necessarily limited. What is more, in limited time there is a tendency for tutors to refer to the appropriate elements of the Code of Conduct rather than to explore the underlying values. If that were not addressed there would be a failure to meet the Bar Council's requirement: teaching and learning must be designed to enable students to appreciate the core principles that underpin the Code (Bar Council, 2001b: S. 3: 27).

Addressing this problem requires attention to the whole structure of the course ensuring that the activities are sufficiently integrated and varied.

Integration and diversity

Underlying the values identified above is a fundamental matter of developing students' responsibility for their own learning. In the induction programme, the perception that this is the 'first year of your professional life' and the change of approach from university can be stressed. Students can be introduced to a greater understanding of the learning process, their own learning preferences (Honey and Mumford, 1986) and how they can gain mutual benefit by learning how to give (and receive) constructive feedback.

Another element of the change from university is the expectation of a greater degree of active participation in classes of all sizes. It is now widespread for 'lectures' to be designated 'large groups' with the symbolic function of demonstrating that they are as much a place for active engagement as smaller classes. Large groups need not involve significant didactic presentation. Instead students can be given prior reading and then placed in situations, which require the application of that prior reading (Inns of Court School of Law (ICSL) uses a set of manuals, written by staff at the School and practitioners). They should then be expected to participate actively in the work of the class to develop their expectation that that is how to behave in such large groups.

In the 'knowledge' subjects (on the BVC these are Civil and Criminal Litigation and Evidence) students may have been given directed reading and a set of problem questions to research. Case studies may be presented visually and the students asked to work in small groups to prepare responses, thus encouraging cooperative working methods.

In the skills classes they may be given the papers in a case to prepare before the class and then be expected (for example) to sit in opposed pairs and conduct a negotiation. In large groups, the object of this is not to allow a teacher to give individual feedback on the quality of their performance but to inform them sufficiently of the demands of that particular problem so that they are better able to critique a demonstration of a negotiation in the same case. While many students respond well to this approach and gain enormous benefit from it there are others who never overcome the assumption that lecture halls are places where they receive information in a passive manner.

Individual learning and feedback

In small groups students may be given opportunities to perform the skills on which they will ultimately be assessed and to engage in collective work. With the oral skills the focus is likely to be to give each student individual feedback on the quality of their performance and an indication as to how they might best improve. That can be done in part by encouraging peer feedback, which itself can be structured by the use of questionnaires (see box on page 118).

Example of a feedback questionnaire

This example is to be used after students have sought to settle a civil dispute; initially to encourage self-reflection and then to provide the basis for peer feedback as they compare perspectives on their experience.

1. How closely did the agreement reflect:
   – your client's objectives;
   – your planned optimum outcome;
   – your worst realistic outcome?
2. Could/should you have achieved more for your client in respect of: [each of the six identifiable items that were subject to negotiation]?
3. In which order did you deal with the above items? With hindsight, would it have been more beneficial to adopt a different structure?
4. Identify your:
   – most effective argument;
   – least effective argument;
   – opponent's most effective argument;
   – opponent's least effective argument.
5. Identify the first concession you made. Was it too generous? Did you make it too early?
6. What strategy did you plan to adopt? Did you modify this during the negotiation?
7. What did you find most difficult?
8. With hindsight, how could you have planned it more effectively?

These classes are supported by sessions where students receive detailed personal feedback on the quality of their work from their tutor. These performances do not form part of the formal assessment as experience suggests that students respond better to feedback from a tutor who is not also perceived as assessing a (possibly disappointing) performance. They take away a videotape that contains their performance and their tutor's feedback, both oral and written. To encourage them to reflect on that they receive a self-appraisal questionnaire. In the box on page 119 is one from the Negotiation course.

Self-appraisal questionnaire form

This form is designed to assist the process of critical self-appraisal and requires you to think reflectively on your own performance. **IT DOES NOT FORM PART OF THE FINAL ASSESSMENT OF NEGOTI- ATION**. You will gain the greatest benefit from this exercise if you are honest with yourself, being neither too generous nor too critical.

Complete the form after you have reviewed your performance and had time to absorb the feedback from your tutor. Take time to complete the form; you will need to set yourself realistic and achievable goals. The areas you focus on need not necessarily be the same as those that have already been addressed in the tutor's feedback.

Identify two strengths in your preparation for and conduct of the negotiation:
1.
2.
State why they are strengths and how you will maintain and develop these strengths:
1.
2.
Identify two weaknesses in your preparation for and conduct of the negotiation:
1.
2.
State what you will do differently next time to improve on these weaknesses:
1.
2.
Once completed return this form to your Negotiation tutor. Retain a copy for your records – it will assist you to chart your progress on the course.

Similar exercises are carried out in respect of the written skills, which will obviously not involve video-recording. This integration of learning methods across large and small group sessions needs to be reflected in respect of the skills being developed and the ethical issues being addressed. Thus underlying analytical and research skills need to be reinforced in different contexts and a variety of ethical dilemmas need to be built into the different skill and knowledge development programmes in order to reinforce the underlying values in different contexts. The twin development of personal responsibility for one's own learning and the ability to respond to dilemmas in an ethical manner can be further facilitated by other learning approaches.

Collaborative learning

One innovation designed to develop students' responsibility for their own learning and development is the collaborative learning group. These are timetabled sessions where students meet in their regular groups to conduct directed activities. In order to achieve a high level of participation it is important that these sessions be closely integrated into the existing skills programme and that each session has a clear and tangible outcome. They may be completely unstaffed or they may have a degree of staff input. They should not, however, become like a conventional staffed tutorial where the tutor is seen as taking responsibility for the conduct of the session, or the function of developing individual (and collective) responsibility for learning may be lost.

Presentation is important. At ICSL, we organise these sessions into streams: Research and Analysis; Critical Appraisal and Reflection and Group Learning and Preparation. This reflects the approaches that are most significant for effective development on a professional course, but other ways of organisation may be appropriate in different contexts.

One way in which this will help to overcome some of the admitted limitations of the approach to professional legal ethics presented earlier is to allow exploration of values underlying the Code. In the box below is an example of one of the collaborative learning sessions within the Negotiation course and within the 'Critical Appraisal and Reflection' stream. Students are required to e-mail their group response to their tutor who will then respond with feedback on their response. Student instructions are as follows in the box. The Negotiation Manual referred to is ICSL 2001c.

An example of a collaborative learning session

The ethics of negotiation

Before the session:
Read Chapter 8 of the Negotiation Manual.
Check your understanding of how conditional fee arrangements work (see Bar Council Web site – 'Rules and Guidance' – then choose 'Conditional Fee Agreement' from top menu).

At the session:
Below you have two tasks. Divide your time approximately equally between the two of them. In each case, seek to come to a group view as to the answers. There may be dissenting views.
One member of the group should log on to the PC and between you, you should write down the group view (with any dissents). E-mail that to your Negotiation tutor.

Task 1

The Negotiation Manual (p 88) says:

Never deliberately deceive or mislead your opponent in order to achieve a more favourable offer of compromise, for example, by pretending that you have a witness to support your client's version of events when you do not. It is, however, acceptable to use 'bluff', allowing an opponent to form an impression without positively misleading him.

1. Do you agree with the above paragraph?
2. What underlying values do you think it represents?
3. Did the group arrive at a consensus view as to the paragraph's ethical propriety?
4. If not, what were the dissenting views?

Task 2

You are representing the Claimant in a personal injury case where a defence has been entered that also alleges contributory negligence. The case is funded by a conditional fee arrangement drawn up by your Instructing Solicitor and signed by your client. This provides that if you win you will receive your normal fee (£2,000) plus an uplift of 40 per cent (based on your initial risk analysis). If you lose you will receive nothing. You consider it likely that if you go to court there is a small risk that you will lose altogether, that you could win outright, but that a finding of contributory negligence is the most likely outcome. You estimate that £18,000 is the most likely final award. In negotiation at the court door your opponent offers £15,000. This will constitute a 'win' for the purposes of your fees.

1. Would you explain your own personal interest to the client?
2. Why/why not?
3. Is there anything wrong in advising the client to accept?
4. What underlying values influence your view?

Outcome:

One e-mail (from the whole group) to your Negotiation tutor, presenting your answers to the above questions, indicating dissent where appropriate.

There is scope to develop this approach (for example to explore further the underlying values thrown up by the Conference Skills example given above) in other collaborative learning sessions. Thus, it is possible to combine reflection on the underlying values with an activity, which in itself requires students to take more responsibility for their own learning. The identification of one stream as 'Critical Appraisal and Reflection' should, at both a symbolic and practical level, encourage a more reflective approach to student learning.

Reflective practice and professional development

One day each week is designated a 'Professional Development Day' and students are encouraged to undertake a variety of activities in it. These include a series of court visits (some arranged by the School, others by the individuals themselves) after which they need to prepare a reflective report to discuss with their personal supervisor. This is structured with specific questions designed to draw students' attention to the issues they are learning about on their course: procedural matters, the quality of the advocacy etc. Some examples of headings and students' responses follow in the box below.

Sample headings and student responses in a reflective report

In County Court possession proceedings by a large Housing Association against eight tenants:

- **Could you follow the reasons? Do you think that the parties could?**
  'Yes. The judge took great steps to explain the decision and his rationale both to counsel and to the defendants.'
- **Please comment on any other procedural aspects.**
  'Little by way of argument was presented, as the judge was predominantly interested in whether the regulations of the Housing Acts had been complied with. All proceedings followed a set "menu" of questions and answers.'
- **Any other observations about your visit?**
  'Although the judge was working quickly through the cases, one or two of the defendants expressed their disappointment at the progress of the proceedings and that it was a "waste of time". I have doubts on whether this style of hearing serves to convey or portrays the correct approach to the application of the law particularly through the eyes of those defendants for whom this will be their first contact with the judicial system and the trial process.'

In a busy Magistrates' Court:

- **Any other observations about your visit?**
  'Whilst we were waiting for the magistrates to come back to give the judgement in respect of another case concerning driving without due care and attention, the barrister from the CPS came over to where we were and started discussing the merits of the case (in particular that the defendant will lose his licence) when the defendant was present and could hear what was being said.'

Before a District Judge in the Magistrates' Court:

- **Could you follow the reasons? Do you think that the parties could?**
  'Yes. The magistrate spoke very quickly and I think that sometimes the defendant would have difficulty following the procedure. In particular one defendant had learning difficulties. The magistrate knew this but made no attempt to clarify his instructions.'
- **Please comment on any other procedural aspects.**
  'On occasions the stip. mag. (now District Judge [Magistrates' Court]) gave his common sense opinion, for eg: A defendant had left a hotel refusing to pay for his breakfast – charged with theft of £11.70. He opted for Crown Court – he was represented. Mag. said he was going to block it going to the Crown Court as a waste of public money – £2k per case. Party told to see sense!'

These responses may then form the basis for individual and group discussions, which take place with personal supervisors in the 'Critical Appraisal and Reflection' stream described above.

The other main activity students are encouraged to undertake is to work with the School's Pro Bono Unit. There is some evidence that working with real clients during the educational experience increases the likelihood that students will go on to work in fields of law that provide a service to the general public rather than exclusively commercial concerns (Maresh, 1997). However, experience suggests that working with real clients is a powerful motivator. It helps to put the skills and knowledge learnt on the course into perspective and encourages students to develop the skills of independent research. The School provides three approaches to pro bono work.

ICSL runs an in-house advice clinic where students work in pairs to interview clients who have made appointments to see them. They work under supervision but otherwise take responsibility for advising their client.

A partnership programme is also in operation whereby we work with a variety of agencies. These include general advice agencies such as advice centres; specific interest groups such as the Terence Higgins Trust and Shelter and other groups such as ProHelp London, which provides an advice service to other charities. This latter opportunity can provide a great experience for students interested in the corporate field. Thus they might find themselves advising on the formal docu mentation for a charity seeking to establish itself as a company limited by guarantee. One partner provides an opportunity to give a full representation service. The Free Representation Unit (FRU) provides representation in a variety of tribunals, most notably the Social Security and Employment Tribunals and the Criminal Injuries Compensation Authority. This gives students full responsibility for representing a client before one of these tribunals.

The third pro bono opportunity is also with FRU but is integrated into the BVC course itself. This is the FRU Option, whereby instead of undertaking a programme of study followed by a simulated assessment task, students undertake an employment tribunal case and submit their work on that case for assessment. FRU and ICSL work closely together on this as FRU takes responsibility for the initial training and ensuring that the individual is ready to undertake a case, both share the supervision of students and ICSL conducts the assessment process.

An alternative approach is street law. This involves students in providing education and training to those in the community who need to understand about their rights and how to realise them. This may take place in schools, prisons or with community groups.

These pro bono activities appear to have a powerful influence on students' learning. They encounter at first hand (often for the first time) the real significance of limited access to justice and the way in which the law impacts upon ordinary people. They face head on the ethical problems that have been introduced in the simulated setting of the skills classes. Previously published in Brayne, Duncan and Grimes (1998) the extract from students' reflective journals in the box below provides clear evidence of the ethical issues faced.

Case study from a student's reflective journal

In an employment tribunal case where the client had been paid without deduction of tax the student was carrying out a telephone interview with his client using the client's daughter as a translator. The student (who spoke the client's language to a fair degree) overheard the client resisting his wife's suggestion that he should lie about his understanding of the tax situation. He pre-empted the daughter by indicating that he had heard the conversation. His reflective journal records:

'In a sense I had averted an embarrassing situation by shooting first and not letting them tell me lies. On the other hand, should I not have waited until they came back to me with an answer (albeit a lie) aimed at me? Or would that have been unethical? Maybe I was exaggerating my ethical duty and should have just pretended not to hear. But then again maybe they should not have spoken that loudly (I could not *not* hear).'

On a more general level students regularly respond to their experience with comments such as: 'It has helped me understand civil procedure in context, fact management, conference and negotiation skills in reality and the power we possess over people's lives'.

These approaches are an attempt to provide a diverse range of learning activities, which students can use to develop their sensitivity to ethical issues, their ability to deal with them properly as they arise in practice and their ability to look critically at existing practice.

Values at the undergraduate stage

ACLEC (1996: 18) identifies the need for these issues to be developed from the earliest stage of legal education. It would certainly give vocational students an easier transition to the requirements of professional and lifelong learning values. A moment's reflection will see that they are qualities that will be of value in any of the fields into which law graduates might direct themselves. Indeed, it can be argued that they constitute an element of what is essential to 'graduateness' (Bell, 1996: 13) and will assist university law schools to meet the benchmarking require- ments of the Quality Assurance Agency (QAA, 2000). How might these values be effectively addressed in the undergraduate curriculum where the interest in professional ethics is critical and academic rather than oriented towards practice?

Theoretical approaches abound. Many fascinating suggestions are presented in Economides (1998). Gill, for example, presents how fundamental issues were debated in classical times, opening a rich mine of ideas and analysis (Gill, 1998). Dare presents a stimulating example of the use of literature analysing the dilemmas in *To Kill a Mockingbird* to explore fundamental ideas as well as entering a rigorous debate about the limits of the Codes and how one might respond (Dare, 1998). Rosen explores how a deontological approach encourages cynicism and a retreat into a craftsmanship, whose only value is that of craftsmanship (Rosen, 1998). Such discussions, however, are often sidelined into a Jurisprudence course, which is usually available only as an option and in 1996 was only offered by 61 per cent of law schools (Harris and Jones, 1997).

There is considerable support for the view that ethics should be taught perva- sively rather than being seen as an add-on (particularly an optional add-on) and this is even more true of the underlying values if they are to be recognised by students as of genuine significance to their understanding of the law. Rhode (1994) gives many examples of how this might be done in the US context. Giddings (2001) suggests how it might be done in the context of teaching Criminal law. One aspect of his approach is to use clinical methods, either simu- lated (where students role-play value-laden problems) or working under proper supervision with real clients (see Chapter 2).

This is a field that has enormous potential. At the Pro Bono Conference in London in March 2001 (SPBG, 2001) a network of student, staff and interested professionals was established to assist in the development of opportunities for students to become involved in providing advice and representation to those in need and in developing 'street law' projects, which involve working with schools, prisons and community groups to develop their understanding of the law that affects them. These provide powerful learning opportunities to students and give them direct experience of the inequalities in society, which inform many of the values they should be considering. Practical assistance may be available to those interested in such developments either through the Solicitors' Pro Bono Group (pro.bono@virgin.net) or the Clinical Legal Education Organisation (law-clinic@shu.ac.uk).

Conclusion

Suggestions of this sort represent a radical change for many law teachers and while research demands remain dominant, the impetus for change may be lacking. If, however, initiatives such as the UKCLE and Institute for Learning and Teaching are effective, there will be a stronger motivation to develop a broader range of learning methods. This book indicates something of the wealth of variety available. Different institutions may, if they choose, develop distinctive learning cultures. This will be most effectively achieved if law teachers themselves develop a reflective approach to their experience of students' learning (see Chapter 2) and use it to develop their own professionalism. In this way, they will be mirroring their students' experiences and providing a foundation for intellectual, critical and professional development at both undergraduate and professional stages. This can only be good for the prospects of developing strong personal and professional values.

The author would like to thank colleagues and students at the Inns of Court School of Law for granting permission to reproduce the fruits of ideas and work.

References

ACLEC (1996) *First Report on Legal Education and Training*, Lord Chancellor's Advisory Committee on Legal Education and Conduct, London

Bar Council (2001a) *Code of Conduct of the Bar of England and Wales*, 7th edn [Online] http://www.barcouncil.org.uk/document.asp

Bar Council (2001b) *BVC Revalidation Requirements and Guidelines*, 4/1/01

Bell, J (1996) General Transferable Skills and the Law Curriculum, *Contemporary Issues in Law* II (2), p 2

Bennett, M (2000) Assessment to Promote Learning, *The Law Teacher*, **34** (2) pp 167–75

Bloom, B (ed) (1956) *Taxonomy of educational objectives: the classification of educational goals. Handbook One: Cognitive domain*, David McKay, London

Boon, A and Levin, J (1999) *The Ethics and Conduct of Lawyers in England and Wales*, Hart, Oxford

Brayne, H, Duncan, N and Grimes, R (1998) *Clinical Legal Education*, Blackstone, London

Dare, T (1998) The Secret Courts of Men's Hearts, Legal Ethics and Harper Lee's *To Kill a Mockingbird*, in *Ethical Challenges to Legal Education and Conduct*, ed K Economides, pp 39–60, Hart, Oxford

Economides, K (ed) (1998) *Ethical Challenges to Legal Education and Conduct*, Hart, Oxford

Evans, A (1998) The Values Priority in Quality Legal Education, *The Law Teacher*, **32** (3), pp 274–86

Giddings, J (2001) Teaching the Ethics of Criminal Law and Practice, *The Law Teacher*, **35** (2), pp 161–80

Gill, C (1998) Law and Ethics in Classical Thought, in *Ethical Challenges to Legal Education and Conduct*, ed K Economides, pp 3–19, Hart, Oxford

Harris, P and Jones, M (1997) A Survey of Law Schools in the United Kingdom, *Law Teacher*, **31** (1), pp 38–126

Harris, P and Tribe, D (1995) The Impact of Semesterisation and Modularisation on the Assessment of Law Students, *The Law Teacher*, **29** (3), pp 279–95

Honey, P and Mumford, A (1986) *Manual of Learning Styles*, Honey, Maidenhead

Hutchinson, A (1998) Legal Education in a Fragmented Society: Between Professional and Personal, *International Journal of the Legal Profession*, **5** (2/3), pp 175–92

ICSL (2001a) *Professional Conduct*, ed A Turtle, Blackstone, London

ICSL (2001b) *Conference Skills*, ed R Samwell-Smith, Blackstone, London

ICSL (2001c) Negotiation, ed M Taylor, Blackstone, London

Kaufman, A (1986) A commentary on Pepper's The lawyer's amoral ethical role, *American Bar Foundation Research Journal*, **1986** (4), pp 651–55

Koh-Peters, J (ed) (1998) *Reflections on Values for Clinical Teachers*, proceedings of the AALS Conference on Clinical Legal Education, Portland, Oregon, 5–9 May 1998

Law Society (2001) *Law Society Guide* [Online] http://www.guide.lawsociety.org.uk

Law Society/Bar Council (1999) *A Joint Statement issued by the Law Society and the General Council of the Bar on the completion of the initial or academic stage of training by obtaining an undergraduate degree* [Online] http://www.lawsociety.org.uk

Luban, D (1986) The Lysistratian prerogative: A response to Stephen Pepper, *American Bar Foundation Research Journal*, **1986** (4) pp 637–49

Luban, D (1988) *Lawyers and Justice: An ethical study*, Princeton University Press, USA

Maresh, S (1997) The Impact of Clinical Legal Education on the Decisions of Law Students to Practice Public Interest Law, *Educating for Social Justice: Social Values and Legal Education*, ed J Cooper and L Trubek, pp 154–66, Ashgate, Dartmouth

Pepper, S (1986) The Lawyer's Amoral Ethical Role: A Defense, A Problem, And Some Possibilities, *American Bar Foundation Research Journal*, **1986** (4) pp 613–35

Pepper, S (1986a) A rejoinder to Professors Kaufman and Luban, *American Bar Foundation Research Journal*, **1986** (4) pp 657–73

QAA (2000) *Quality Assurance Agency for Higher Education. Benchmarking statement for Law* [Online] http://www.qaa.ac.uk/crntwork/benchmark/law.pdf

Rhode, D (1994) *Professional Responsibility: Ethics by the Pervasive Method*, Little Brown, Boston

Rosen, R (1998) Devils, Lawyers and Salvation Lie in the Details: Deontological legal ethics, issue conflicts of interest and civic education in law schools, *Ethical Challenges to Legal Education and Conduct*, ed K Economides, pp 61–81, Hart, Oxford

6

The Human Rights Act and
the UK law school

Andrew Williams

Introduction

If the wealth of academic and media debate is anything to go by, the introduction of the Human Rights Act 1998 (HRA) has already had a massive impact on the United Kingdom. In particular, it would seem that human rights concerns have become all pervasive in legal practice. Whether judicial reaction will encourage such a movement will always be in dispute but there can be little doubt that lawyers will become increasingly aware of human rights considerations in their work. They are already learning how to adapt to the new environment through trial (literally) and error.

We can take it for granted that law schools will not ignore this important development. Several institutions may respond by looking to introduce HRA-related issues across the curriculum. Others will leave them for individual teachers to adapt their courses where necessary whilst ensuring that traditional subjects such as English Legal System and Constitutional Law now incorporate the HRA into their programmes. Equally, courses devoted to human rights may well deal with the Act as an important addition to the subject of 'civil liberties' in the United Kingdom.

Whichever method is adopted, the problem for law schools could reflect those faced by the legal profession in general. Is the HRA to be treated as the introduction of just another strategy to be employed by lawyers in the pursuit of their clients' interests? Or can it fulfil those aspirations attached to its introduction that envisaged a change in the whole legal culture of the United Kingdom? The very uncertainty associated with the HRA therefore has significant implications for the legal academy. The question remains whether the envisaged approaches to teaching the subject are a sufficient response.

The purpose of this chapter is to consider this question and the implications for teaching and learning human rights in the light of the highly unpredictable legal environment that now subsists. It is divided into three sections. Section 1 reviews briefly the teaching and learning issues related to human rights following the HRA's introduction. It also examines the responses that law schools are likely to adopt and the tensions that might appear as a result. Section 2 then suggests that other approaches may be considered within the legal academy, approaches that respond more to the notions inherent in human rights than simply the recent jurisprudential aspects of the subject. Finally, Section 3 considers some practical examples of how these other approaches may be implemented.

Section 1
The challenge of the HRA

The Human Rights Act 1998 is not an isolated piece of legislation. Its very design recognises the incorporation into UK law of an international human rights instrument. By placing the European Convention on Human Rights (ECHR) within the constitutional framework of the United Kingdom, the HRA explicitly enshrines the link between the English common law traditions of civil liberties with the internationally promoted human rights movement. 'Bringing rights home' was the rhetoric that accompanied the introduction of the Act (Fenwick, 2000: 1).

The incorporation of the ECHR into UK law is, of course, not just of academic importance. There is a real possibility that the scope and definition of human rights actionable in law will undergo immense scrutiny if not change. Indeed, we may well be at 'a turning point in legal history' (Clayton and Tomlinson, 2000: 1). Human rights activists, interest groups from corporations to charities, individuals, public and private lawyers, academics and, of course, the judiciary, will test the frontiers of human rights law both within and outside the courts. The range of responses will be extensive both from a practical and academic perspective. Even if legal professionals react to the new conditions in a cynical or instrumental fashion, using the HRA and any other source as an extra weapon in their legal armoury, the impact of their actions for others will still be crucial. The precedents that may be developed could alter drastically the relationship between state and individual as well as prompt a continual re-examination of values that underpin the United Kingdom's political and legal system.

Equally, by acknowledging the relevance of the European human rights system the possibility of drawing on wider inspirations other than the ECHR may well be encouraged (Clayton and Tomlinson, 2000: 3–5). This could entail examination of the whole spectrum of human rights issues that have taxed the international legal community particularly since the formation of the United Nations. Tensions that have arisen with regard to the merits of collective rights as opposed to those of the individual, of economic, social and cultural rights as opposed to traditional civil and political rights, may be encountered directly within the UK legal system.

The practical implications of the introduction of the HRA may therefore be of central importance in the development of law in the United Kingdom as well as the whole of the legal culture of the country. As a result, it is hard to imagine any institution involved in the teaching of law ignoring the actual and potential change in landscape that the HRA heralds. The difficulty arises in *how* teaching and learning human rights might now be approached. What strategies, based on what appreciations, present themselves to law teachers?

At first glance, the new environment poses no great problem for the legal academy. Indeed, some institutions are unlikely to oversee a dramatic change in their curriculum for some time, if at all. Current courses will be adapted as jurisprudence and debate evolves. The distinction between the international law of human rights and UK laws may well be maintained, albeit with some degree of cross-reference. In particular, the ECHR will act as a bridge to other interpretations of human rights and even enable access to some of the philosophical debates that surround the evolution of the subject. Equally, human rights issues may appear more generally in those courses dealing with the United Kingdom's constitutional framework and the English Legal System. However, the focus will naturally rest upon the development of UK law.

This approach has already been instituted in many university law departments. Kent Law School, for instance, offers an undergraduate module that aims to, 'develop a sound knowledge and understanding of the nature and extent of "human rights" as they are recognised in English law' (Kent Law School Web site). Essex, similarly, offers a UK Human Rights Law course on its LLB providing 'students with a theoretical base from which to examine the legal protection of human rights' (University of Essex Law Department Web site). Although both courses look to wider interpretations of human rights, international perspectives and the whole human rights discourse provide a backdrop rather than the context. Similar course options and constructions are likely to be ubiquitous in UK law departments if they have not already attained that status.

This particularisation of the teaching of human rights in the United Kingdom is less a reflection of the Act's radical impact than of a distinction traditionally drawn between civil liberties within the United Kingdom and human rights outside. Admittedly, strong references will be made in a UK course to the theoretical and international dimensions of human rights law, in particular the European dimension, but familiar approaches to the subject are likely to persist. Consequently, we should still expect to see the national–international dichotomy continue. Indeed, the National Centre for Legal Education's publication on teaching human rights reflects the central distinction (Bell *et al*, 1999).

Whilst acknowledging the efficacy of the above approach, other law schools will wish to respond to the challenge posed by the HRA by employing perhaps more dynamic means. Recognising that specialist courses might fail to reach the whole student body, it might be considered necessary to ensure that the Act's underlying philosophy (if one can indeed be discerned) is reflected *throughout* the curriculum. Such an approach might not only look to coordinate the teaching of the HRA but also ensure that human rights *sensibilities* were inculcated across all subjects. This could raise significant problems, however. On the one hand, accusations might be levied that academic freedom was being fettered. Human rights principles are by no means uncontested; thus it may be argued that values that relate to human rights were being imposed irrespective of subject area. As a result, a curriculum-wide application of human rights could be seen to hinder some teachers in the content and delivery of their courses. Alternatively, in order to avoid such an accusation, any coordination may end up reproducing an anodyne response to the issues involved. In other words, a pragmatic approach to the HRA and human rights may be taken that is more likely to be reactive to judicial decisions than critical of them. Consequently, there may be a tendency to treat case law as merely one more strategy to be deployed where necessary to support a particular legal argument.

The pervasive approach to the teaching of human rights would therefore face significant difficulties in fulfilling the promise of the HRA. Too cautious and the concentration on the techniques of human rights law might neuter any attempts to encourage deeper reflection on the meaning of values and their impact on legal practice. Too bold and a law school might be affected by accusations of proselytization. Such a dilemma may well push law schools to favour the safer option of the specialist course at first. Unfortunately, this would also fail to consider both the radical nature of the HRA and the students' need to understand its potential all-encompassing effect. It is highly predictable therefore that, whatever the difficulties, 'mainstreaming' human rights across the curriculum will be undertaken by law schools.

Should that prove to be the case and a culture of human rights appreciation was to be assumed by the legal academy, the question of assessment of the students' appreciation of those related values and understandings would arise. In the specialised course, no such difficulty presents itself. All assessment would be infused with these issues. In contrast, to prove its effectiveness the pervasive approach would need to look to more creative methods. Bearing in mind that HRA considerations would remain ancillary to the subjects within which they were considered, this may not be so easily achieved. It would be a question of balance. Paying lip service to HRA sensibilities would undermine the purpose of the exercise. Equally, forcing HRA questions to the fore might destabilize the nature of the topic being studied. For these reasons, deliberate assessment of the human rights issues across the curriculum could well be evaded. Each subject would claim that human rights formed part of the essential elements to be imparted and thus examined without providing a mechanism for ensuring that that would be the case.

Faced, therefore, with the limitations imposed by both the specialised course and the pervasive imposition of the HRA and human rights, law schools might consider a third path; the compulsory course. Although this may result ultimately from pressure applied by the professional bodies (when dictating the content of a qualifying law degree, for instance) it would more likely arise from an institution's particular appreciation of the importance and potential of the HRA. However, few law schools are likely to volunteer such a change to their curriculum. Rather, any compulsory element that related to the ethos of human rights would be consigned to a constitutional law course. That would be the least objectionable strategy. It is inconceivable in any case that the Act would not appear in this context thus perhaps rendering any call for a compulsory human rights course devoid of support.

All of the above present clearly legitimate responses to the HRA challenge. All can also be considered as complementary rather than mutually exclusive. They could be instituted together or separately. However, there is little to suggest from these likely strategies, whether employed individually or collectively, that the radical alteration in the legal system posed by the HRA will be reflected in the teaching models adopted. In many respects, they will reapply traditional methods, reactive to legal developments rather than encouraging new attitudes. They will be didactic in character, instructing rather than necessarily providing the environment for imaginative reflection and deeper understanding. They will pose a danger of the HRA acting as a constraint on learning about human rights, the subject sealed by limited judicial decision, ever awaiting developments, endlessly guessing directions. Such restrictive methods cannot be sufficient. They will not do justice to the potential of the HRA and, indeed, those possible conceptions of human rights within that context. Nor will they do justice to the ethos that might lie behind the adoption of human rights as core value-expressions.

Consequently, in order to query the orthodox approaches already outlined an alternative needs to be considered. Before examining some examples of possible initiatives in this direction, the next section attempts to provide a different perspective for the teaching of human rights in the UK law school.

Section 2
Human rights education as inspiration

In itself, the HRA is not revolutionary. It provides another source of law and interpretation. It suggests new avenues for legal argument. But it does not even begin to address or acknowledge the subject of human rights in all its complexity. Consequently, the contested site that is human rights continues to throw up questions; on conflicts between rights; on cultural perspectives, on the extent of rights. Undoubtedly, Parliament intended to avoid such questions. They were left, as perhaps they must, to practice, the unwritten supplement to the law.

The extent of that impact through practice will depend, if only in part, on the ability of lawyers to appreciate the possibilities that the HRA unveils. And the extent of that appreciation will depend on how human rights can be understood *in* practice. This does not mean only in the practice of law. Rather, it means in the practice of people, their lives and the values, needs, beliefs that people hold and wish to protect, or promote, or advocate.

This message has been sustained for some time by the international movement concerned with human rights education (frequently shortened to HRE). Although subject to as much disputation as those questions posed about human rights above, it is possible to discern two core appreciations redolent within this discourse. First, that human rights education has to be 'participatory and operational, creative, innovative and empowering' (UNESCO, 1993). This requires active cooperation between educators, learners, and community. Second, that it has to be relevant, it must 'engage learners in a dialogue about the ways and means of transforming human rights from the expression of abstract norms to the reality of their social, economic, cultural and political conditions' (United Nations, 1995, Article 6).

These perceptions tell us that the role of experience and dialogue in the understanding of human rights is of acute importance. It implies an acknowledgement that monological means of teaching human rights cannot alone lead to their deeper appreciation or their potential application. It suggests that educating human rights is a dialogical and continual process, ever evolving and in constant need of reappraisal. The education of human rights is thus preferred as a collaborative enterprise, one that requires the student and educator to be engaged within communities, to experience the lived-lives of people, to become immersed in the messy world of ethics and justice. It is no coincidence that such an approach echoes Zygmunt Bauman's appreciation of the postmodern mind, one that is now aware that:

[t]here are problems in human and social life with no good solutions, twisted trajectories that cannot be straightened up, ambivalences that are more than linguistic blunders yelling to be corrected, doubts which cannot be legislated out of existence, moral agonies which no reason-dictated recipes can soothe, let alone cure.

(Bauman, 1993: 245)

Similarly, the anthropological perspective adopted by Clifford Geertz suggests that law can only be understood in the context of its local application (Geertz, 1993: 167–234). The philosophy behind HRE could be said to reflect both Bauman's and Geertz's appreciations. It is defined by communication through experience. Exposure to people's practice is a prerequisite to insight. Without that engagement one has to question seriously the ability for learners *and* teachers to understand the complex arena of human rights, to appreciate the conflicts and dilemmas that underpin any dispute about the rights of one person against others.

If one widens this approach, we might say that practice is therefore not separable from the law. But rather, as has been suggested, it is the necessary supplement to the law, the experience that gives law its definition and its scope. Consequently, the presumption that telling stories about human rights law in the law school, in whatever course and whatever form, can really hope to introduce students to the totality of their possibility is suspect. Such stories may be a necessary precursor to experience (although even that might be doubted) but ultimately it is the disclosures that may emanate from encounters with practice that will encourage deeper understanding about the very notion of human rights and the consequences of their application. Enabling the student to become 'involved' in the messiness of practice, of others' lives, might then enhance their capacity for action, perhaps through the HRA, perhaps through other means. Regardless, the experience is the key.

If such realisations are accepted, clear implications for the teaching of human rights and the HRA result. The argument that it is not the law school's place to pre-empt practice cannot be a satisfactory response. Nor will it be convincing to suggest that the theoretical study of the law and human rights does not require any direct experience of either. Rather, if the supplement of law defines the law then an early exposure to that supplement through teaching and learning experiences at the law school must be preferable. In the case of human rights law, the supplement exists locally in the community.

This is not to say that a law school can hope to provide a total education in the supplement. That would be by definition impossible. But what the institution can do is provide the student with perspectives honed from experience. By working with students in the community, the law school can encourage reflection and analysis as a part of practice. It can promote an understanding of the meaning and possibilities of human rights (whether that be in conjunction with the HRA or not) that might otherwise be submerged within the constraints and pressures of professional and commercial life. In other words, the law school can help students acquire strategies to pursue the potential offered by the human rights discourse, strategies that are thoughtful and creative rather than purely reactive. The value of such experience for deeper thought about human rights may therefore be incalculable.

The argument presented above leads us to conclude that exposing students to active engagement with human rights in the community might be an invaluable means of their teaching and learning. But what programmes might achieve this aim? The final section of this chapter considers two possible responses to this challenge. They are not confined to the UK experience but are connected by the involvement of Warwick Law School. Neither example can claim to fulfil all the requirements suggested by the above analysis. However, in both cases they are intended as supplements to more traditional human rights teaching, not substitutes. They also demonstrate perhaps two ends of a spectrum or rather a range of possibilities available to a law school determined to place human rights close to the heart of the study of law.

Section 3
Experience in practice

Teaching as learning: Warwick human rights project

The first example, although by no means novel in approach, has the value of having taken place soon after the HRA was introduced. The Act was both the project's focus and its inspiration. Conducted at Warwick Law School in the first half of 2001, it involved seven final year students undertaking an assessable module or half course. The central premise was that through teaching human rights in the community, students would be encouraged to learn more about human rights and be exposed to different perspectives and problems that people had with those rights.

Copying the notion of what has been termed 'street law' programmes (a term that has been used to signify the education of people 'in the street' about the law and their rights), the project aimed to introduce the HRA in particular and human rights in general to sixth formers in a local school through the delivery of a workshop (consisting of two one-hour seminars). Each student was obliged to plan, design, research and implement this workshop. In doing so, they worked in teams of two or three and were required specifically to address the following:

- setting objectives;
- assessing needs;
- planning the project;
- conducting research;
- designing the project;
- delivering the project;
- evaluating its success;
- reflecting upon that evaluation and introducing change.

Although the students were encouraged to approach the exercise in their own way, these criteria formed the parameters for their project. From this point of view, it was stressed that the criteria had wider application than purely the delivery of their own project. Seminars were given to the students throughout the term to emphasise this possibility as well as to discuss the details of their workshops, teaching techniques and assessment criteria (both for the course and the students' own evaluation of the workshops they were intended to deliver). Issues related to human rights and the HRA were also covered. In total, therefore, the students were introduced to and explored more general notions of human rights 'advocacy'.

A school local to the university agreed to cooperate in the venture and made available a member of their sixth form staff to help with the arrangements. Coundon Court School and Community College in Coventry generously gave their time and facilities to enable the project to take place. In this respect, it is noteworthy that schools are becoming increasingly open to joint enterprises such as this. Through the school, it was agreed that the students' workshops would be included within the General Studies 'A' level studies. It was a matter for the students to liaise with the school so as to assess need, agree content and all other administrative details.

The students were encouraged to approach their project in their own style. They did so imaginatively and sensitively. They were made aware of responsibilities that flowed from the activities they planned. Key ethical questions were therefore raised and drawn into their project planning: how to deal with differing perspectives on the nature of human rights; the impact of using illustrative material concerning human rights abuses to an audience that might contain a victim of such abuse; how to engage with principles of participation in any advocacy enterprise. One response was for a preliminary meeting between the students and the school staff member assigned to the project as well as with a representative group of pupils. This established: the numbers of pupils involved; the multicultural environment of the school; the teaching methods that the pupils preferred; the issues related to human rights they had already covered within their studies, and the issues the pupils were interested in discussing. Equally, there was an opportunity to confirm that the pupils had no objection to the workshops being observed by assessors from Warwick Law School.

On completion of the workshops, the students were then asked to reflect upon their experiences. They were each required to present a written and oral report for assessment. Through those mechanisms they demonstrated a vast array of appreciations: the possibilities and constraints of human rights teaching; the potential range of meanings of human rights; the difficulties of translating people's life-views into a legal forum (in this case the HRA); the tensions associated with such legal interpretations.

Clearly, the scope of the project was limited. But even so, the reflections that were produced by the students indicated a deep appreciation of complex issues involved in human rights practice as well as theory. Without exaggerating its claims, the project did prompt several important developments for those students involved. In particular, it required an engagement with the subject and people who presented different perspectives and demonstrated different understandings and values. It is difficult to conceive of a situation in the law school classroom where such revelations could have been replicated. Not impossible but the threat of contrivance and thus irrelevance might always have been present.

Similar 'street' enterprises, therefore, involved with different sections of the community (the students suggested providing workshops for prisoners, the elderly, other identifiable groups), could expand the experience of human rights for students. Throughout, the educational premise is simple and was expressed in one of the students' reports:

> I feel I have learnt far more by actively teaching human rights than I could ever have learnt by passively observing a series of lectures on the subject. [D]ue to the responsibility of teaching in a real-life scenario, one cannot escape from the fact that if you do not have an adequate knowledge of the subject then you will be doing a disservice both to yourself and to your students.

Deeper realisations as to the nature of human rights, the problematics associated with their co-option by the law and how they might affect our life-worlds were an evident progression from this base. Indeed, the exercise seems to have challenged many of the preconceptions that the students had about the universality of human rights. Merely engaging with an audience holding different views on the sanctity of rights, for instance, drew out the distinction between teaching human rights and advocating for their promotion. Clearly, therefore, there is immense scope for developing these possibilities within the curriculum. In particular, such a street law exercise could well be combined with a more traditional course on human rights that seeks to play on the appreciations that arise. Equally, the exercise could be extended to a large number of students, perhaps outside the confines of the degree programme, working with local schools and community groups.

Human rights immersion: a model from the Philippines

The second example suggests a more complete approach to the teaching of human rights through experience. It is a model that requires a large-scale institutional commitment placing human rights firmly at the heart of a law school's operations. The example appears in the Philippines but the model is no less instructive for all that.

The Ateneo Human Rights Centre (AHRC) was set up within the Ateneo de Manila University School of Law shortly after the revolution that unseated President Marcos from power in 1986. As such it is hardly surprising that it was invested with an ethos that promoted human rights advocacy for its transformatory and emancipatory potential. However, this message found a natural home with the notions of liberation theology that lies beneath the Ateneo de Manila University's teaching, it being a Jesuit-based establishment of long history. The philosophy of 'social concern and involvement' permeates through the University's literature culminating in a commitment to 'a faith that does justice' (Ateneo de Manila University Prospectus, 1998). The AHRC implements such tenets through the integration of education and practice.

On the foundations of this religious and philosophical commitment (which echo much of the motivational rhetoric that has, historically, given impetus to human rights' movements and actions), AHRC has developed a programme that seeks to fulfil a number of intersecting aims. These have been described by Carlos Medina, the Executive Director of the Centre, as to: '(a) form human rights advocates; (b) make justice accessible to poor victims of human rights violations; (c) monitor government compliance with human rights instruments; and (d) educate the public on law and human rights' (Medina). For our purposes, a primary goal is the 'formation of human rights advocates' to include not only law students but also practising lawyers and members of 'grassroots' or 'base' communities. This is to be achieved in the context of a Centre that acts in a number of interrelated spheres. It is engaged in legal advice representation for individuals and community groups on human rights issues through its legal aid clinic. It undertakes research and publications into human rights concerns in the Philippines, thus providing a monitoring service on the current conditions of human rights implementation and observance in the country. It conducts training programmes in human rights for government and non-government organisations as well as 'street law' projects aimed at providing information to sectors of society vulnerable to human rights abuses. More recently, it has also become involved in the Working Group for an ASEAN Human Rights Mechanism thus elevating its work to the international as well as local sphere.

Although the Centre employs a number of permanent qualified lawyers to undertake these operations, all their activities involve the active and continual participation of students from the Ateneo Law School. This involvement is a conscious acceptance of the equal importance of active legal education and the promotion of human rights through law. This balance is redolent throughout everything the Centre does. However, it is of particular importance within its core 'Human Rights Internship Programme'.

The main purpose of this programme is to help address a perceived need for human rights advocates who 'know' the law and the workings of the legal system. 'Knowledge' is not confined to awareness of constitutional protections for human rights but rather requires the student lawyer to *understand* the possibilities for, and actualities of, abuse still present in the country. Armed with this understanding, the advocate can then apply the skills and strategies available through the legal system, which are also the subject of their education, to effect change.

To this end the internship programme has a fluid structure, which seeks to fulfil these concurrent aims of clinical legal and human rights education in practice. However, its identifiable components can be described as follows.

First, the student is introduced to grassroots communities with particular human rights interests through a series of immersion projects. These range from one-day preparatory visits to two-week courses held between-semesters. During the latter, the student spends one week living with a tribal or community group in an attempt to obtain some experience of any relevant poverty and human rights issues, and one week undergoing an intensive group reflective process, held by all the student participants and a tutor, in order to evaluate the lessons learnt.

Following this immersion programme, the student is able to take up the option of a two-month summer internship with an NGO active in human rights work. This is the mainstay of the educative scheme. The student undertakes an induction organised by the Centre (although most of the training is provided by ex-interns under the supervision of the intern Director) and then works within an organisation carrying out litigation, paralegal training, local lobbying initiatives etc. Ultimately, the student might continue this practical experience after graduation by accepting a one-year internship with a similar organisation.

The internship programme has to be seen as integral to the remainder of the Centre's activities. Students invariably graduate to the internship scheme after working within the Centre's other areas of operations. Thus, they will have been involved in the Legal Aid Clinic or the research and public education programmes from an early stage of their law school careers. Indeed, the students' engagement in the Centre's work is a fundamental requirement for its continuing effectiveness. Students assume many of the administrative responsibilities and work together to ensure that the programmes remain operational. They are given opportunities to introduce their own initiatives. One such example was the publication of a comic in association with a consortium of NGOs. Inspired by an ex-student of the Centre, the comic was designed to assist in the promotion of democracy and justice at a local and accessible level.

Once the students have undergone the internship programme they continue to assist in the induction and training of future interns. Whatever the ambitions of the Centre, whether it be the promotion of law reform, or the conduct of new actions of legal action, the students are seen as an essential working component without whom it could not continue.

As a result, the Centre looks to generate a sense of commitment that seems to endure beyond the college life of the student. Indeed, many ex-students who have become practising lawyers continue to maintain a close relationship with the Centre. Whether this has succeeded within the Centre's own remit of producing effective human rights advocates in a legal setting would require further empirical study. One might also ask whether the model is translatable to other settings such as UK universities, particularly given the inevitable resource constraints. However, the example provides an indication of what may be possible given the will and commitment of both institution and students. Some law schools have adopted clinical approaches that bear resemblance to the Ateneo structure. Kent Law School and Sheffield Hallam University are two notable examples. The potential is therefore open to realisation. The argument that initiatives are constrained by resources is a smokescreen. Ultimately it is a question of institutional and personal choice. If human rights are to be treated seriously and with imagination by law schools, as a subject and as an activity, the means could be found.

Conclusion

The Human Rights Act offers new challenges both for the law and lawyers. That much should be uncontroversial. Equally, how law schools now respond to this new environment must be seen as relevant in determining whether the legal culture of this country will be altered radically.

Should such new challenges and responses therefore necessitate new strategies for teaching and learning in human rights? It would be naïve and perhaps complacent to answer automatically in the negative. If that is the case, it will not be sufficient to experiment indiscriminately. First, there must be a consideration of the ethos behind any approach adopted. Without such an underpinning theoretical appreciation it is difficult to imagine how one can argue that human rights *are* being treated seriously within the legal academy. This chapter has therefore been an attempt to articulate one perspective, one approach buttressed by a theoretical understanding. Its implementation, however, wholly depends on the willingness of law schools not only to accept the premise but also to provide the resources and the support it requires. The decision to do so would alone represent a momentous transformation for some institutions. Then the choice as to how academic study might be supplemented by practical action can be undertaken. Whether that entails electing to incorporate 'street law' or similar small-scale operations into the curriculum, embarking on a major institutional project involving externships, legal aid clinics and the like, or adopting activities that fall somewhere between the two, will be a matter for discussion preferably with the students *and* with the local community.

References

Andreopoulous, G and Pierre Claude, R (eds) (1997) *Human Rights Education for the Twenty-First Century*, University of Pennsylvania Press, Pennsylvania

Bauman, Z (1993) *Postmodern Ethics*, Blackwell Publishers, Oxford

Bell, C et al (1999) *Teaching Human Rights*, National Centre for Legal Education, University of Warwick

Clayton, R and Tomlinson, H (2000) *The Law of Human Rights*, Oxford University Press, Oxford

Fenwick, H (2000) *Civil Rights, New Labour, Freedom and the Human Rights Act*, Longman, Harlow

Geertz, C (1993) *Local Knowledge*, Fontana Press, London

Medina, C [accessed 5 December 2001] *Legal Aid Services in the Philippines* [Online] http://www.pili.org/library/cle/1...ices%20in%20the%20philippines.htm

UNESCO (1993) World Plan of Action on Education (the Montreal Declaration)

United Nations Organisation (1995) Draft Plan of Action of the United Nations Decade for Human Rights Education

University of Essex Law Department [accessed 5 December 2001] [Online] http://www2.essex.ac.uk/law/

University of Kent Law School [accessed 5 December] http://www.ukc.ac.uk/law/
Wadham, J and Mountfield, H (2000) *Blackstone's Guide to the Human Rights Act 1998*,
  Blackstone Press, London

Useful Web sites
Amnesty International
http://amnesty.org

Council of Europe Human Rights Web
http://www.dhdirhr.coe.fr/

Human Rights Network established by the British Council
http://humanrights.britishcouncil.org

Street Law Online
http://www.streetlaw.org/

United Nations High Commission for Human Rights
http://wwwunhchr.ch

Human Rights Education Associates
http://www.hrea.org/

The People's Decade of Human Rights Education
http://www.pdhre.org/

Human Rights Resource Centre
http://www.hrusa.org/default.htm

7

Law teaching for other programmes

Linda Byles and Ruth Soetendorp

Introduction

This chapter is intended to support law teachers involved in the delivery of such diverse programmes to students whose main discipline is not law. It acknowledges that the contribution of law teachers is not confined to unit design and delivery, but may also involve advising, supporting and collaborating with colleagues in a different discipline field. In the post-compulsory sector, law is taught across a wide range of programmes and discipline areas. The time allocated to delivery can vary enormously as too can the level to which it is taught. These points are illustrated at a micro-level here at the University of Bournemouth, where a recent survey identified that law was being taught across 12 different programmes and to disciplines ranging from computing to nursing, from media to archaeology. Teaching inputs varied from 4 to 33 weeks and the nature of the student cohort covered a wide variety of interests and learning needs. This diversity of disciplines and student profiles has a significant effect on approaches to the learning and teaching of law. These issues will be explored by focusing on two key questions: 1) how can students, whose main discipline is not law, be best supported in their learning of law? and 2) what approaches to teaching and learning are best suited to these students?

In addressing these questions we start from the underlying principle that teaching students from non-law disciplines needs to be done in the context of their own subject area. We shall explore this by discussing approaches to teaching, the identification of learning outcomes, assessment strategies, decisions on content, and finally student skills. Throughout the chapter, we refer to students for whom law is not their main discipline. We recognise that they do not form a uniform category of students, having significant differences in their discipline backgrounds, and approaches to study.

As a starting point, it may be worthwhile reflecting on why law appears in the curriculum of so many programmes. Suggestions identified at two workshops on 'Teaching Law to Non Lawyers' run by the authors and organised by the UK Centre for Legal Education (UKCLE) included:

- ensuring accountability;
- application to the discipline;
- effect on the operation of work;
- requirement of professional body;
- knowing when to bring in a legal advisor;
- background to the main area of study;
- concept of citizenship;
- knowing how the law works;
- creating opportunities to change and shape the law;
- ability to communicate across disciplines.

This list is not exhaustive, rather an illustration of the need to identify a rationale for the inclusion of law in the curriculum. Those who taught accountancy students, for example, cited the requirements of professional bodies. In contrast, those who taught politics students stressed the importance of the concept of citizenship. Whatever the rationale, it is important that all persons involved, particularly the students, understand why the study of law is included. The following extract highlights the perceptions of a business law teacher:

> It was decided that the main objective of business legal education is to prepare students for the business world. Graduates should be able to operate a business within the parameters of the law, consider the legal implications and risks inherent in business decisions, and identify legal issues at a preliminary stage. A person involved in business should not only be able to suggest possible solutions to disputes but also to distinguish circumstances in which it would be more appropriate to seek professional legal advice.
>
> (Skwarok, 1995: 190)

Approaches to teaching

Three factors seem of particular importance to us in deciding on approaches to teaching law students:

- knowing your own values and experiences –'where you are coming from';
- understanding the relevance of law to the discipline that you are working in;

- identifying strategies for supporting student learning that focus on context rather than content.

In addressing the first point you may wish to consider the strengths that you bring to your teaching, the challenges that you might face and the benefits that might accrue to you. See the box below.

Strengths of and challenges and benefits for the academic/practitioner in law

Strengths

- conceptual legal framework;
- knowledge of sources;
- application of legal principles.

Challenges

- scope of discipline;
- linkages to disciplinary themes;
- identifying appropriate level.

Benefits

- a fresh approach to law as a discipline;
- opportunity for cross-faculty/inter-disciplinary work.

You may also need to consider the strengths, challenges and benefits as they relate to your colleagues with whom you work with in their discipline area. They will bring a different perspective to the study of law, which can help you identify a focus for your own teaching. See the box on page 147.

Strengths of and challenges and benefits for the discipline subject specialist

Strengths

- knowledge of subject context;
- application;
- perspective on level.

Challenges

- knowledge of broader legal framework;
- keeping up to date;
- locating appropriate sources.

Benefits include a wider perspective of the discipline in professional practice.

There is a valuable synergy between your own approaches to teaching and that of the colleagues that you work with in their discipline area. This can help you shape your own understanding of the values and experiences that you bring to your teaching and more importantly help you understand the needs of your students. As one law practitioner from a Scottish university teaching technology students identifies: 'It was strange at first to minimize legal terminology and Latin usage, moving away from traditional legal teaching to a more progressive innovative approach with a strong emphasis on the vocational needs of these students'.

The importance of understanding the nature of the discipline is illustrated by a study done with focus groups of business studies students at Middlesex Business School. The students concluded that they did not enjoy studying law because it was boring and involved too much to learn and remember (Jin, 2000). What the students found difficult was that the style of teaching law was mostly content-driven. While these views may accurately describe their learning experience, they may not reflect trends in current law teaching, where there appears to be a move away from a content-driven approach.

What is significant about this example is the students' perception of the stark contrast between the approaches to teaching law and that of their main discipline area. They explained that they were used to their main discipline, business studies, being taught in an analytical way, eliciting principles and applying knowledge. This different approach had called for a role alteration in student learning and it had been difficult for them to adjust. 'The wider the gap (or the greater the difference) between taught disciplines, the more effort should be put into addressing the potential difference of lecturing styles in order to achieve educational/learning objectives.' (Jin, 2000: 31)

In addition to recognising and working with the approaches to teaching in specific disciplines, a balance needs to be struck between delivering content and focusing on the context. Too great an emphasis on content can make the study of law appear as a process of learning the right rules in order to avoid costly or dangerous mistakes. In our experience, encouraging students to integrate their experience with legal concepts, and to make greater use of the skills and knowledge that they bring with them, can result in deeper learning. It also brings an understanding of the significance of law in its own subject domain. This student-centred focus requires the teacher to support student learning by emphasising a resource-based approach. The following example of the BA course in Financial Services and Accounting illustrates this.

BA Financial Services/Accounting

Level one undergraduate students are taught law by a legal practitioner, who uses the Web as the prime means of delivering content. The Web-learning environment contains 'lecture' notes, case and statutory references and a range of links with information sources. There are no lectures; instead, seminars are used to explore and discuss legal themes. This is supplemented by computer conferencing using 'First Class', where students can follow up the seminar activities by posting questions or sharing information with their peers. It requires the students to take a high level of responsibility for their learning, in particular to prepare for the seminars. It requires the teacher to reconsider how previous teaching methods, which were all delivered face to face and relied on printed resources, need to be adapted for electronic delivery. More importantly, it has forced a radical rethink in terms of the relationship between staff and student.

Getting the learning outcomes right

All participants in a law programme need to be clear about why law is present in the curriculum. Law study can be extremely demanding, not least because its language, its discourse and its resources can be fundamentally different from the students' own discipline area. Helping students come to some understanding of this, and hence helping them engage effectively in their own learning, is to a great extent achieved through appropriately articulated learning outcomes. They inform the student what they can expect to learn and what they can expect to get out of their study. Learning outcomes have a hugely motivational role, by highlighting what has to be learnt in order to succeed (Ramsden, 1992).

Learning outcomes play an important part in shaping teaching, learning and assessment strategies. In the design of teaching activities, the teacher decides on what teaching/learning activity best achieves the intended learning outcome. Similarly, the assessment strategy must consider what type of assessment method is best suited to demonstrating that the learning outcome has been met. As Table 7.1 illustrates, all three factors must work in harmony (see also Chapter 3).

Table 7.1 BSc Software Engineering, Level II, Law and Business unit

Learning Outcome	Learning Activity	Assessment Strategy
to work collaboratively with legal advisor	role-play focused round a case study	reflective account of the nature of the interaction between the legal advisor and the client

Identifying learning outcomes

There are many ways of classifying learning outcomes. They range from the cognitive to the affective, psychomotor, perceptual, attitudinal and experiential (see Rowntree, 1981: 45–53 for a fuller discussion). The following is an example from an undergraduate social work programme:

At the end of the unit the student will be able to:

- critically examine a pathway for specific practice issue with legal and ethical dimensions;
- demonstrate the ability to engage in balanced and reasoned debate on legal practice issues;
- evaluate personal and professional value systems in practice.

The students are expected to demonstrate both cognitive abilities as well as oral skills. There is an emphasis on attitudinal outcomes which, it could be argued, is appropriate to the domain of social work. Whatever types of outcome are chosen, it will be important to set them appropriately in the discipline domain.

It will also be important to take a holistic view of the learning outcomes set for the law element in relation to the learning outcomes set for other parts of the programme. This will be especially significant for the learning experience of the student. In particular, issues of potential duplication need to be addressed. It may also be necessary to provide opportunities to reinforce individual outcomes; for example, 'report writing' skills may need to be highlighted across the curriculum.

Meeting the outcome challenge: professional bodies, benchmarking and level

Learning outcomes may need to take into account requirements imposed on programmes by professional bodies, in particular those that grant exemptions from the overall qualification (see Chapter 1). These restrictions can be seen as limiting. In gathering data for this chapter the following quote typified the response of many teachers of law to the constraints imposed by professional requirements:

> Part of my remit is to teach Company Law to accountants and other non-lawyers. The unit is an exempting unit for CIMA and therefore has to cover an enormous amount of ground. The accountants struggle, the other non-lawyers grumble at the amount to study and it is a constant challenge to keep this unit on an even keel. Other units I teach do not have the exempting requirements and so they are much more relaxed and there is a little time to explore issues of interest.

> (anonymous law teacher in a post–1992 university)

There is much debate on the effect professional bodies have on curriculum content and delivery (for an example in the area of accountancy and law, see Ward and Salter, 1990). The influence of professional bodies needs to be viewed creatively with consideration given to the extent to which the specified outcomes must be adopted literally or may be interpreted imaginatively.

Meeting benchmark statements poses another problem for teaching law to non-lawyers. A decision must be made about which benchmarks are applicable for the law unit: those of the subject discipline or those of law. This needs to be discussed amongst the programme team.

As well as clarifying the types of learning outcomes, it is equally, if not more, important to establish them at an appropriate level. Finding the right level can signal to the student the value placed on them by the tutor or professional body. Some outcomes for example will appear more important than others because they require the student to engage with subject themes in complex ways (see Hospitality examples below). Less important topics may only require a level of engagement sufficient to be able to list, recall or record. Biggs (1982) describes this differentiation as a series of hills. His SOLO taxonomy (Structure of Observed Learning Outcomes) identifies four different levels of understanding in ascending order of cognitive complexity. This is outlined in Figure 7.1.

Some examples of different levels for BA Hospitality Management, level I, Hospitality Law unit students are given below:

- Identify the statutory provisions of the Licensing Acts that relate to the restaurant sector (unistructural).

- Describe the key features of the Licensing Acts that relate to the restaurant sector (multistructural).
- Apply the provisions of the Licensing Acts to the running of the restaurant sector (relational).
- Reflect on the validity of the Licensing Acts in the context of the restaurant sector (extended abstract).

Setting the appropriate level of outcomes is a unique activity for each programme. It needs to be done, however, in the context of the discipline, taking account of the prerequisite knowledge and skills of students, time allocated to delivery, and the complexity of the topics being taught.

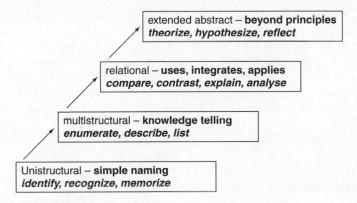

Figure 7.1 SOLO taxonomy

Writing learning outcomes

It may be difficult to identify sources to assist the law teacher in writing learning outcomes, particularly if the discipline domain is unfamiliar. Newble and Cannon (1995) give some pointers to address this issue:

- teacher's own knowledge and skills and attitudes;
- student needs, interests and characteristics;
- subject matter as reflected in published literature, particularly textbooks;
- requirements of professional bodies;
- requirements of department or faculty;
- ways of thinking and problem solving of particular discipline;
- relevance to context of subject.

The output from these sources can be complex and putting ideas together can be problematic. However, once the learning outcomes have been set then the rest of the unit planning can take place. Each outcome can then be matched with an appropriate teaching and learning activity and with a valid form of assessment.

Assessment strategies

Students' commitment to learn about law may be simply driven by the fact that they will be assessed. While we may not be able to change this view, we may as well try to work with it. In particular, assessment can be used to inform the ways in which students learn. The case study example in Table 7.1 directly links into the assessment task. It utilises a student-centred approach to learning and requires the student to apply their learning experience to an assessed piece of work. This linkage between the *learning activity* and *assessment* is ultimately shaped by the *learning outcomes* that have been set.

Assessment tasks

Assessment tasks need to allow students to demonstrate their respective strengths. These will vary from discipline to discipline and it will be important for the law teacher to acknowledge this (see Student skills, page 158). Creating assessment tasks can prove a liberating experience, especially for the lawyer who may have been limited to the traditional essay or question-style exercises. Some examples are given in Table 7.2.

Table 7.2 Examples of assessment tasks

Subject Discipline	Assessment Task
Media Studies	reviewing/writing a journal article on a legal theme
Business Studies	writing a report on the legal implications of specific employment practices
Leisure and Tourism	devising an entry on a legal theme for a subject handbook
Conservation Science	critique of legislation affecting archaeological digs
Nursing	guidance note on drug administration
Product Design	preparation of a model patent specification
Information Technology	develop an expert system on aspects of the Data Protection Act

Table 7.2 continued

Whatever the discipline, a selection of generic tasks could include:

> compilation of annotated bibliography for new practitioner
>
> debate/group presentation on relevant legal issues
>
> a quiz – to be answered in class, with material in support of correct answers to be supplied, or collected by students
>
> reflective log on legal representation of an issue in professional press
>
> multiple-choice questions on legal concepts
>
> critique of media (print or broadcast) presentation of relevant legal issue

In all of these examples, the student will need to be supported by clear criteria. This should include guidance on what is being tested, clarification on the breadth and depth required and instructions on how it is to be presented. Consideration will need to be given to whether the task lends itself to being completed individually or collaboratively and, where appropriate, whether it should be presented orally or electronically. In deciding on these issues, reference needs to be made to the learning outcomes, the time and resources available to the teacher and the nature of other assessment tasks undertaken by the student.

Teachers not located in the students' faculty can find themselves isolated in terms of knowing what is going on in the rest of the programme, particularly where they may only form a small element of it. Where students have to make several assessed presentations or write a number of journal reviews for different topics for different teachers, the effect can be disruptive and demotivating. It will be important for the law teacher to work with other programme colleagues to complete an assessment matrix, which identifies the range of assessment tasks (see Chapter 3).

Self- and peer assessment

Involving students in the assessment process can also have a significant influence on their motivation. In self- and peer assessment the students are involved in the same issues as the teacher in deciding how the subject of law relates to their main area of study. Students can be encouraged to keep a log of how law relates to other areas of the curriculum. If, for example, computing students are designing or critiquing software for customer records, then you would expect them to be able to understand the impact of data protection or copyright issues. This may promote reflective learning for the student and encourage linkages across the curriculum, while at the same time developing evaluative skills. This can be '*rewarded*' in the students' eyes by linking it to the final assessment, in particular by allowing the students to allocate for themselves an element of the mark. To ensure reliability this can be matched against the marks given by their peers and tutors and with the final say being given to the tutor where there may be disagreement.

Peer assessment can work well where it is specifically targeted at assessment activities, which lend themselves to students sharing their knowledge and expertise, and where it encourages further discussion and review. (For a fuller picture of the uses of peer assessment see Chapter 3 and Brown and Dove, 1991.) Where potential law topics are diverse, and time is limited to cover them, students making presentations on topics which they select for themselves can give an element of self-directed learning to the students. It also allows others to comment on and add to the knowledge of students. An element of peer assessment in the process, on agreed criteria, can further give ownership to the student. The following example in the box illustrates another use of peer assessment in the context of cross-disciplinary learning.

Cross-faculty peer assessment: BA Product Design students working with LLB students (criteria are in bold)

Students on the Design programme work with students on the full-time Law degree. The engineers describe their products, and ask the lawyers for intellectual property advice. The lawyers' advice has to be **user friendly** but authoritative (supported by an appendix from the tutor). The engineers' letters have to be **clear and coherent** in the way they describe their innovations. An element of peer assessment ensures that both groups of students retain these **objectives** in mind when completing the tasks.

Not all tasks need be part of the summative assessment process. Short, frequent, challenging assessments, including exercises such as getting students to identify key legal concepts from a previous session and sharing them with fellow students, can provide a useful feedback mechanism. Use of multiple-choice questions can have a similar effect. The questions can be used with other cohorts if they are part of the formative process. When students mark them in class and explain to each other their choice of answers, this adds no further marking burden on the teacher. If all assessment is left to the end of the programme, this may reinforce the perception that law is something that needs to be passed but does not have any wider significance for the rest of their studies.

Deciding on content

Earlier in the chapter we identified sources of information, which could be used to write learning outcomes. These same sources can be used to identify curriculum content. In particular, the published literature of the discipline can yield a rich source of ideas from which to develop the indicative content of a law unit.

Textbooks

Textbooks provide a useful starting point, especially if you are unfamiliar with the discipline. Their contents pages can provide a list of key legal themes that can be compared across a selection of core textbooks. A pattern will emerge of the common legal elements and, equally important, highlight those themes that are less frequently included or even left out. This data can be used as a framework from which to start considering content. This process is illustrated below from the field of nursing, in Table 7.3. The template of subject themes was drawn up from a review of nursing textbooks.

Internet

The Internet can provide a valuable resource not only in identifying key legal themes but also as a means of supplying legal data. This may be an issue, particularly where law students do not have access to law libraries. Some important sources currently available are UK statutes, UK decisions (in all courts), European legislation, European Court of Justice, Court of Human Rights, Patent Board of Appeal. Keeping up to date in this area can be problematic but sources such as Holmes (1997) can provide a useful overview. Similarly, Web links such as Sarah Carter's at the University of Kent [www.ukc.ac.uk/library/lawlinks/default.htm] and the Legal Information Service at the University of Warwick [www.law.warwick.ac.uk] can provide an invaluable source of legal information.

Some sites are freely available, while others are available on subscription. Free services are increasingly forthcoming from law firms whose sites provide accessible, user-friendly information on the premise that potential clients will expect to find this information, prior to them paying for a more specialised consultation and advisory service. Similarly, the sites of official government or professional bodies that relate to the students' discipline area can provide a useful resource. The Patent Office Web site for example [www.patent.gov.uk] supports both teachers and students by providing comprehensive coverage of the intellectual property matters in the United Kingdom. This includes information on copyright, designs, patents and trademarks. In addition, they have made available a teaching resource, the Patent Office Micromodule that is devised to enable discipline subject specialists with little or no knowledge of intellectual property, to introduce their students to

Table 7.3 Template of subject themes from a review of nursing textbooks

Introduction Legal Environment	Nursing Negligence	Patient Complaints	Legal Aspects of Expanded Role	Consent to Treatment	Confidentiality and Access to Health Care Records	Nurse and Employment Relationships	Clinical Research	Reproductive choice	End of life
law and legal system	liability in tort	complaints and patient confusion	developments in nursing practice	types of consent	general obligations	employment rights	framework of regulations	contraceptive services	ending of life criminal liability
structure of the law	criminal liability and negligent conduct	handling complaints	advanced practice situations	capacity	grounds for disclosure	safety in the workplace	regulation of research	reproductive techniques	death
structure of health care provision	litigation process	practice based complaints	nurse prescribing	criminal law liability	specific obligations	liability for unsafe conditions	policing trials	regulating the conduct of the mother	organ transplants
	damages in clinical nursing	health service commissioner		civil law liability	confidentiality and standards		compensating research subjects	abortion	
	importance of records			children	health care records				
	risk management and defence of clinical negligence			mentally ill					

intellectual property concepts. The resource is presented on a Web-enabled CD ROM, with links to the Patent Office Web site.

Professional/trade journals/press

Discipline subject specialists who are teaching law will know the titles of, and have access to, the relevant professional and trade journals. For the academic or practitioners in law, these sources can be a way of immersing in the culture of the students' discipline. Trade and professional journals often contain legal up-to-date information, legal advice columns, and articles highlighting problems encountered in a particular professional field. All of these provide useful classroom material. They will probably be pitched at a level the students can engage with because they will be dealing with material with which the student is familiar. In particular, they will give currency to the legal content of a programme and embed it very clearly in the context of the students' own discipline area.

The general press, both tabloid and broadsheet, all have the potential to carry stories that have learning and teaching potential. Once you know that you are teaching in a particular discipline, it is important to become sensitized to potentially relevant teaching material. Encourage the students to be on the lookout for relevant topics. This can help them take ownership of their learning by identifying legal issues in their own discipline field. You may be surprised at what they bring! BA Media Studies students identified the following legal themes:

'Sampling' of tiny extracts of recorded music to produce popular music products was an issue in the industry, and had been the subject of academic legal discussion, but no disputes had made it to the courts. A student provided a cutting from a popular music magazine, listing about 20 'sampling' disputes between major artistes and their recording companies, and the independent artistes and labels that had sampled their music. The cutting was a useful resource from which to discuss the legal status of sampling, and the issues involved in deciding whether or not to litigate.

'Napster' was a dispute that did make it to the courts, in the United States. It involved issues of infringing electronic copying of music. By encouraging students to bring to class published comment on 'Napster', from consumer and professional sources, it was possible to explore and consider the legal issues involved in a wider context.

Breadth versus depth: linking to programme design

Sometimes there will be a conflict for the teacher between the breadth unit content must cover, and the depth to which it 'should' be covered. Resolving this conflict is not easy. Some themes will require more attention than others. If the law element is part of an accredited programme, then breadth and depth may be dictated by the professional body. More often, the conflict is resolved as the result of a series of negotiations, which link into the design of the programme as a whole. If the law teacher is part of the development team then the significance of law within the curriculum and hence the importance of individual subject themes can be identified. But the reality is often not so neat. Where the programme design is well established, then opportunities to influence the scope of the curriculum can be limited. Strategies to overcome this problem can include the following:

- Aim to establish a rapport with the programme leaders. They can be a vital link to making the programme relevant to the students.
- Study the programme documentation. It can provide an insight into the nature of the programme.
- Find out if the programme is due for review. This is particularly important if your involvement with the programme is long term. Decide upon what contribution you could make to design prior to revalidation.
- Identify other units in the programme that link to your own. Offer to act as a visiting speaker and suggest reciprocal teaching activities. Think about complementary assessment activities.
- Think laterally about the indicative content. If it was written by a discipline specialist, it may be sufficiently vague to allow the incorporation of more relevant material.
- Consider if the indicative content needs revision. If it was written more than two years ago, it may need to be significantly changed to reflect the current legal position.
- Look outside the programme for inspiration. Examine the outputs from professional bodies and government organisations. Gain an awareness of the research profile of the discipline field. These can all highlight the significance of legal themes.
- Most importantly, work with the profile of the students. Identify their areas of interest and build on them.

Student skills

We have stressed the need to make law teaching fit the context of the subject discipline in which it is applied. There is a corollary to this, however, in that the students must also have an appreciation of the culture of law and the legal skills necessary to engage with it. This is particularly important if a student-centred approach to delivery is taken. A list of key skills for any law student may comprise the following:

- research;
- problem solving;

- oral skills;
- written skills;
- group work;
- IT skills;
- self-management.

It is hard to imagine any discipline for which these skills are not relevant. The significance for law teachers is to assess the extent to which these need to be developed within their own curriculum and whether they need to be given a specific legal slant. This needs to be done in conjunction with an awareness of the skills set that the law students may bring from their own subject domain. The following skills appear to us to be particularly important.

Research

The law student needs to be able at minimum to find a way through legal materials, and know where to retrieve such material from a variety of sources. This may be limited in scope, but the important focus should be that they reflect the discipline area of legal study. Once appropriate resources have been identified, the student will need to be guided as to how to read, evaluate and integrate what has been read. There is a need also to demonstrate what has been assimilated, and to incorporate research into written work. Understanding the relevance of different materials will be important, particularly the status of primary and secondary sources. As Boston College Law Library recommends: 'If you are writing about an area that is new to you, it is often best to start with a secondary source. Finding one or two law review articles on your topic is a good place to begin. They may even provide you with all you need for your project.' (Non-law school courses information guide 11, revised June 2000.)

Finally, students need to recognise the importance of regular updating of legal information. This point may also help them realise that they will not need to learn the content of a piece of legislation by rote, but that they will need to know how to find out what is the most up-to-date version. Ultimately the range of legal research activities undertaken by students will depend on access to legal resources and the depth to which law is studied.

Problem solving

Here the student should be able to apply skills from their own discipline in order to approach a problem in a logical manner, to identify it and apply the relevant law. A key lesson to take on board is that there is no 'right answer' in law (as evidenced by dissenting judgements in cases at all levels of the court system). Students should be encouraged to identify the problem, apply the relevant law, and generate a solution, at the same time recognising that a variety of approaches can be applied to finding an answer. In helping the student engage with the issues presented in a problem, encouragement needs to be given, not simply to view them from a legal perspective, but also take on board the ethical, ecological, business, social, political, commercial, economic, and policy dimensions as illustrated in the following example in the box below.

BA Public Relations coursework assignment

This assignment requires you to prepare two reports for senior management. For both you will need to draw upon your understanding of the relevant law and additionally upon your skills as a public relations officer:

1. Draw up a report for the information of the Board indicating the legal implications for the company with regard to product liability in the event of any defect in an imported product causing damage/injury to a consumer/customer.
2. [following purchase of a defective product that has caused damage and injury] Advise the Board as to their legal position in this matter. Draw up a notice for a media publication aimed at advising persons in possession of similar articles as to what action they should take.

Analysis

Analytical skills are a requirement at all levels of undergraduate and postgraduate study and in all disciplines. In a legal environment, analytical skills focus on the ability to separate law from fact and fact from assumption. The challenge for law teachers is to support students in this process. Critical analysis and application of abstract concepts, synthesizing from different sources, will be made easier if the problems with which the students presented are in a context with which they are familiar. For BA Social Work students, the following assignment tests their analytical skills: 'Critically evaluate the implications for Social Service departments of the introduction of new asylum seeker regulations'.

Oral and written skills

Here the focus is on enabling the student to dialogue effectively with professional advisers. Whilst an understanding of the language of law, and an ability to present unfamiliar material to a lawyer, orally and in writing, will have a direct financial benefit to students in their later careers, that ability will also prove useful in dealing with other professionals. A student's understanding of the legal context of their core discipline will enhance future encounters with, for example, accountants, tax and financial advisers, patent and trademark agents, surveyors and architects, health and social workers.

This is highlighted by a Patent Agent who was consulted by two graduating BSc Engineering Business Development students, who had taken a patent law unit as part of their programme of study:

> During their visit, they demonstrated their prototype. We would like to say how impressed we were by the skill and knowledge of these two people and the way in which they were able to explain their invention and its commercial potential. As a result, the billable time they had to spend with us was considerably reduced.

Where oral and written skills form a major element of the assessment strategy, there is a greater need to focus on the development of these skills with the student. They could take the form of presenting reports, writing memoranda, essays, videos, presentations and electronic media. Their choice will depend on the learning outcomes for the law input, alongside strategies being used for assessment in other units of the programme.

Information Technology skills

Law students will appreciate an introduction to legal databases and e-journals. The ability to utilise these sources will enhance their research capabilities and support the development of their transferable IT skills. The support of the information specialist within the library services can assist in this process. They may also need to be competent in a range of IT skills, particularly where programme delivery utilises online learning technologies, such as Web-delivered materials, electronic mail, and Web-based assessment. The Legal Multimedia Simulation Shell (LMSS) illustrates some of the ways in which law students may engage with online resources.

The Legal Multimedia Simulation Shell, developed at University of Melbourne Law School, comprises an authoring environment, which enables teachers to write exercises for use within the system, and a simulation system, which students see and with which they work through exercises. 'Introduction to Business Law' is taught by the law faculty to non-lawyers. The exercises simulate the work of an in-house lawyer in a small computer hardware company. Scenarios revolve around, for example, change of delivery date in a wholesale purchase contract, or liability of the employer for potentially misleading information given to a customer. The student receives the correspondence file embodying the scenario within the system. Because it is based on HTML and XML, and served over the Web, scenarios can incorporate any content that can be delivered over the Web, including graphics, attachments, audio, video (Aikenhead, Williams and Hunter, 2000).

Conclusion

Ten commandments for teaching law to non-lawyers (with acknowledgements to Rowntree, 1981)

1. *Establish outcomes.* Identify learning outcomes, which clearly indicate what students will be able to do as a result of completing the programme.
2. *Question your own values and experience.* This will help you assess ways in which you can approach your teaching practice.
3. *Identify your students' approaches to study.* What are the discipline-specific ways in which your students learn?
4. *Use active learning techniques.* Make it student-centred and involve the students in taking responsibility for their own learning.
5. *Put legal concepts in context.* Ensure that legal themes are explored with examples from the discipline area of study.
6. *Recognise the importance of assessment.* It will play an important part in motivating your students.
7. *Consider breadth versus depth.* You cannot cover everything so use colleagues, sources from the discipline coupled with your own knowledge and judgement to identify priorities.
8. *Work alongside discipline colleagues.* Establish your influence on the teaching programme by sharing with colleagues issues relating to assessment strategies, student characteristics and general approaches to teaching.
9. *Support the development of student skills.* Foster skills development that enhances the learning experience for students.
10. *Keep improving your practice.* Be reflective about your own practice and be open to feedback from both students and colleagues.

References

Aikenhead, M, Williams, C and Hunter, D [accessed 2001] *Teaching Law to the Nintendo Generation*, BILETA 2000 conference papers [Online] *http://www.bileta.ac.uk/00papers/hunter.html*

Biggs, J and Collis, K (1982) *Evaluating the quality of learning – the SOLO Taxonomy*, Academic Press, New York

Boston College Law Library [accessed 2000] Legal sources for Non-Law School courses [online] *http://www.bc.edn/bc-org/avp/knu/lawlib/guides-h/nonlawyer.html*

Brown, S and Dove, P (1991) *Self and Peer Assessment*, SEDA Paper 63, Birmingham, UK

Holmes, N (1997) *Researching the legal Web: a guide to legal resources on the Internet*, Butterworths, London

Jin, Z (2000) The Learning Experience of Students in Middlesex University Business School (MUBS): Why do they enjoy some modules/lectures and dislike others?, *The International Journal of Management Education*, **1** (1), pp 22–36

Newble, D and Cannon, R (1995) *A handbook for teachers in universities and colleges: a guide to improving teaching methods*, Kogan Page, London

Ramsden, P (1992) *Learning to Teach in Higher Education*, Routledge, London

Rowntree, D (1981) *Developing Courses for Students*, McGraw-Hill, London

Skwarok, L (1995) Business Law for Non Lawyers: setting the stage for teaching, learning and assessment at Hong Kong Polytechnic University, *The Law Teacher*, **29** (2), pp 189–212

Ward, J and Salter, M (1990) Law for Professional Accounting Education, *The Law Teacher*, **24** (3), pp 208–28

8

The new advocacy: implications for legal education and teaching practice

Julie Macfarlane

Introduction

In the United States, a significant cultural change is taking place in legal practice as a result of the widespread introduction of court-connected and private ADR (Alternative Dispute Resolution) programmes, which aim to resolve litigation matters as early as possible by party agreement (Macfarlane, 1997; Sander, 2000). The most complex and far-reaching of these changes is a challenge to the traditional model of the lawyer as a manager of war – the strategic and skilful facilitation of peace now appears to be equally important. The increasing acceptance of ADR processes within civil litigation has immediate practical consequences for legal practice.

Clients, especially repeat users, are starting to expect early efforts to explore settlement, using mediation or other consensual processes wherever possible. Assumptions about timelines in the management of civil litigation have been significantly affected by case management, which generally sets timelines for filing and the production of documents. No longer does litigation get filed away for months or years while counsel gathers information; instead work is often 'up front' as parties scramble to get ready for an early settlement discussion. Developments within the profession itself include the emergence of specialist 'settlement counsel' (Coyne, 1999); the establishment of 'ADR departments' in big litigation firms; and the development of 'collaborative lawyering' networks, where lawyers are retained to settle but not to litigate (Sholar, 1993). Similar court-based reforms and private sector initiatives in the management of civil disputing are being implemented – although not yet on the same scale – in the United Kingdom and throughout Europe (CEDR, 2000). As a consequence, similar patterns of change in the practice of litigation seem likely to be repeated.

This chapter addresses some of the implications of these changes for legal education and training by exploring the following questions:

- What vision of lawyering practice and dispute resolution does the legal curriculum presently promote and sustain?
- How does the increasing acceptance of ADR processes challenge these assumptions about the lawyer's role in conflict resolution, and how might these be modified to reflect consensual, interests-based approaches to resolving disputes?
- What does the changing culture of legal practice mean for the way that teaching and learning takes place in law schools?

Legal practice and pedagogic change

Before turning to an examination of the impact of ADR on legal education, a threshold question for many teachers is the relationship between legal practice and the law curriculum. There has been a long and continuing debate within legal education over the extent to which the law curriculum should be driven by the exigencies of legal practice – for example, whether law school should teach practical professional skills along with conceptual tools for analysis and reflection.

The tendency has often been to assume that a choice must be made between two dichotomous goals for legal education – on the one side vocational training and on the other intellectual development. The fallacy of this dichotomy is immediately obvious if one recognises that the law always draws its meaning from the context in which it is applied (Macfarlane, 1997). Any level of legal studies – whether basic or advanced, theoretical or applied, jurisprudential or interdisciplinary – *must reflect the ways in which law is understood, used and practised in the real world*, whether the programme focus is academic analysis or vocational applications (Twining, 1988). The conceptual and the practical dimensions of learning about the law are inextricably linked.

The implications for legal education of the growth of ADR and institutionalised consensus-building processes within legal practice are also both conceptual – the models of conflict analysis and resolution that law schools promote via the informal curriculum – and practical – the skills and knowledge that they teach via the formal curriculum. Our understanding of the way in which the tool of the law is used is affected by a number of factors. These include: the increasing frequency with which litigators utilise third party mediators, appear at settlement conferences or pre-trials and resort to neutral fact-finding or other early evaluative processes. In addition, these factors impinge upon the skills and knowledge of those who use the law as advocates.

In reconceptualising the law school curriculum from the perspective of 'alternative' dispute resolution philosophies, the objective is not simply to substitute or to displace the adjudicative rights-based model, which casts its shadow over civil disputing. Rather, the assumption is that there is space for more than one approach, and that in teaching conflict analysis and skills development from the perspective of one model only, legal education is incomplete as a preparation for legal practice in the 21st century.

The present focus on one particular disputing model (adjudication) and a single approach to dispute analysis (rights-based) fails to foster the capacity for creative problem solving and reflexivity that might be a worthy goal for legal education in and of itself (Schon, 1995; Lerner, 1999; Reno, 1999). Allowing for alternatives to the 'one size fits all' assumptions of the adjudicative model also creates new epistemologies of knowledge and learning, which have implications for the whole enterprise of legal education. In addition to the selection of materials for a 'complete' syllabus, these include the choice of appropriate teaching pedagogies that challenge the 'givens', and an evaluative model that valorizes different types of learning outcomes than those traditionally assessed in law school (Macfarlane, 1998). In short, there is a crucial relationship between theories of conflict and meaning-making, and between meaning and action in the form of educational pedagogies (Lyons, 1994).

The relationship between the world of application and the world of learning about law means that the law curriculum must reflect – not necessarily uncritically – the cultural changes taking place within the practising profession. The impact of ADR on the practice of law requires legal education to adapt and adjust both its substance and its objectives, and to develop pedagogies of teaching and assessment that appropriately reflect these changes in assumptions, scope, and emphasis.

To some extent, this process of adaptation and adjustment has already begun. There is a growing recognition among legal educators at all levels of the need to respond to changes in both the expectations and the realities of the lawyer's role with an enhanced curriculum that more fully equips lawyers to operate successfully in the new milieus of settlement conferences, mandatory mediation, case management and so on. This is most immediately evident in the widespread provision of continuing legal education courses and other commercial training programmes aimed at lawyers, which offer a 'crash course' in mediation advocacy or negotiation strategies, and introduce the basic vocabulary of ADR.

Most lawyers presently in practice have received little or no legal education in the use of alternative, informal dispute resolution processes (Zarkiski, 1997). This too is changing, with courses in ADR and negotiation increasingly becoming an assumed component of undergraduate legal education (Watson-Hamilton, 1999). In addition, there is a marginal but growing recognition of the impact of these changes on traditional doctrinal courses such as civil procedure, administrative law and family law (Mitchell et al, 1995). But the changing face of legal practice as it responds to developments in ADR presents a challenge for legal education, which extends well beyond the development of discrete, supplemental courses – or segments of courses – which introduce students to the use of consensus-building processes to resolve contentious litigation. A simple 'add-on' approach does not address the fundamental normative assumptions of legal education, in particular the traditional emphasis on mastery of substance, competitive individualism and the enduring culture of dichotomies (right/wrong, moral/immoral, win/lose, lawyer/client, and so on). How might these be adapted to reflect the evolving reality of legal service and practice in the 21st century?

Reconceptualising conflict and conflict resolution

Despite many changes in both pedagogy and substance, which reflect a growing diversity (and acceptance) of approaches to learning – for example, movement away from traditional assessment methods and towards some adoption of peer and self-assessments, and the introduction of multi-disciplinary, diversity and critical materials into course syllabi – the law curriculum appears to un-self-consciously reinforce a model of conflict that remains largely unchanged.

A rights-based model of conflict produces an epistemology that understands knowledge as the power to win. Can legal education promote an alternate approach to knowledge – as contextual, dynamic and fluid rather than as 'given truth' (Macfarlane, 1992, 1995) – and a related transformation in the ways that information is used and exchanged between disputing parties? Numerous tacit assumptions about the nature of conflict and its appropriate resolution presently dominate the law curriculum, and are reflected in pedagogic practice. The next three sections explore three of these core values, providing some examples of their influence on teaching and learning practices, and considering the implications of introducing alternative perspectives on conflict and conflict resolution, which might challenge and modify these values – and in the process, better reflect the changing realities of litigation practice.

Assumption one: conflict is always about principle and rights

When students are introduced to the principles of Contract law, Tort, Property law or any other substantive topic within the law curriculum, they appear at first glance to be studying disputes and the process of dispute resolution. In reality, what they are introduced to in any of these subjects is not disputing as a phenomenon, or a range of potential processes for dispute resolution. Instead they are taught the rules that will be used to resolve such conflict (Silbey and Sarat, 1989). Furthermore, the assumptions made by these rules about the sources of conflict, and about how conflict develops and evolves, are never questioned; indeed, they are not a subject of discussion in law school classrooms. Instead, a particular analysis of conflict – and with it, a particular dispute resolution process that logically fits this analysis – permeates doctrinal teaching at law school.

The rights-based model of Western justice systems emphasises an individualist approach in which the rights of the individual will be recognised and upheld – or the converse, the individual will be protected against the oppressive assertion of another's rights (Kidder, 1980). This model assumes that the source of conflict is an uncompromisable moral principle, or an indivisible good. Once the conflict becomes 'objectified' in this way (sustained by an appeal to allegedly objective moral standards, and beyond merely partisan preferences) it becomes inevitable that the aggrieved party will press their moral claim (Simmel, 1955). What may be a natural tendency to elevate our conflicts to the level of 'a matter of principle', is further aggravated in a litigation model (Aubert, 1963), and reinforced constantly in law schools by classroom debate, which focuses on the resolution of competing principles of rights, typified by mooting. In this model, information is gathered and analysed in order to advance the merits of one side's argument, not to provide clarification or enhance the range of possible outcomes (see the further discussion below). Within a zero-sum game where the potential outcome is either winning or losing (as in a trial or via positional negotiations played out in the shadow of a trial), there is clearly only one acceptable outcome for the competent professional: winning.

This message is clearly communicated to law students as they are taught the principles of appellate judgements in Contract, Tort, Property courses, and so on. If conflict is understood as essentially normative – in other words, as always being fought over values and principles – the rational way to resolve incompatible aspirations is to adjudicate on which has the strongest moral appeal, or in law the strongest 'rights' claim. Thus the adjudicative model, which is taught in law schools, assumes that all conflict must be resolved by an evaluative process in which one or other view is chosen as 'trumping' all others. The winner will be the party whose arguments are judged the most compelling, using criteria (legal norms), which assume the essential moral basis of any conflict.

An adjudicative model that provides moral victors – and holds out such a promise to each and every disputant – strongly reinforces our natural tendency to assume the moral basis of claims and assertions. This assumption permeates legal practice also; while acknowledging that there is a strong pragmatic component to dispute resolution – in particular that many commercial conflicts simply need a 'business solution' – lawyers rapidly assume and assimilate the merit-based arguments that their clients can advance, and feel little discomfort in moving into a highly adversarial mode, especially where they claim that their good faith efforts at consensual resolution have been rebuffed (Macfarlane, 2001).

The unquestioning assumption of the normative basis of conflict, as well as the invidious tendency to assume moral outrage in the face of contrary argument, is exemplified in student mooting, an activity that is seen as one of the rites of passage of undergraduate legal education. Focus shifts away from finding a 'good outcome' towards discovering a 'winning formula', with little attention paid to actual consequences. Although this approach may be valorized and rewarded in law schools, it is incomplete and naive when it comes to dealing with real-life problems and real-life clients. While pervasive adversarial practices continue in some legal cultures, litigators who have had significant exposure to alternative dispute resolution processes are increasingly aware that their clients – and in particular, their repeat user clients – hire them for their skills in facilitating good outcomes rather than producing winning formulae. In the words of one commercial litigator: 'If I see a fair deal I would take it, or I would recommend it, because I'm client-oriented. I want the client to come back and come back happy. If the client wants to go to trial I have no problem doing that. I look at disputing as a fact of life and resolution as a part of life and you don't always have to go to trial to resolve a dispute especially if it's not in a client's best interest' (Macfarlane, 2001). Traditional law school pedagogy, on the other hand, such as the case law method or even the reliance on casebooks, accentuates the emphasis placed on rule-making and application.

Other personal, business, practical and emotional issues that might be involved in the development of the conflict are usually reduced to irrelevancies, because this is not information that bears on a legal outcome. Law students are not taught to or even asked to consider the import of such concerns as the avoidance of negative publicity, the knock-on impact of a business stoppage on third party contracts, the need to save face in both business and personal contexts, the significance of a request for an apology or acknowledgement, or the need for closure in a long-running and bitter family conflict. At best, law students are warned that some 'family' and 'domestic' disputes may contain a significant emotional component, and they are generally advised to try to steer their clients away from emotional (read 'irrational') responses to their conflict.

However, commercial litigators readily admit that more often than not, business disputes are significantly driven by pride or ego or anger on the part of a particular individual. Disputes that originate over resources rapidly transform into disputes over values where one or more parties have a personal investment in the outcome of the conflict. The original substance of the dispute may become overtaken by personal rancour and hostility, making negotiation all but impossible. Traditional legal analysis as taught in law school does not enable law students to understand this process of conflict transformation that is so characteristic to litigation; instead, the psychological and emotional dimensions of conflict are seen, at best, as the 'side show', rather then being integrated into the overall analysis.

Despite the picture painted in law school, many conflicts that turn into lawsuits do not originate in value differences or moral outrage. Instead, they are usually precipitated by incompatible aspirations involving access to finite resources, principally money. For example, how much are these goods or services worth? What will I pay? What value can be placed on my losses that were caused by your acts?

Other types of resource-based conflict, common in commercial, workplace and even family contexts, include disputes over non-monetary resources such as relative status or spheres of influence – for example, access to and competition within markets, status and reputation, and issues of personal control (Moore, 1998; Mayer, 2000). While it is always possible to devise principled arguments for notions of 'fair' allocation of resources (indeed this is what the legal system does), this type of conflict might also be understood as the simple pursuit of self-interest – the desire to maximize one's gains and minimize one's losses. Therefore, in order to avoid total loss by either side, a negotiated compromise may be less risky and more practical. Resource-based disputes enable outcomes in which the resource 'pie' – money, influence, status, market control etc – can be divided between the parties; or even integrative ('win–win') outcomes, in which 'expanding the pie' (Menkel-Meadow, 1984) and/or prioritizing different aspects of settlement enables both sides to achieve some of their objectives.

Integrative solutions or trade-offs are usually possible – for example, repayment of monies owed in instalments, division of markets, renegotiation of relative status and areas of control, or an undertaking to compensate based on externally derived criteria. Therefore, law students should be learning about how to develop creative, pragmatic, and potentially integrative outcomes for their clients as well as how to assert their legal rights. They cannot make sense of how to do that if conflict is always presented as a normative struggle. Instead they need to be challenged to think through hypotheticals and case studies with a view to analysing conflict other than using a purely normative lens, and developing creative and integrative outcomes, rather than simply presenting principled winner-take-all arguments. The case study provided on page 171 and the questions that follow are an illustration of this type of alternative approach. It is important to note that since there is an entrenched – although rarely articulated – assumption in law school that the learning that is most valued is exclusively focused on winning, teachers need to be both clear and explicit about setting up different expectations and assessments.

How then might one practically introduce such ideas into the traditional syllabus? Take Contract as an example. Hypotheticals that are presented for classroom discussion or as questions on the final examination in Contract can of course be analysed from any number of perspectives. If I were to present a classic Contracts hypothetical (minus the final lines instructing students to 'Advise X') to a mediation workshop of non-lawyer professionals, they would likely have questions about the motivations of the parties, how the conflict arose in the first place, what the various needs and interests are, what expectations the parties might hold about a 'just' outcome to the dispute, what is the best possible outcome and what type of outcome might provide an acceptable level of satisfaction to allow for closure, and so on.

These individuals are not training to be lawyers, and their preoccupations are clearly different, but this type of discourse about conflict is strikingly absent from the law school classroom or examination hall. In law school, it is the clear expectation that students are to provide doctrinal analysis; they are not expected (or rewarded) for any efforts to analyse the sources of the conflict or even (other than exceptionally) to present non-adjudicative alternatives for resolving it. Law students should be asked to consider these questions also, which are of practical relevance to their future work as dispute resolvers. For the same reason, it is also instructive for law students to conduct a 'reality-check' between a doctrinal analysis and a practical problem-solving strategy. For example, students might be asked to consider questions such as, 'What if X could not afford to continue with legal action?' 'What if X could not let the damage to his business continue for a single day longer?' 'What if X could not sleep at night and urgently needed to resolve this issue with Y?'.

The limitations of the traditional approach could easily be addressed if the Contract curriculum were to incorporate a selection of ideas drawn from conflict theory, along with some tools for conflict analysis. This would require teachers to include some additional expectations for approach and analysis in classroom exercises and final assessments. For example, see the case study below.

A case study in conflict – an alternative approach

Mrs A has a chronic back injury suffered in a motor vehicle accident two years ago. She has been advised by her physiotherapist that the regular use of a whirlpool with massage water jets before she goes to bed at night would help her to sleep. Mrs A acquires several estimates and finally settles on one from X Co. She has previously met and become friendly with Mr X in an adult education programme on Parenting Skills that they both attended. X Co will remodel the bathroom as well as install the new whirlpool. Mrs A can recover the cost of the whirlpool installation from her insurance company.

Mrs A tells her friends and neighbours that she is having a 'dream bathroom' installed in her home. X Co commences the job in May and very quickly Mr and Mrs A become concerned about the standard of workmanship. Mr X and his co-workers are often late and leave early, usually without cleaning up. The tiling looks untidy and the new wiring, instead of being built into the walls is stapled on the outside. The skirting for the new whirlpool does not seem to fit properly. When Mr X is questioned by Mr and Mrs A he brushes off their concerns and assures them that if they will only be patient, he knows what he is doing and the bathroom will look lovely when the work is completed. Mrs A begins to watch Mr X at work all the time, hanging over his shoulder and constantly questioning him about what he is doing. This serves to irritate Mr X who feels that his professionalism is being called into question by someone who, he believes, 'knows nothing' about bathrooms.

> The work is completed in July but Mr and Mrs A are not satisfied. They have since called in an architect who has inspected the bathroom and has provided them with a report listing a number of deficiencies – both aesthetic and safety-related – which she estimates will require $5,000 to put right. Meanwhile a balance of $8,000 is owing on the bathroom. Mr X acknowledges that there are some problems but says that he will not do any further work before he is paid in full.

This hypothetical case study might ordinarily simply be used to ask students to provide the legal rules that would form the basis of a case for either Mr and Mrs A or Mr X. Instead or as well, students might be introduced to some simple models for analysing the sources of conflict (for example, Moore's Circle of Conflict, 1998) and ask:

1. What appear to be the causes of this conflict – for example, is there a relationship conflict here? A data conflict? A conflict of interests? A conflict over values or principles?
2. How might the different sources of this conflict be reflected in different ways for resolving it?
3. What role might a lawyer play in the resolution of this dispute? How might your analysis above be reflected in your advice to your client?
4. What is the 'shadow of the law' here, ie what might be the resolution if the matter were to be decided by a judge?

These questions would focus discussion on the potential of a negotiated outcome to this conflict (including possible non-legal remedies such as an apology or acknowledgement, agreements over privacy, and the future of the friendship between Mrs A and X). Students could assess the significance and weight of outcomes other than simply 'winning', where one or other party was ordered to pay the other. Exploring the potential of a negotiated outcome would also allow for discussion over the value of a face-to-face meeting between the disputants, and the appropriate role for the lawyer in a range of possible circumstances (for example, Mrs A and X refuse to talk directly, either party sets preconditions to direct negotiations, either party asks for a meeting without lawyers present, etc).

The discussion could be underpinned by relevant conflict theory (for example, Rubin, 1993) in order to obtain broader insights into the nature of conflict escalation and the relationship between the sources of conflict, the design of resolution processes, and possible outcomes. Students could also be asked to reflect on the level and type of resolution that the parties might need, not a question that law schools generally pose. For example, do these parties need a behavioural resolution so that the bathroom can be completed to their satisfaction, or would some monetarized version of this be an equally acceptable outcome? Does Mrs A need an emotional closure on their conflict, including perhaps some kind of rapprochement with Mr X? The answers to these questions will affect the type of resolution that is possible, acceptable and, above all, best for these parties (Mayer, 2000). Finally – and crucially – students can be asked to locate their analysis within the context of the potential legal outcome, which inevitably casts its 'shadow' (Mnookin and Kornhauser, 1979) over the consensual resolution of the dispute.

An analysis of bargaining scenarios also leads inevitably into a discussion of how much information the parties will share, and how much they will hold back, in their efforts to reach an acceptable resolution. It will raise questions about what the 'facts' are in this case and how, if at all, they might be determined. It is important that law students are challenged to evaluate what types of information may be valuable in trying to reach resolution, and how that information might be used to build an acceptable settlement. The next section explores the reasons why.

Assumption two: knowledge and information is for winning

The epistemological basis of litigation in an adjudicative model flows from, and then reinforces, the assumption that conflict is inherently normative. Information is gathered in order to substantiate a particular version of events; all other information is discarded or ignored. Evidence is generated to enhance a particular rights–based argument, and anything that does not bear on this is deemed irrelevant. Presenting information as evidence means presenting it as 'fact', and requires the denial of any ambiguity, circumstances or context (unless self-serving). In a rationalist, zero-sum model, the side with the most complete and well-constructed information edifice looks best placed to carry the day. In this paradigm, information is for winning, not for sharing, and certainly not for enhancing the possible options available to the parties.

The way that law is taught uncritically reflects these same assumptions about the nature and value of information in a singular adjudicative model. 'Winning' means having the most, and the best, information, preferably of a kind that one's peers do not possess. Information is understood to be 'right' or 'wrong'; students are often encouraged to search for a magic 'bullet' that will enable them to 'solve' the problem.

The extent to which law students buy into this epistemological framework, and the norms of secrecy and concealment it encourages, is reflected in the lengths to which students will go to monopolise resources (even to the point of tearing pages out of case reports) and compete on an individual basis with one another. The dominant pedagogy of legal education and its rationalist epistemology perpetuates passage through law school as a highly individualistic endeavour. Although there are some moves towards the inclusion of peer or self-assessment (Tribe and Tribe, 1986; see Chapter 3) in the United Kingdom, there remains an almost exclusive emphasis on individual graded work with choices over assessment rare. Law students are rapidly assimilated into this highly competitive and hierarchical culture. Assimilation increasingly includes adopting a competitive attitude and avoiding any cooperation, which might reduce one's chances of being scored over a peer by a professor. The manner in which a rights-based, normative approach to dispute resolution both understands and uses information, fosters these attitudes among law students – the assumption of knowledge as 'truth' or 'fact', an ethos of solitary individual endeavour, and a culture of competitive concealment

This understanding of the nature and function of information is inherent to traditional notions of zealous (and responsible) advocacy (Simon, 1978). A frequently advanced explanation of the historical tendency to late settlement (Trubek *et al*, 1983; Kakalik *et al*, 1996) has been that a better negotiated outcome will result if the advocate has had the fullest possible opportunity to develop a theory of the case (conducting the necessary fact-finding, legal research, extensive discoveries and so on), and to appraise the case made by the other side.

In the ritual dance of traditional settlement negotiations between lawyers, an emphasis on rights-oriented case development discourages early exchange of information about needs and interests. Traditional settlement negotiations between lawyers – consistent across a wide range of practice areas – are characterised by the exchange of highly positional arguments based on each side's appraisal of their best legal case. The reliance of rights-based arguments on the development of legal theories means that even once serious negotiations are underway, they are inhibited by the obvious reluctance of each side to disclose their best arguments before trial. In Canada, civil litigators report being unwilling to commence 'serious' negotiations before discovery (in the United States discoveries usually include examinations under oath), other than in exceptional cases (Macfarlane, 2001). The consequence of this style of bargaining is that negotiations will only take place once the lawyers on both sides are confident that they have obtained as much legally relevant information as possible; that is, post-discovery or possibly even later, depending on how quickly discovery material is read and digested (Barkai and Kassenbaum, 1989).

What might law schools do to challenge the assumption that knowledge is power, but only if kept secret from the other side? Can legal education promote a different approach to the collection and sharing of information to enhance communication and the potential for settlement? The dominant 'techno-rationalist' epistemology of professional education (Schon, 1983, 1995; Macfarlane, 1992) assumes that learning about the law or learning how to be a lawyer can be framed within an epistemology of absolute 'truth' and a set of professional 'routines', rather than multiple and flexible practices of context and circumstance, need and outlook. If knowledge and information in a legal paradigm can be freed from the constraints of these assumptions, it is possible to reconceptualise not only the character, but also the strategic uses of information.

Where interests-based or business solutions are sought, the need for secrecy around particular pieces of legally significant information is often greatly reduced. Litigators experienced in ADR processes (in which information is shared in a confidential, without prejudice environment in the hope of avoiding or reducing the costs of discovery) recognise the ability to identify information essential to early resolution – both for their own client and for the other side – as a critical skill.

This does not mean that all information should be shared, but that assumptions regarding the 'blanket' witholding of data need to be examined, and quite frequently rebutted. Being able to discriminate between data in this manner is not a skill that is taught at law school; characteristically, law school teaches what to hide, not what to show. This points to the need for enhanced law school teaching on negotiation, and in particular teaching on value-creating negotiation strategies for creating 'power with' rather than 'power over' outcomes (Chornenki, 1997). These types of outcomes are highly dependent on the good faith exchange of information in a non-adversarial process.

If such a radical reconceptualisation of the nature and uses of information – as a shared resource that can be used to advance the interests of all parties and to effect changes in actual practice lawyers need to be able to build trusting relationships with other counsel and with other professionals. There is an obvious need for norms of reciprocity. This is not new, of course – lawyers practising in smaller communities have always been acutely aware of the importance of positive professional relationships – but takes on even more practical importance with the advent of mandated early settlement processes. These processes may be used to great advantage by lawyers who are skilful at interpersonal communication, coordinated problem solving and, generally, cooperation with others; skills that are essential to effectiveness within informal models of dispute resolution.

Achieving faster, mutually beneficial solutions requires lawyers to conceive of solutions and their role in those solutions as a team effort (a team that includes the client; see the further discussion below). The emphasis of legal education, noted earlier, on individual activities, which encourage information to be kept secret and used only as a weapon, clearly works against this. Greater use of groupwork and teamwork activities, in which information is exchanged and shared both within groups and between groups, could begin to enable cooperation, coordination, and relationship-building . In other parts of the university, educators have for some time now been arguing that collaborative and team-building skills should be a pedagogical goal (Astin, 1987). For the lawyers of the 21st century, it should be a professional goal also.

One example of an approach that explicitly valorizes group work and information sharing, both within and between groups of students, is problem-based learning or PBL (see Chapter 2 for further examples). PBL is used widely in medical and other programmes of professional education (Boud, 1985). PBL replaces regular lectures with group work on simulated problems which, in law, usually take the form of a client file. Each group generally represents a client and draws on various forms of real-life documentation, including an originating memorandum with instructions from a principal or supervisor, correspondence, contracts, attendance notes, etc. In some exercises, students might also be asked to interview the 'client' and to negotiate with the student group representing the other party. In these exercises, issues of information exchange become critical, and can be a focal point for later reflection and debriefing. PBL is particularly appropriate for learning about the structure of conflict and informal dispute resolution processes, because it enables both in-depth analysis of a particular client issue or issues and consequent problem-solving (the conceptual dimension described earlier), and the integration of negotiation components into the exercise (the practical dimension).

A typical PBL exercise for the law curriculum presents each student group or team with a set of documents along with a memorandum from a supervisor asking (usually) for a written response. Instructions to the students emphasise creative problem solving as well as substantive research and analysis. In an exercise based on a dispute between a franchiser and franchisee, designed to explore some dimensions of Contract, students were directed as follows in the box below.

Directions for students exploring a dispute – a PBL exercise

I would like you to thoroughly review the relevant documentation and research and advise on the following matters:

Re: *Pantry Donuts* v *Kelly*

1. Is Pantry Donuts entitled to terminate Ms Kelly's franchise for any of their stated reasons?
2. Does Ms Kelly have a basis for any counter-claims against Pantry Donuts?
3. Do you think that the procedures that Pantry Donuts presently has in place to deal with complaints against franchisees are effective in addressing complaints and facilitating early conflict resolution? Can you make some suggestions for some alternative (either formal or informal) steps in this process that you might suggest to Pantry Donuts?
4. Given your client's desire to remain as a franchisee, what negotiation strategy and approach would you discuss with her and what form – including process choices – might that take? And what negotiation options do you see for her? Please include in your answer what you would look at in order to better understand the causes of this particular dispute and how you would ask Ms Kelly about the type of resolution she is seeking here.

This matter is **urgent** as Ms Kelly continues to operate the store. Please have a memo on these points and any others you see arising to me by a week from today. Complete materials are available from the author.

When working in teams, students must learn to work cooperatively. This requires negotiation over the allocation of work and responsibility and sometimes the resolution of intra-group conflict. They must decide what information they need to resolve the problem, and then share that information among the members of the team. Careful and thoughtful listening is as important as the articulate presentation of one's arguments, as they learn also from their colleagues. Effective discussion in the team will improve the quality of the analysis so they must learn how to think critically about team members' work and debate issues constructively, in order that the final collective product is the best possible.

In addition, they will have to decide how to communicate, and what information to share with the opposing group in order to advance their client's best interests in the resolution of the problem. The complex dynamics of teamwork provide a significant opportunity for students to develop a work method, which will enable them to be more effective, both working alone and as team players, in the future. A consistent theme that emerges from student evaluations of PBL is that working with others in this way exposes them to the views and opinions of others and encourages them to listen seriously to their peers in a way that does not occur in class. In task-oriented small groups, students are more willing, it seems, to learn from one another, and to value the exchange (Macfarlane and Manwaring, 1998).

Outside the formal curriculum, law schools could also do more to valorize teamwork and constructive cooperation. The nurturing of informal study groups may also encourage a culture in which information and expertise is shared. The bias against cooperative work with peers is evident in the prevailing assumption that study groups are the refuge of the 'weaker' students, and that the really smart students work alone. Law schools could consciously promote alternative conceptions of exchange, relationship building and cooperative problem solving by valuing and encouraging this type of cooperative study.

Students need skills and strategies to enable them to take responsibility for dealing with these types of issues, which they will inevitably confront in practice. There are further implications here for the assessment regime, with its historical focus on individually graded work – the most sensible and fair outcome of work generated within study groups, like PBL groups, may be an assessment via a collective product (such as videotaped presentations, peer reports or individual reflective statements). Law schools could also include conflict resolution education for law students themselves in the curriculum. Greater self-awareness of how one deals with conflict and the development of more reflective and sophisticated strategies to cope with difficult relationships, for example, seems highly relevant both to this way of working and also to future legal practice.

Assumption three: lawyers 'own' the conflict

A third assumption embedded in the adversarial model of dispute resolution, and hence in legal pedagogy, is that lawyers acquire some form of ownership – more than simply stewardship – of their clients' conflicts as a consequence of their professional expertise. Where the relationship is understood as one of expert/naif, there is little for the latter to do other than to place themself in the hands of their lawyer. An exclusive emphasis on a rights-based paradigm reinforces these parameters, because it identifies the lawyer as technician – fixing the problem by applying the law (Riskin, 1982). As a result, many litigants feel that their original problem has now transformed into something they do not readily recognise, moulded into a 'stock story' via a statement of claim or defence (Mather and Yngvesson, 1980).

Since this assumption of ownership is intertwined with the ideology of rights-based problem solving, it is a critical element of the professional norms promoted at law school. Students are encouraged to expect to 'take charge' in the professional relationship rather than develop a working partnership with their clients.

Because the relationship between lawyer and client is seen as one of expert/naif, little or no time is given to considering how lawyers develop and conduct their relationships with clients. There have been important efforts to develop courses in client counselling (and even an international competition), and this initiative at least recognises that clients may have more to add to the development of a legal theory than their legal representatives may anticipate before meeting them, and in drawing up their narrow list of standard interview questions. Nonetheless, the objective of client counselling generally remains the development of a legal theory to the virtual exclusion of other strategies for problem solving, and as a result only certain types of client input, which are deemed relevant to building a strong legal argument, are sought. Where other issues – such as a client's emotionality or sense of urgency – intrude, the message is that these fears should be assuaged and controlled in order that the lawyer can get back on track.

Now the increasing application of ADR processes, and in particular mediation, to civil litigation is changing the comfortable parameters of this relationship. Clients almost always play some role in mediation – some more active than others – but their presence throughout the process changes the dynamics of what has traditionally been a private negotiation between counsel. Counsel now need to ensure that they prepare along with the client representative in advance of any mediation, even if this means only warning the client to 'say nothing'; an admonition that business clients, at least, are often unprepared to accept (Cooley, 1996). As one senior litigator put it, 'Lawyers do not own this process anymore – it's more a client-driven experience' (Macfarlane, 2001). Moreover, the emphasis on *early* mandated settlement processes means that counsel is often forced to rely less on legal research, which has nicely consolidated into a theory of the case, and more on what their client tells them. For example, one commercial litigator, when asked what difference early mediation made to her working relationship with her client, responded as follows:

> [T]he client really has to be more involved in the sense that as a lawyer, you can't say to them, 'I've had a real good offer, can you accept it.' You haven't had the opportunity to feel what their evidence is going to be like and what the other side's evidence is going to be like. So, the client has to be more involved because you have to rely on the client more to determine what their expectations should be. It changes the dynamic, I think, in the sense that it is a reliance thing – I feel like I have to rely on and trust the client's instinct. But they're more engaged in the process because of that.

(Macfarlane, 2001)

As a result, the types of discussion that are encouraged in mediation and other settlement processes – over interests as well as legal rights, and encompassing non-legal and non-monetary outcomes, which are possible in private negotiation – require the input of the client in a practical fashion, which goes well beyond the traditional role of giving instructions for a legal negotiation.

In domestic matters, the opportunity for face-to-face discussion over needs and interests may relegate legal issues to the sidelines. In commercial matters, solutions may be thrashed out directly between corporate agents with lawyers playing only a marginal role. Institutional and corporate clients in litigation are increasingly coming to expect that they will play a larger role in the conduct and management of litigation. Law firms in the United States – in particular those with large corporate clients – are increasingly expected by their clients to include them in seeking time- and cost-efficient solutions, which match the needs of the parties, not just the legal merits of the case. An increasing appetite for early reporting, strategic settlement planning, and early dispute resolution has been noted in relationships between commercial lawyers and their institutional clients (for example financial institutions, insurance companies and so on). Sometimes this is attributed to the increasing influence of in-house counsel who is obligated to account for and justify all litigation expenditure to their manager (Lande, 2000; McEwen, 1998).

What it is to be an 'expert' also changes in this model of dispute resolution. While the lawyer's primary role continues to be offering legal advice and evaluation, in addition lawyers need new skills in order to use early settlement processes effectively and in their clients' best interests. These include interests-based bargaining skills; an ability to work constructively with their own client and to build rapport with the client on the other side; a familiarity with the process dimensions of dispute resolution mechanisms such as mediation, neutral evaluation and arbitration in order that appropriate design choices can be made; an openness to settlement alternatives that have not appeared, or even been thought of, before; an ability to manage the expectations of their own client; and advocacy skills that are appropriate to the context of settlement discussions, where the other side can simply walk away if they dislike counsel's aggressive tone.

These shifts in the roles traditionally played out in conflict resolution by both lawyer and client raise new dilemmas and issues for each. For example, what is counsel to do if their client wants to accept a settlement that counsel believes to be significantly less than the case is worth? How much pressure does counsel bring to bear on their client in this situation? And how are these actions and behaviours compatible with notions of responsible advocacy?

Law students need exposure to the complex issues that surround the negotiation of the lawyer/client relationship in a changing culture of litigation practice, rather than the simplistic and presumptive paradigm that they are presently offered. This can be done in a classroom setting, by raising these and other questions in the discussion of hypotheticals and real cases, but it can be done most effectively in a clinical setting. This requires some rethinking of the traditional assumptions of clinical legal education.

Law school clinics tend to be very litigation-focused (seen as 'exciting' and 'action-based' training for law students). Alternatives to litigation are rarely canvassed among legal representatives and even more rarely discussed with clients whom, it is assumed, want a lawyer to 'speak up for them'. More serious consideration needs to be given to the integration of a range of practical strategies for client service, including, but not limited to, litigation.

In the area that many law school clinics operate – handling landlord and tenant, social security and small claims matters – most of the administrative tribunals to which their clients are headed are introducing early settlement processes, some of them mandatory, which will further change the advocate's role in these settings. Unless they can respond to these changes with appropriate training and an adjustment away from an exclusive focus on the rights-based adjudicative paradigm, law school clinics are in grave danger of falling into a time warp. Whether a procedural requirement or simply a practical approach, ADR should be properly canvassed with clients and opportunities offered if the experience of law students in these clinical settings is to reflect the reality of litigation practice as it has become. Mediation advocacy training is essential for students representing clients in these new processes. When they represent their clients in a mediation process, students confront head on many of the tensions inherent in the advocate's role.

Another alternative is to develop clinical programmes that focus on the provision of mediation or other ADR services, in which law students act as neutrals under the supervision of faculty or professional staff. Mediation Clinics are widespread in the United States, and are beginning to develop in Canadian law schools (Schulz, 1999). Working in a Mediation Clinic facilitates an entirely different view of the role of the legal representative, from the perspective of a neutral. The involvement of students in the facilitation of a consensual solution between parties who are represented by counsel, highlights the balance of power and control in the lawyer/client relationship. As neutrals, students are exposed to – and must take seriously – a range of partisan perspectives, both legal and non-legal, on the conflict that they are working on. They will see discussions – sometimes arguments – between lawyers and their clients. They may also see strikingly different discourses carried on – one between the clients themselves, and another between the lawyers – within any one mediation session. In the process, the student neutral is able to explore, both practically and intellectually, alternate ways for advocates to work with clients in constructive partnership.

Conclusion

It could be argued that the assumptions of the traditional legal curriculum that are critiqued in this chapter are not uniquely challenged by the growth of ADR – that in fact they have always looked impossibly naïve from the perspective of real-life legal practice. An important difference for legal education in the 21st century is that civil litigators, in particular, are now being required to adjust their practice to accommodate both client and government demands for earlier structured efforts at settlement.

Whether one looks at the growth of private judging, private and court-connected mediation programmes, or the use of ADR by government and institutions, the movement towards 'process pluralism' (Merry, 1988) – an array of different dispute resolution process choices, both public and private, formal and informal – is evident in the United States and in Europe. Process pluralism is characterised by '... the availability and acceptability of a wide range of goals, norms, procedures, results, professional roles, skills and styles in handling disputes involving legal issues' (Lande, 2000). As a result, legal education's long-time assumption of legal centralism, in which rights-based legal processes were the primary and preferred means of dispute resolution, is no longer either self-evident or realistic.

Despite these widely recognised changes, the law curriculum – no matter what its subject area – continues to reinforce the assumptions of legal centralism and the 'one size fits all' adjudicative model. While rights-based theory will remain the cornerstone of legal education, just as legal rights and remedies remain the cornerstone of legal negotiation, it is important that law schools begin to effect a more appropriate balance between these assumptions and some alternate perspectives. Legal education's traditional focus on appellate judgements and doctrinal analysis needs to be augmented and enriched by other insights, tools and practical skills to enable context-sensitive case appraisal, creative and pragmatic problem solving, and relationship building with clients and other counsel. The addition of 'specialist' ADR courses is, by itself, a wholly inadequate response to the underlying conceptual challenges of an alternative dispute resolution paradigm. The argument made here is for an integrated approach that incorporates 'alternative' perspectives on conflict and conflict resolution ADR into all parts of the law curriculum – changes that are both substantive and pedagogic, conceptual and practical.

References

Astin, A (1987) Competition or Co-operation?, *Change*, **19** (5), p 12

Aubert, V (1963) Competition and Dissensus: two types of conflict and conflict resolution, *Journal of Conflict Resolution*, **7**, pp 26–42

Barkai, J and Kassenbaum, G (1989) Using Court-Annexed Arbitration to Reduce Litigant Costs and to Increase the Pace of Litigation, *Pepperdine Law Review*, **16** (S5) pp 45–74

Boud, D (ed) (1985) *Problem-Based Learning in Education for the Professions*, HERDSA, Australia

Centre for Dispute Resolution (CEDR) (2000) Report for the financial year April 1999 [Online] http://www.cedr.org

Chornenki, G (1997) Mediating Commercial Disputes: Exchanging 'power over' for 'power with', in *Rethinking Disputes: the Mediation Alternative*, ed J Macfarlane, pp 159–68, Cavendish Publishing and Emond Montgomery

Cooley, J (1996) *Mediation Advocacy*, National Institute for Trial Advocacy, Washington DC

Coyne, W (1999) The Case for Settlement Counsel, *Ohio State Journal on Dispute Resolution*, **14** (2), pp 367–413

Kakalik, J et al (1996) *Just, Speedy and Inexpensive?*, The Rand Institute for Civil Justice, Santa Monica, CA

Kidder, R (1980–81) The End of the Road? Problems in the Analysis of Disputes, *Law and Society Review*, **15**, pp 717–23

Lande, J (2000) Getting the Faith: Why lawyers and executives believe in Mediation, *Harvard Negotiation Law Review*, 5, pp 137–231

Lerner, A (1999) Law and Lawyering in the Workplace: Building better lawyers by teaching students to exercise critical judgement as creative problem-solvers, *Akron Law Review*, **32**, p 107

Lyons, N (1994) Dilemmas of Knowing: Ethical and epistemological dimensions of teachers' work and development, in *The Education Feminism Reader*, ed L Stone, Routledge, London

Macfarlane, J (1992) Look Before You Leap: Knowledge and learning in legal skills education, *Journal of Law and Society*, **19**, p 291

Macfarlane, J (1995) A Feminist Perspective on Experiential Learning and Curriculum Change, *Ottawa Law Review*, 26, p 357

Macfarlane, J (1996) The Legal Skills Movement: Triumph or Compromise? *Review of Teaching Lawyers Skills*, ed J Webb and C Maughan, Butterworths, London, in *Journal of Law and Society*, **24** (3), pp 440–49

Macfarlane, J (ed) (1997) *Rethinking Disputes: The Mediation Alternative*, Cavendish Publishing and Emond Montgomery

Macfarlane, J (1998) Assessing the Reflective Practitioner: Pedagogic principles and certification needs, *International Journal of the Legal Profession*, **5** (1), pp 63–82

Macfarlane, J and Manwaring, J (1998) Using Problem-Based Learning to Teach First Year Contracts, *Journal of Professional Legal Education*, **16**, pp 271–98

Macfarlane, J (2001) *Culture Change? Commercial Litigators and the Ontario Mandatory Mediation Program*, Law Commission of Canada

Mather, L and Yngvesson, B (1980–81) Language, Audience, and the Transformation of Disputes, *Law and Society*, **15** (3–4), p 775

Mayer, B (2000) *The Dynamics of Conflict Resolution*, Jossey-Bass, San Francisco

McEwen, C (1998) Managing Corporate Disputing: Overcoming barriers to the effective use of mediation for reducing the cost and time of litigation, *Ohio State Journal on Dispute Resolution*, **14**, p 1

Menkel-Meadow, C (1984) Towards another View of Legal Negotiations: The structure of problem-solving, *UCLA Law Review*, **31**, p 754

Merry, S (1988) Legal Pluralism, *Law and Society Review*, **22** (5), pp 869–96

Mitchell *et al* (1995) And Then Suddenly Seattle University Was On Its Way To A Parallel, Integrative Curriculum, *Clinical Law Review*, **2** (1), pp 1–35

Mnookin, R and Kornhauser, C (1979) Bargaining in the Shadow of the Law: The case of divorce, *Yale Law Journal*, **88**, p 950

Moore, C (1998) *The Mediation Process,* Jossey-Bass, San Francisco

Reno, J (1999) Lawyers as Problem-Solvers, Keynote address to the American Association of Law Schools, *Journal of Legal Education*, **49** (1), p 5

Riskin, L (1982) Mediation and Lawyers, *Ohio State Law Journal*, **43**, pp 29–60

Rubin, J (1993) Conflict from a Psychological Perspective, in *Negotiation Strategies for Mutual Gain*, ed L Hall, Sage Publications, London

Sander, F (2000) The Future of ADR, *Journal of Dispute Resolution*, **1**, pp 3–10

Schon, D (1983) *Educating the Reflective Practitioner,* Jossey-Bass, San Francisco

Schon, D (1995) Educating the Reflective Legal Practitioner, *Clinical Law Review*, **2**, pp 231–50

Schulz, J (1999) The University of Windsor Mediation Service: A model for Canadian law schools, *Interaction*, **11** (3), p 7

Sholar, T (1993) Collaborative Law – A Method for the Madness, *Memphis State University Law Review*, **23**, pp 667–82

Silbey, S and Sarat, A (1989) Dispute Processing in Law and Legal Scholarship: From institutional critique to the reconstruction of the juridical subject, *Denver Law Review*, **66** (3), pp 437–89

Simmel, C (1955) *Conflict*, New York Free Press, New York

Simon, W (1978) The Ideology of Advocacy: Procedural justice and professional ethics, *Wisconsin Law Review*, **29**, p 29

Tribe, D and Tribe T (1986) Assessing Law Students, *The Law Teacher*, **20**, p 160

Trubek, D *et al* (1983) The Costs of Ordinary Litigation, *UCLA Law Review*, **31**, pp 72–127

Twining, W (1988) Legal Skills and Legal Education, *The Law Teacher*, **22**, p 4

Watson-Hamilton, J (1999) The Significance of Mediation for Legal Education, *Windsor Yearbook of Access to Justice*, **17**, pp 280–94

Zarkiski, A (1997) Lawyers and Dispute Resolution: What do they think and know (and think they know)? Finding out through survey research, *Murdoch University Electronic Journal of Law*, [Online] http://www.murdoch.edu.au/elaw/issues/v4n2/zaris422.html

Zweibel, E (1999) Where Does ADR Fit into the Mainstream Law Curriculum?, *Windsor Yearbook of Access to Justice*, **17**, pp 295–303

9

Space, time and (e)motions of learning

Abdul Paliwala

Introduction

This chapter deals with the processes of transformation of relationships between students, academics and institutions, in physical and virtual learning spaces and props, and in learning times. It suggests that the transformation is influenced by changes in the ideologies of learning and wider environmental factors such as commodification, globalization and digitisation. I suggest that the situation is not clear-cut; possibilities exist for changes that can be either constructive or destructive of educational values. It therefore considers the ways in which creative teaching/learning strategies can protect and promote values in legal education. Relying on the issues raised in this chapter as well as previous chapters in the book, the chapter suggests guidelines to academics involved in the negotiation of change.

Changing geography

One approach to locating change is to use geographical metaphors such as mapping (Economides, 1996; Blomley, 1996; Twining, 2000). However, commentators on the geography of law have also urged caution against the simplistic use of mapping metaphors. Harvey (1996: 4), for example, suggests that 'maps are typically totalising usually two-dimensional Cartesian, and very undialectical devices with which it is possible to propound any mixture of extraordinary insights and monstrous lies' (see also Santos, 1995: 541; Twining, 2000: 141). The subject of this chapter is not law, but the changes in spaces and times, including multi-dimensional physical space (such as cyberspace), social and institutional relationships and cognitive spaces and processes within which legal education occurs. The chapter therefore makes a cautious use of the mapping and other geographical metaphors but in the multi-dimensional sense preferred by Harvey (1996).

The core relationship in legal education is that between students and academics, but this works within the context of wider relationships within and without educational institutions. These relationships operate in and assist in the constitution of learning spaces and times. Classrooms, real or virtual, are merely theatres with props and actors, which are constituted by and yet also provide the spaces and times for the interplay of power relationships between students and lecturers involved in the processes of learning and teaching. These power relationships are further bounded by institutional power relationships between educational institutions, students and staff.

If we go further afield, there is need to take into account relationships between institutions and educational funders and regulators, as well as competitive and cooperative relationships between educational institutions at both national and global level. The relationship between students, the academic institution and their approach to studies is greatly affected by the way their studies are funded. In the United Kingdom, the abolition of student grants and the imposition of fees has empowered students as consumers, while at the same time forced many into the part-time job market, thus creating a mass of part-time student-workers. Furthermore, the way students study is affected by the job market. Yet, somewhere in the middle of it all are the cognitive processes involved in student learning or, to cautiously use a mapping metaphor, a student's own learning map.

While discernible changes are taking place at all levels, it is a moot question whether we live in an age of paradigm change. On the surface, most academics still teach in the same old way. This consists for the majority of students in the United Kingdom, for example, of talk and chalk lectures and more discursive 'seminars', 'tutorials' or 'small group' sessions. Class sizes may have grown with the massification of legal education (Harris and Jones, 1996) but otherwise the standard fare has not changed. Students rely on set texts to do most of their learning.

And yet, there are distinct winds of change in the geography and political economy of learning, which are likely to have deep impacts in the future. The geography of classrooms is changing. To take physical spaces as an example, class sizes have grown, the ratio between small and large group teaching is changing, as is the organisation of physical classroom spaces, with the introduction of innovative teaching methods such as group and clinical work. Classroom props are changing as well, as 'talk and chalk' are supplemented by multimedia.

Learning beyond the classroom is also changing as a result of digitised libraries, courseware and electronic communications. Increasing global flows of students induces a different change in learning spaces. At the same time, the growth of distance learning challenges the concept of campus universities. Learning times also change with development of asynchronous and synchronous extra-classroom interaction whether within on-site or distance learning environments.

Learning times and spaces change in another way as well – the increasing flexibility of learning provision together with demographic changes in career structures and funding of legal education enables changes in the ages and times at which students learn. These affect the key relationship between lecturer and student. Power shifts are also occurring in learning institutions with a dilution of academic autonomy and governance. Strategies such as quality assurance audits, which are apparently intended to improve research, teaching and learning, also promote managerialism and surveillance.

At both national and global level a variety of factors are influencing changes in institutions in relationships, spaces and times of learning, in particular towards greater competition and diversity of provision. These include commodification, globalisation, digitisation and changes in pedagogy. It is therefore necessary to look at these factors before going on to consider the wider changes in geographies of learning.

Commodification

Processes of commodification of learning and the development of consumer power are affecting the relationship between law lecturers, law schools and universities on the one hand, and between lecturers and students on the other (Martin, 2000; Paliwala, 2001). For example, Lyotard (1992: 4) suggests:

> The old principle that the acquisition of knowledge is indissociable from the training of minds… is becoming obsolete and will become ever more so. The relationship of the suppliers and users of knowledge to the knowledge they supply is now tending… to assume the form already taken by the relationship of commodity producers and consumers to the commodities they produce and consume – that is, the form of value. Knowledge is and will be produced in order to be sold, it is and will be consumed in order to be valorised in a new production: in both cases, the goal is exchange. Knowledge ceases to be an end in itself, it loses its 'use value'.

The commodification of knowledge has been powered by the growth of IT induced exponential growth in information, easier accessibility and greater choice for those wanting to acquire it.

At a practical level, such commodification arises both from the external market, which increasingly demands that students be embodied as skilled deliverables, and from the fact that students are becoming financially responsible for their education – and thus become consumers. Arthurs (1998: 21) relates how in Canadian law faculties, students exercised their consumer power to vote against these innovations in faculty council debates, ignored them when selecting optional courses, and if enrolled, passively resisted them by not taking them seriously. Likewise, students often favoured the appointment of new faculty recruits with apparent promise as teachers and mentors rather than those who displayed the most impressive intellectual credentials.

However, the important learning contract in the consumer relationship is not between the lecturer and student, but between the student as consumer and the university as seller. This is further mediated by two powerful relationships. The first is between the law school and the legal professions, which although liberal in form, enforces compliance because of its professional hold on the products of the law school (see Chapter 1). The other powerful relationship is between the universities and other providers of legal education and the state as the provider of funds. This relative monopoly power enables the state to engage institutions within disciplinary relationships that promote compliance with regulatory frameworks and ensure competition for funding among the sellers of legal education. Of course, this power is not absolute, as increasing commercial activity by institutions (especially in non-state funded programmes) enables relative escape and a commercial diversity of provision.

One tendency of commodification is to separate out the relationships involved in research, teaching and learning as separate production-consumer transactions. It may alienate the student as consumer from the academic as teacher. It may separate out the roles of the academic as teacher and researcher in most disciplines, especially in a professional discipline such as law where there is a specific distinction between academic courses and professional training. The power demands of students, academic institutions and national surveillance agencies in relation to teaching may pull in different directions from the equally important power demands from academic institutions and national research surveillance agencies.

Globalization

Globalization has become common currency, but it is a highly contested term underneath the simple assertion of intensification of relationships at a global level (Giddens, 1990). Its claims of global improvement in living standards and conditions are increasingly contested as part of the march of global corporate culture or, as Silbey (1996), Santos (1995) and Hardt and Negri (2000) respectively describe it, 'post-modern colonialism', 'globalised localism' or postmodern 'empire'. In relation to legal education, there is significant evidence of intensification of global interaction in flows of students across the globe, the development of global distance learning, relatively lesser flows of academics and great increases in academic interaction (Scott, 1998). It is clear that metropolitan legal education institutions already play a dominant role in the global flows.

This process of globalization of Higher Education is likely to increase as a result of enforced economic liberalisation through agencies such as the General Agreement on Trade and Services (Rikowski, 2001). Free trade in services could promote equality in learning. However, this equality is deceptively limited to those with ability to pay. In practice, globalisation may do less to promote a uniform spread of global legal culture, and more to produce dissonance between a global legal elite schooled in the West and deschooled in local legal cultures and local legal personnel. This may be particularly so in developing countries, where all but the few who escape to on-site or virtual metropolitan institutions learn in institutions that are increasingly impoverished and deprived of leading scholars and resources (Global Joint Task Force, 2000). The result may be another form of local deschooling. As Appadurai (1990) suggests, the processes termed globalisation do not produce uniform intensification effects, but complex, chaotic incoherence.

Digitisation

At a surface level, information and communication technologies (ICT) do not seem to have had much impact on the day-to-day relationships in legal education. Learning and teaching are very much lecture and discussion shows. However, there are already symptoms of change at the interstitial level in the props and communications systems used in the organisation of learning. The most dramatic change has been in the digitisation of libraries. More significantly, ICT is at the heart of potential fundamental changes, whether it is at the level of electronic distance learning, electronic virtual classrooms or in the transformation of physical classroom spaces through the introduction of teaching and learning props (Martin, 2000; Paliwala, 2001; Woods, 2001). Digitisation has the potential of not only transforming the actual learning experience in the classroom, but also of providing effective management systems to enable the very shifts in spaces and times of teaching and learning that are consequent on globalization.

Changing relationships

The factors outlined above articulate with contemporary learning and teaching theory to affect important changes in the most significant relationship in legal education – that between lecturer and student. Learning and teaching theory has been affected by apparently contradictory goals. On the one hand is the Platonic ideal of learning as acquisition of knowledge. Rousseau (1991) substituted this with learning as personal development of the student. A twist is given by Freire's notion of learning as personal liberation (Freire, 1970; Shor and Freire, 1987). Finally, there is learning to meet social needs (Dearing, 1997). Each approach can be problematic. The acquisition of knowledge can become a shallow exercise in the hands of unimaginative teachers. In ivory tower mode, it can be too abstract and not related to the learning needs of the student. Personal development can, in consumerist times, easily become a cloak for anti-intellectualism. Learning as personal liberation can alienate the teacher's intellectual role as communicator of ideas. Social needs are easily translatable by governments into the production of trained technicians. Yet, these goals can be combined to produce approaches that enhance intellectual values, personal development and a social fit between students and society.

Recently, there has been a shift of emphasis away from the academic to the student. The focus has shifted to student cognition, personal development and market potential in theoretical approaches, which emphasise a shift from instructional to constructional, from passive to active, surface to deep, from the authoritarian lecture to student-centred or independent learning, and finally to the development of student skills.

Moon's (1999) map of learning charts learning pathways in terms of student cognition, starting progressively from a low point of *surface learning* and reaching the highs of *deep learning*. See the box below.

The five types of learning

Moon (1999) charts learning pathways by representing this in terms of five types of learning including:

- noticing;
- making sense;
- making meaning;
- working with the meaning;
- transformative learning.

The first two stages involve surface learning under which the student's cognitive processes are used to take cognisance of and to catalogue and order the information. The three deeper learning stages involve processing of the material in ways that reshape the cognition processes themselves (Moon, 1999: 137–39). The ways in which these processes take place depend both on the nature of the learner and the learning environment. Crudely, the shallower learning processes are effected by *instructional learning* and deeper learning processes are supported by *reflective learning*. Moon's map has all the weaknesses of cartographical metaphors in suggesting specific routes to specific forms of learning when learning processes are likely to be much more complex and chaotic than those resulting from highly structured learning systems.

The focus on student as learner has another effect. Thus, Le Brun and Johnstone's (1995: 56) concept of the student is 'a self-determining agent who actively selects information from the perceived environment, and who constructs new knowledge in the light of what that individual already knows'.

The envisioned shift towards the new learning methodology involves a range of learning/teaching approaches, including resource-based learning, problem solving, problem-based learning and experiential or clinical learning, which are covered in Chapters 2, 4 and 8. These new learning techniques emphasise another aspect of student development, that of the development of skills.

A balanced treatment of the shift in focus towards the student can be compatible with the best ideals of teaching and learning. Deep and reflective learning and the emphasis on independent learning can promote Platonic ideals while enhancing the student's personal development. What is required is a clear understanding of the value of intellectual skills as an appropriate corrective to shallow notions of the marketplace. Learning ideologies derived from school education and operating in an era of commodification undervalue the nature of the academic community as a teaching/learning community in which both academics and students are learning and sharing knowledge – whether as researchers or students. Underlying this change in power relationships is a fundamental shift in the concept of knowledge and the knower with the commodification of knowledge itself (Lyotard, 1992).

The commodification of roles within the academic community as disarticulated researchers, teachers and learners undermine the value of the link between what is researched and what is learnt by the student. This is particularly the case with legal education where there is a historical conflict between the wider academic concern with understanding of the law and a pragmatic concern among legal practitioners and students for technicist lawyering.

An underlying issue is that of academic power. Webb (1998: 149) provides a criticism of authoritarian teaching:

> Its symptoms may include an apparent unwillingness to negotiate large elements of the teaching and learning process; a lack of reflexivity about the curriculum and its delivery; disinterest in the students' subjective experiences of learning; a lack of transparency of the criteria governing, say, learning outcomes and assessment processes, as well as the small daily acts of intellectual and personal arrogance, of unthinking discrimination and discourtesy which can sometimes mark out the respective statuses of student and teacher.

New teaching/learning techniques attempt to dethrone the 'authoritarian' lecturer, whether they perform using the Socratic case study method involving an interrogative dialogue between academic and student (Friedland, 1996; Rhode, 2001) or the 'instructionist' lecture. Laurillard (1993: 87–90) criticizes both forms as being authoritarian. However, apart from the issue of power, they are very different. In one case, the lecturer tells the 'truth' to the students, in the other the lecturer imposes authority by making students into mouthpieces for their version. By contrast, in the new language of problem-based learning the lecturer becomes a 'facilitator' of student learning. A more democratic medium is Laurillard's (1993: 86) concept of dialogue between the teacher and student involving the following steps:

1. clear explanations of phenomena, structures and goals for learning;
2. problem solving and feedback to appreciate student cognition;

3. resetting of learning tasks based on analysis of student responses;
4. prompting reflection from students.

There is a shift towards an obligation of greater transparency and clarity by the teachers. They have to make their learning/teaching objectives clear. A process of course appraisal surveillance is instituted that constitutes an alliance between the student consumer, the institution and the university system. While such quality measures reduce authoritarianism, they also have an impact on the freedom to teach as they constrain the teacher within approved forms and approaches to learning.

The relationship of power between academic and student has psychological implications. Borrowing Lacan's terminology, traditional teaching involved either the imposition of the teacher's version of truth on the student as an authoritarian exercise in power (master discourse) or of engaging the student in the teacher's version of truth through a process of seduction (university discourse) (Ragland, 1991: 1111). Neither process was democratic, however: in an era in which students only attended classes as a matter of choice, and academics were free to teach what they wished, they had to engage in a process of seduction to involve students in their version of truth. The new relationship of commodity exchange is one in which the student is required to attend class. However, academics are not free to teach what they wish. This is psychologically fundamentally different from that of the past.

In the process, in the will to depart from the authoritarianism of the master discourse, we might be abandoning the process of intellectual stimulation, the seduction of academic discourse. Such seduction might be further threatened by virtual learning systems. As O'Donnell (O'Donnell and Hackney, 1995) [the University of Pennsylvania Web site accessed in 2001] suggests in an interview, as a consequence of such routinization and bureaucratization 'we might end up missing something of the authentic experience of face-to-face encounter between youth and age, between wisdom and what's the counter, chutzpah – between tradition and innovation'.

Changes in learning spaces

Learning spaces provide theatres for the working out of the key power relationships between academic and students. However, these spaces and relationships operate within a context provided by the wider institutional factors described above and are subject to significant changes.

Changing classrooms

The geography of classrooms remained nearly constant for decades, and in the case of lectures, perhaps for centuries. The instructional lecture remains dominant in Europe (see Thomas, 2000 for a contemporary guide to lecturing in law). In the United States the interrogational Socratic lecture holds sway (Friedland, 1996; Rhode, 2001). Both forms were premised on the authority of the lecturer, but the latter was interactive. The interactive seminar or tutorial formed a supplement to the lecture. The physical spaces in which these activities took place were taken for granted. The lecture rooms were large and preferably tiered, in which all attention was focused on the lecturer, and the seminar rooms were smaller and flat, in which the space was ideally intended to promote interaction between the students, but all authority was located at the head of the table. This may not have been the precise pattern in the immediate post-war expansion of provincial universities in the United Kingdom. Small student numbers meant small, flat lecture rooms.· Nevertheless, it is still not unusual for seating in seminar rooms to be arranged in rows as in lecture rooms. The props remained standard – the blackboard (or increasingly the white board) and chalk. The raised platform symbolized authority and the lectern performed simultaneously the role of the autocue and defence from student gaze.

Interestingly there is an older Oxbridge tradition of law lecturing that eschews chalk and the lectern. A prominent academic has been known to state that 'notes are the crutches of an intellectual cripple'! For the students, the props were their notebooks and perhaps the textbook. The props in the seminar room were no more exciting! The difference between the two modes was the absence of the lectern. Nevertheless, it is not unknown for seminar teachers to spend most of their time talking *at* students who are unprepared to engage in discussion (Alldridge and Mumford, 1998).

These spaces have seen some changes in recent years. The tiered lecture theatre has not disappeared. Indeed, there is growing demand for larger lecture rooms as class sizes have grown with the massification of legal education (Harris and Jones, 1996). However, there is also the rise of large seminar rooms. This is partly to accommodate larger classes and partly to provide for teaching that is primarily 'seminar-based'. Mushrooming of course options has resulted in enrolments in individual modules of between 20 and 40 students.

The second is the growth of postgraduate teaching, both academic and professional levels, which is also increasingly seminar-based. Thirdly, forms of teaching and learning such as clinical education, role-play, games etc can only be accommodated effectively in flat interactive spaces. Increasingly, students have to do their negotiations etc outside the bounded classroom; so the diversification of learning spaces results from the diversification of learning. These transitions are not smooth, and personal experience of law teachers at different institutions suggests that the inability of university architecture to cope with innovative teaching is a significant constraint.

The stage props are changing as well. Chalk and blackboards have been supplemented by overhead projectors (OHP) for lecturers and large poster boards for students. Again these symbolize the changing interaction between lecturer and student. The poster boards are there to represent the results of student group work for full class discussion. Even greater transformation is taking place in the classroom props through the use of technology (Thomas, 2000). See the box below.

Classroom props in the typical US law school

A typical lecture room in Harvard or other major US law schools will now include the following:

- white board and pens;
- poster boards;
- OHPs;
- multimedia projection facilities for laptops linked to university intranet and Internet, video, TV and audio;
- laptop and Internet connections from each student desktop. In some cases, there is also potential for the student to be able to display directly onto the large display facility;
- within five years, videoconferencing facilities will also become common in each room.

The transformative potential of these is enormous. However, the props can be used in very different ways by different lecturers. The following in the box below is sound advice from the JTAP Application of Presentation Technologies Programme Presentation Tools Web site (JTAP 2001; see also Thomas 2000, section 6).

Advice on the use of Presentation Tools

Computer-based Presentation Technologies (PT) such as PowerPoint are simply *a way of helping you to communicate more efficiently and effectively*, not only to a live audience but also now via the World Wide Web.

The move towards computer-based presentation approaches of course has wide-reaching administrative and technical implications for institutions. Although quick and easy to produce, they need an expensive infrastructure (computers, projectors...) to deliver. Changeover from traditional means of presentation such as overhead transparencies and 35 mm slides is usually gradual and of course *computer-based tools are designed to work alongside and not necessarily replace these*. However, one of the most commonly reported benefits of using computer-based techniques is *their flexibility*, particularly the possibility of making 'last minute' amendments.

Effective communication means having a well-defined and structured message. Also your message needs to be clear, understood and convincing. Presentation technologies will not help you a lot with content, of course, but it *can help you organise and develop your thoughts, and express them in a more structured and engaging way*.

You do not need to be a specialist in a Presentation Tool. Today's Presentation Tools make your introduction to their world fast and painless. Another central point about these technologies, especially for academics, is that *you do not have to spend a lot of time (on average) developing your presentation*. A minimal Presentation Tool nowadays provides a relatively wide variety of pre-defined templates, and wisards with pre-defined outlines and colour schemes. Most of them have galleries with resources (art, photos, animation, sound, video...) you can add or even post-edit within your presentation to illustrate or reinforce your message. They include built-in facilities to create your own resources quickly (eg easy-to-use drawing tools), and enable you to import external resources created using other applications. Visually appealing 'slides' can be produced easily, fast, and with next to no artistic ability (provided you stick to a few simple rules of thumb!). You can even add live demonstrations of other software. With modern tools, the main limit becomes our imagination!

However, Presentation Tools are maximally efficient if you keep in mind that *they serve your aim of communicating a message to an audience*. So please *don't get driven by technology*! Students report, for example, that a non-relevant sound that is included, eg in an animation, oppresses or annoys them rather than keeping their attention.

Last but not least, Presentation Tools allow a great variety of delivery modes, from the traditional 35 mm slides, acetates and handouts to live projection, distribution on floppy disks, via mail and even publishing full multimedia and interactive presentations on the Web.

While there is welcome emphasis on the need for appropriate infrastructure in this message, very little work has been done on the changes taking place in the learning environment. Increasing use of sophisticated and technical props require techniques and skills that are relevant to theatre. For example, the effect of new props may not be uniformly towards greater interaction. The OHP and its digitised descendant, direct projection from the computer typically using PowerPoint, can sometimes have a disturbing effect in the classroom.

A third force or 'crutch' is introduced that can change the relationship between the lecturer and student. Ostensibly the projection system is there to make things clear, but for the student the need to take down notes becomes an imperative, which may distract from the attention being given to the lecturer's words. This is the reason why those using OHPs are instructed to make them succinct and effective links to what is being said. Those using OHPs also increasingly provide handouts of slides to students to avoid this problem.

It is difficult for those using slides to be spontaneous and to improvize when a structured path has been created in advance. The use of media can also enshroud the performance in darkness. Even the best projection facilities require dimming of lights. Very good systems provide illumination of the lecturer's body. Depending on the quality of projection system and quality of stage lighting, the lecturer becomes relatively disembodied – a mere voice-over with the key facial and other expressions being disguised. The lecturer can be decentred by the very media used to enhance student understanding. The students also become a disembodied dark mass whose body language is lost to the lecturer. This situation can be ameliorated by the use of higher quality projection devices and stage-type lighting.

These cautions are not intended to suggest abandonment of the new props, but to encourage their use to produce higher arts, greater performances in teaching and learning. An exciting mediated lecture could bring up key passages of text of cases, statutes etc and provide comparison through hypertext. The lecture could be illustrated by graphic images, photographs or film of the events and processes and video film of key speeches. Imagine the smooth addition of videoconferencing to this. A class can be further heightened by a live discussion between key academics or practitioners on a subject. Furthermore, new media provide an enhanced capability for classroom interaction. A 'Socratic' or non-Socratic dialogue can be enhanced by use of the new media (Byrnes, 2001; Woods, 2001). In the typical case method lecture, the key passages under dispute can be brought up on screen. More significantly, where students want to produce an argument, they can take over the screen.

Role-play and group work exercises can be further enhanced by the new media. If students are given access to intranet and Internet resources to prepare their presentations, for example with their networked laptops, they can do research on the spot, and provide much better illustrated arguments than can be done via points on a poster board. The main drawback is that writing points on a poster takes very little time, and you can enhance the argument with your oral presentation. Preparing a multimedia presentation beyond basic PowerPoint slides can take much longer. At some point one has to consider the relationship between time spent on the media and time spent in intellectual work. The way to ameliorate the problem is to restructure preparation outside the classroom and presentation in the classroom.

Virtual classrooms

The media's intrusion into the classroom challenges classroom-focused teaching. Of course, the classroom has never been the sole location for teaching and learning. The classroom is merely the space for communal learning. Students spend the vast majority of their learning time in individual learning activities. In the days when there were few books, this was done in the library. As more resources became available to students, the library became a less exclusive but still important repository of knowledge. Before the onset of IT, students had access to three resources – text and cases and materials books, photocopied materials distributed by the course teacher and the library. In the contest of convenience, the library lost out relatively. Students mainly used to read prescribed texts, which they generally acquired as part of their personal libraries or occasionally in the university library. In a predominantly exam-based culture of law schools, they needed to do little more than this. The ratio of effort to marks was insufficient for most students. The library provided a public workspace. The librarian was the collector, cataloguer, arranger and lender of books with very little role in relation to individual students. The era of IT has introduced a different potential of learning beyond the classroom. This includes online:

- commercial and free datasets;
- courseware varying in complexity from interactive multimedia systems (such as Iolis) to video lectures to lecture notes on screen;
- communications systems including e-mail, discussion lists, e-conferencing and videoconferencing.

These developments have been accompanied by a relative growth in student-centred teaching, learning and assessment approaches. As a result, there has grown a need to provide access to new technology and training in its use. More significantly, there is a growing need for day-to-day advice and support to enable students to negotiate the information maze.

The legal education community has not yet satisfactorily resolved the physical delivery of electronic resources nor the responsibility for their delivery. The physical delivery was initially based on the concept of the dedicated computer work area. This shifted to a wider delivery on university networks (BILETA, 1991, 1996). However, as students increasingly have access to their own equipment in their study rooms and as Internet access becomes easier, the attention has shifted to providing this access via university intranets. This process has been assisted by the development of Virtual Learning Environments (VLEs) to enable easy management of student learning resources and administration.

Such potential changes need not necessarily disrupt the flow of traditional teaching. In most institutions, they could be absorbed into the 'individual learning' part of student studies, without disturbing the system of lectures and tutorials. However, as Chapter 4 on resource-based learning (RBL) indicates, creative use of e-learning resources can introduce new approaches to beyond classroom teaching and thus displace some of the traditional teaching/learning methods.

Multimedia electronic material such as Iolis raise the prospect of reducing seminar time or changing seminar content by enabling high quality auto-learning prior to class. Electronic negotiation exercises can transform seminar, group work and clinical teaching. Electronic lectures raise the prospect of competition with traditional lectures. The former can involve additional notes, commentaries and hypertext links to primary and secondary material, which the students can access from their own study rooms at their own time.

On the other side, one-off deliveries by institution-based lecturers provide students with a sense of immediacy, interaction and community. In principle, resource-based learning puts the emphasis on student learning as opposed to teachers teaching. If student learning and assessment is geared towards RBL, then the role of the traditional lecture and seminar is challenged. Yet, the problem lies in seeing the new methods as substitutes for traditional teaching. If they are seen as complementary, then they provide students with a plurality of learning resources from which they select the ones most suitable to their learning style. The underlying issue is not simply to maintain traditional structures in the face of changing realities, but to ensure the maintenance of academic values in the process of change.

Virtual institutions

Once learning transcends the physical classroom, the question is raised whether the geography of time and space can transcend on-site learning by promoting the virtual classroom. Until now, there has been very little suggestion that distance learning is a qualitative substitute for on-site learning. Most commentators have stressed the value of personal contact, on-site learning (Dearing, 1997). Distance learning is seen as the medium for those who cannot have access to on-site methods. The success of distance learning institutions such as the UK Open University depends on the provision of significant personal contact tutorials (Daniel, 1996). However, this tends to be of a very different nature to personal contact in the on-site universities. This is because the underlying functions of on-site universities go beyond mere learning of content and skills and promote forms of socialization and personal development.

The significance of digitisation in this type of development is that it promises to bridge the gap between the on-site learner and the global distance learner. Digitisation promotes distance learning strategies in a variety of ways (Paliwala, 2000), highlighted in the box below.

Some ways in which digitisation promotes distance learning strategies

- *Learning Resources.* Digital libraries have gone a considerable way towards bridging the gap between on-site and distance learning students (see Chapter 4). This can be further supported by digitised catalogues and lending systems for hard copy works. As Web access becomes ubiquitous and efficient, this process will be further enhanced.

- *Courseware.* The growth of multimedia courseware provides interactive learning. A student of the London University External programme in law has access to the Iolis course materials, which provide students with text, materials and interactive exercises that provide feedback. Electronic lectures provide another form of courseware, which transcends the problems of time and space. Furthermore, digitisation and the resources released from massification enable performance material to transcend the concept of 'lecture' by providing wide variety of performances, for example discussions between leading scholars, recordings or re-enactments of important legal events.
- *Communication.* Students can have discussions among themselves and with members of staff. Significantly, e-communication promotes the feeling of community among distance learners by putting them in touch with one another in times and virtual spaces, supplementing the all too infrequent personal contact tutorials. Digitisation also provides the exciting prospect of discussions, which involve learning in active, clinical modes.
- *Learning chunks.* Digitisation enables learning to be delivered in learning chunks, which may be individualised to the knowledge, skills, space/time needs of students or groups of students. Learning packages in the form of fixed period degrees can be supplemented by all types of learning chunks to meet a variety of educational needs. The ability to support 'just in time' learning delivery to meet lifetime learning needs raises questions about 'Who is a Law Student?'
- *Organisation.* Virtual Learning Environments enable a much more complex organisation of learning than was possible previously.

While there is very little likelihood that in the next 10 years there will be a fundamental substitution of on-site learning with distance learning, digitally enhanced distance learning will have an increasing role to play in legal education. This is because of fundamental changes taking place in the wider institutional geography of learning.

At the institutional level, the main influence is commodification. As indicated in the earlier statement of Lyotard (1992), knowledge ceases to be an end in itself and becomes an exchangeable commodity. There develops a market in learning in which on the one hand are the students as consumers and on the other are academic institutions as providers. Status-based rules of access such as quota systems and national preferences are increasingly challenged in a globalized education market. On the other hand, three values become crucial in the new market: the cost of provision, the ability to pay, and the brand value of the education product. The cost factors increasingly promote the development of virtual 'mega-universities' (Daniel, 1996). The provision of spaces, people and resources at on-site universities costs considerable amounts of money. Moreover, live (non-virtual) performances, just as theatre and opera, can be very expensive as the costs are recurrent. The costs include academic salaries and facilities needed to sustain them, maintenance costs of learning spaces and equipment and support staff.

In contrast, investment in IT infrastructure in a virtual campus can be considerable and may be difficult to justify for small-scale operations (Blumenstyk, 2001). However, a mega-university can afford such investment because of student numbers (Daniel, 1996). A virtual lecture by a leading international expert may cost £5,000, but the lecture forms part of a permanent stock. Annual recurrent costs of updating can be considerably less.

There is insufficient data comparing costs of IT-based teaching with traditional teaching. In the United Kingdom, such an exercise to do just that has produced a costing methodology, although no actual cost comparisons (Bacsich, Ash and Heginbotham, 2001). In the United States the Technology Costing Methodology Project (TCM) has carried out case studies and concludes that technology-mediated delivery is more expensive than face-to-face instruction, at least within the parameters of course enrolments and methods tested. There were no instances in which this finding was not true. Research and modelling in other projects has found that scale matters – there are conditions under which technology-mediated delivery is less expensive than traditional classroom instruction. Continued efforts must be made to identify those conditions (WICHE, 2001).

The ability to pay grows in significance in the globally commodified education market as education becomes increasingly privatized and governments reduce their subsidies of institutions. An important consequence is that leading institutions play the market by putting up their cost in accordance with their brand value. However, while the institutional brand can command a high price, the maintenance of its value demands that not all rich students should be let in (unless of course they can buy their way through appropriate endowments!). It is likely that the highest brand values will reside with on-site learning institutions.

Should institutions such as Harvard and Oxbridge or even metropolitan institutions of lesser brand value enter the distance learning market as a supplementary activity, the quality of their brand value may challenge that of on-site learning at institutions of lower brand value and resources across the globe. Leading US institutions such as Columbia, Cornell, New York University and University of Maryland have already created profit for companies. However, there is no guarantee of success, as some who have dipped their toes in the water have had to withdraw (Blumenstyk, 2001).

Learning futures

It was suggested at the outset that apparent continuities in approaches to learning and teaching mask discernible changes of great significance, which affect all aspects of legal education including relationships, times and spaces. The complex interaction between wider forces of commodification, globalization and digitisation and historic values and conditions of legal education communities produce ambivalent potentialities for legal education. There is the potential for a decadent fracture of academic communities that produces:

- students who are consumers of economically relevant skills and institutional brand values;
- decentred academics who are disempowered by the technologies they use and by pedagogical attitudes that make them mere facilitators of learning;
- teaching institutions whose main role is to produce missionaries and mercenaries of globalization (Braithwaite and Drahos, 2000);
- other, more local institutions that do not have the intellectual or physical resources to enable relevant learning for their students.

Nevertheless, there is the potential of using the very same technologies to produce communities of learning in which students have a dynamic and critical awareness of, and engage actively with, legal issues, skills and values and are as steeped in the local as in global awareness. The academics in these communities are active researchers, whose research infuses their teaching, and who shed their authoritarian tendencies and yet do not allow themselves to be decentred as a consequence of consumerist demands from students and bureaucratic surveillance and control of their institutions.

Conclusion

This chapter, and this book, provides a number of ideas about new challenges and initiatives. However, those of us who are hitchhikers in the legal education galaxy are sorely in need of a guide, however inadequate. There is no mathematical answer, but there are some principles – see the box below.

Hitchhiker's guide to some principles

1. *Beware of forces surrounding you.* Our ivory towers have been impregnated by factors such as commodification, globalization and digitisation. Yet, the relationship between these forces and educational communities is not a deterministic one. Instead, according to Bourdieu (1977), educational structures and environments are involved in dynamic interrelationships. The function of the academy has historically been to provide the imagination for change (Martin, 2000; Arthurs, 1998; Paliwala, 2001). At the institutional level, it requires safeguarding the principles of democratic academic governance against the power of managerial bureaucracies. In practice, this calls

for careful engagement of academics as intellectuals (not administrators) in major issues relating to change. This may be particularly important in relation to changes such as those involving ICT, which are frequently introduced as technical and economic rationalizations or modernizations.

2. *Be sensitive to students, be sensitive to academics.* Authoritarian master discourses rightly need to be displaced by sensitivity to the needs of student development and liberation, but this does not require submission to consumerist pressures. Law academics have a dual role as safeguarders of the values of academic responsibility and freedom, of promoting student development and liberation and of supporting ethical values in the legal system (Chapters 1, 2, 5, 6 and 8). This role requires a pedagogy that focuses on student development and liberation, but in ways that promote student imagination through dialectical dialogue of mutual respect and understanding between academic and student (Webb, 1998: 139).

3. *Safeguard the value of the link between research and teaching.* A key value of Higher Education, which makes it different from other education, is that it is a community of learning in which one set of learners, the researchers, teach another, the students. In this relationship, the academic is no mere facilitator, but an active presence in providing the environment for learning, communicating ideas and troubleshooting. The 'independent' learning student is also no mere receptacle for pouring in of knowledge, but themself a producer of ideas and knowledge whether at the undergraduate or postgraduate stages. To be truly professional, the legal educator has to be both an expert in the field and an expert teacher. This requires a combination of active research in their subject with a deep knowledge of how best to promote imaginative student learning.

4. *Transcend the differences between 'academic' and 'professional' legal education.* As outlined in Chapter 1, legal education exists within a range of diversity. However, the chapter proposes a unity in terms of professionalism in the legal education process. A key vehicle is reflective experiential learning which is relevant to both the academic and professional stages (see Chapters 2, 5 and 8). I suggest a further transcending factor – the relevance of research. The research task is as important to the professional stage as to the academic stage. Institutions teaching professional courses in a way that meets the needs of the changing professions (as, for example, suggested in Chapter 8) need to become laboratories of research into changes in the way lawyering is done, if they are to effectively communicate the imagination and skills required of the future lawyer.

5. *Continually reassess the relationship between teaching and assessment.* It is important to appreciate the process of assessment as an intrinsic part of the learning process as well as a form of certification. Therefore, the forms of assessment need to transcend the notion of education as mere knowledge transference and become adapted to wider pedagogies (see Chapter 3).

6. *Resist exclusive pedagogies.* In the legal education context, skills have a dual connotation. They refer to values that are part of the wider educational

process as well as to the specific technical legal skills required to maintain the status quo of lawyering. Skills in the first sense provide an appropriate framework for understanding legal education. Skills education in the second sense may be important, but only, as Chapters 2 and 8 indicate, when skills are infused with wider value-laden methodologies. There is need for careful balance between pedagogies of learning as the search for knowledge, personal development, acquiring appropriate skills and liberation of the self within society.

7. *Neither a Luddite nor a starry-eyed technocrat be.* Effective use of ICT requires careful attention to pedagogic as well as technical issues. Sound pedagogy requires careful understanding of new techniques: for example, that PowerPoint slides in a lecture can be disastrous or effective teaching tools depending on how they are used and the environment in which they are used; that careful attention needs to be given to all aspects of intro-duction of new stage props in the theatre of lecturing; that simply making students read lecture notes on Web pages or even video lectures can produce 'boxed' minds.

This is not just singing praises of more independent or interactive forms of learning such as the electronic negotiation exercises described in Chapter 4. Without an underlying framework for critical analysis of the ethical aspects, such skills training can have equally perverse effects. On the other hand, a careful appreciation of the variety of forms of communication available to an academic, including their management, resource, pedagogic and ethical implications, can provide fulfilling value for both students and academics involved in the process.

8. *Beware that learning law has moved beyond the law school and into society.* Learning law has never been the exclusive preserve of law schools teaching potential professional lawyers. Many law graduates do not become lawyers, a considerable amount of law is taught to 'other disciplines'. More signifi-cantly, and particularly with the rise of the Internet, law is moving away from being the arcane preserve of the professional and becomes more accessible to the lay person. There is likely to arise a new species of legal educator – the electronic public legal information provider. Such providers have the responsibility of making law accessible and deliverable in digestible chunks.

9. *Engage with global forces in order to safeguard local learning needs.* There is much to be gained through global interchange between learning commu-nities. In particular, this can counteract the isolation of academics belea-guered by lack of resources and by authoritarian politics. Corporate globalization of legal education is, however, a very different dimension. It can promote corporate global values at the expense of local legal needs and easily become part of processes similar to the transplantation of Western legal systems in former communist and developing countries. There is a difference between forming strategic democratic alliances between institutions and the development of a new empire of academic mega-corporations.

References

Alldridge, P and Mumford, A (1998) Gazing into the future through a VDU: Communications, Information Technology and Law Teaching, *Journal of Law and Society*, **25** (1), pp 116–33

Appadurai, A (1990) Disjuncture and Difference in the Global Cultural Economy, *Global culture, nationalism, globalization and modernity*, ed M Featherstone, pp 295–309, Sage, London

Arthurs, H (1998) The Political Economy of Canadian Legal Education, *Journal of Law and Society*, **25** (1), pp 14–32

Bacsich, P, Ash, C and Heginbotham, S (2001) *The costs of networked learning Phase Two*, Sheffield Hallam University, Sheffield [Online] [accessed 21 November 2001] http://www.shu.ac.uk/cnl/report2.html

BILETA (1991) *Report of the BILETA Committee of Enquiry into Information Technology in Legal Education*, CTI Law Technology Centre, Warwick University [Online][accessed 21 November 2001] http://www.bileta.ac.uk/B1/b1.html

BILETA (1996) *Information Technology For UK Law Schools: The Second BILETA Report into Information Technology and Legal Education*, CTI Law Technology Centre, Warwick University [Online accessed 21 November 2001] http://www.bileta.ac.uk/B2/b2.html

Blomley, N and Clark, G (1990) Law, Theory and Geography, *Urban Geography*, **11**, p 433

Blumenstyk, G (2001) Temple U shuts down for-profit distance-education company, *The Chronicle of Higher Education*, 2001 July 20, pp A29–30

Bourdieu, P (1977) *Reproduction in Education, Society and Culture* (Nice, R tr), Sage, London

Daniel, Sir J (1996) *Mega-Universities and Knowledge Media: Technology Strategies for Higher Education*, Kogan Page, London

Dearing, Sir R (1997) *Report of the National Committee of Inquiry into Higher Education*, HMSO, London [Online] [accessed 21 November 2001] http://www.leeds.ac.uk/edcol/ncihe/

Economides, K (1996) Law and Geography: New Frontiers, *Legal Frontiers*, ed P Thomas, pp 180–207, Butterworths, London

Freire, P (1970) *Pedagogy of the Oppressed*, Continuum Basic Books, New York

Friedland, S (1996) How We Teach: A Survey of Teaching Techniques in American Law Schools, *Seattle University Law Review*, **20** (1), p 4

Giddens, A (1990) *Sociology*, Polity Press, Oxford

Global Joint Task Force (2000) *Higher Education in Developing Countries: Peril and Promise*, World Bank, Washington

Hardt, M and Negri, A (2000) *Empire*, Harvard UP, Cambridge, MA

Harris, P and Jones, M (1996) *A survey of law schools in the UK*, The Legal Education Research Project (LERP) and Sweet & Maxwell, London. Association of Law Teachers Web site [Online] [accessed 6 December 2001] http://www.lawteacher.ac.uk/1996report/index.html

Harvey, D (1996) *Justice, Nature and the Geography of Difference*, Blackwell, Oxford

JTAP (2001) Presentation Tools, in *The Application of Presentation Technologies in UK Higher Education*. JISC Technology Applications Programme (JTAP) UMIST University [Online accessed 21 November 2001] http://www.umist.ac.uk/apt/ptoolkit/ptools/ptools.htm

Laurillard, D (1993) *Rethinking University Teaching: A Framework for the effective use of Educational Technology*, Routledge, London

Le Brun, M and Johnstone, R (1994) *The Quiet (R)evolution: Improving Student Learning in Law*, Law Book Co, NSW, Australia

Lyotard, J (1992) *The Postmodern Condition: a Report on Knowledge*, Manchester University Press, Manchester

Martin, P (2000) Impermanent Boundaries – Imminent Challenges to Professional Identities and Institutional Competence, *The Journal of Information, Law and Technology (JILT)*, 2000 (2) [Online] [accessed 21 November 2001] http://elj.warwick.ac.uk/jilt/00–2/martin.html

Moon, J (1999) *Reflection in learning and professional development: theory and practice*, Kogan Page, London

O'Donnell, J and Hackney, S (1995) Humanities in the 21st Century, *University of Pennsylvania Web site* [Online accessed 21 November 2001] http://ccat.sas.upenn.edu/jod/hackney.html

Paliwala, A (2000) Leila's Working Day, *The Law Teacher*, **34** (1), pp 1–16

Rousseau, J (1991) *Emile On Education*, Penguin, Harmondsworth

Santos, B (1995) *Toward a New Common Sense: Law, Science and Politics in Paradigmatic Transition,* Routledge, London

Scott, P (ed) (1998) *The Globalization of Higher Education*, Open University Press, Buckingham

Sheppard, S (1997) Casebooks, Commentaries and Curmudgeons: An Introductory History of Law in the Lecture Hall, *Iowa Law Review*, **82**, pp 547–629

Shor, I and Freire, P (1987) *A Pedagogy for Liberation,* Bergin and Garvey, New York

Silbey, S (1996) 'Let them eat cake': Globalization, post-modern colonialism and the possibilities of justice, Presidential Address, *Law and Society Review*, **31** (2), p 207

Thomas, P (2000) *Learning about Law Lecturing*, National Centre for Legal Education, University of Warwick

Twining, W (2000) *Globalization and Legal Theory*, Butterworths, London

Webb, J (1998) Ethics for Lawyers or Ethics for Citizens? New Directions for Legal Education, *Journal of Law and Society*, **25** (1), pp 134–50

WICHE (2001) Western Interstate Commission for Higher Education Web site. *Technology Costing Methodology Project* [Online accessed 21 November 2001] http://www.wiche.edu/telecom/projects/tcm/proj-findings.htm

Woods, R (2001) Order in the Virtual Law Classroom... Order in the Virtual Law Classroom – A Closer Look at American Law Schools in Cyberspace: Constructing Multiple Instructional Strategies for Effective Internet-based Legal Education, *The Journal of Information, Law and Technology (JILT)*, 2000 (3) [Online accessed 21 November 2001] http://elj.warwick.ac.uk/jilt/01–3/woods.html/

Index